Post-award Interest in the Asia-Pacific

Post-award Interest in the Asia-Pacific

Edited by

Kevin Kim
John Bang

Associate Editor
Sameer Thakur

Wolters Kluwer

Published by:
Kluwer Law International B.V.
PO Box 316
2400 AH Alphen aan den Rijn
The Netherlands
E-mail: lrs-sales@wolterskluwer.com
Website: www.wolterskluwer.com/en/solutions/kluwerlawinternational

Sold and distributed by:
Wolters Kluwer Legal & Regulatory U.S.
920 Links Avenue
Landisville, PA 17538
United States of America
E-mail: customer.service@wolterskluwer.com

ISBN 978-94-035-3566-1

e-Book: ISBN 978-94-035-4086-3
web-PDF: ISBN 978-94-035-4096-2

Editors

Kap-You (Kevin) Kim is a senior partner at Peter & Kim in Seoul. He was previously a senior partner at Bae, Kim & Lee LLC, where he worked for the past three decades in various roles, including as the co-founder and head of the International Arbitration Practice and the head of the Domestic and International Disputes Group.

Over the past 30 years, Kevin has acted as counsel, presiding arbitrator, co-arbitrator or sole arbitrator in more than 300 cases of international arbitrations under various arbitration rules. Presently, he is involved in several investment and commercial arbitrations. Among other positions that he holds, Kevin is an Advisory Board Member of the International Council for Commercial Arbitration (ICCA), the Chairman of the Korean Commercial Arbitration Board's (KCAB) International Arbitration Committee and an adjunct professor at the Seoul National University Law School.

In the past, Kevin has served as the Vice President of the ICC International Court of Arbitration (2014-2021), Secretary General of ICCA (2010-2014), member of the LCIA Court (2007-2012) and Vice Chair of the IBA Arbitration Committee (2008-2010).

John P. Bang is a senior partner (foreign attorney) at Peter & Kim in Seoul. He was previously a senior partner at Bae, Kim & Lee LLC, where he worked for 23 years in various roles, including as the co-founder and head of the International Arbitration & Litigation Practice. *Who's Who Legal* notes that John is "the cornerstone of the arbitration space in Korea" and is recognized as "superb counsel" by his peers. He has represented parties in over 250 proceedings under the rules of all major institutions and/or ad hoc arbitrations, including the ICC, SIAC, HKIAC, ICSID, LCIA, AAA/ICDR, UNCITRAL, VIAC, SCC, ACICA, CIETAC, KCAB, CAS, CIAC and JCAA.

He also acts as an arbitrator and is regularly appointed as co-arbitrator or presiding arbitrator by institutions and users. Prior to his work at BKL, John served as a federal law clerk to the Honorable Kathryn C. Ferguson. Currently, he is a member of the SIAC Court of Arbitration, an executive committee member of the Korea Council for International Arbitration and a senior officer of the IBA Litigation Committee.

Sameer Thakur is an associate at Peter & Kim's Seoul office. He is an Indian-qualified lawyer who acts for states and corporations in international disputes. He received his

B.A.-LL.B. (hons.) from NALSAR University of Law, India. He has trained with some of the world's leading law firms in both common and civil law jurisdictions (India, Hong Kong, Germany and Korea) and is equally comfortable handling disputes arising from both legal systems. He has acted as counsel and tribunal secretary in more than 10 international arbitrations (both commercial and investor-state disputes) conducted under the auspices of all major arbitral institutions, often acting as Second Chair for the lead counsel at the merits hearings. He currently serves as a member of the Editorial Board of the ICC Court of Arbitration's Indian Arbitration Newsletter as well as a member of the Steering Committee of the Y-IAMC.

Contributors

Australia

Dr. Janet Walker, CM is an independent arbitrator with chambers at Toronto Arbitration Chambers, Atkin Chambers in London, and Sydney Arbitration Chambers. She has served in commercial and treaty investment arbitrations as sole, presiding and co-arbitrator in ICC, ICDR, DIAC, HKIAC, LCIA PCA, SIAC administered and in ad hoc arbitrations in a variety of seats, covering a range of industries including construction, heavy equipment, M&A, shareholder, distribution, intellectual property, environmental, finance and employment. Janet is a Distinguished Research Professor of Law and former associate dean of Osgoode Hall Law School, York University.

Hong Kong SAR

Michael J. Moser is an international arbitrator and former Chairman of the Hong Kong International Arbitration Centre. Moser received his J.D. from Harvard University, Massachusetts and Ph.D. (with Distinction) from Columbia University, New York. He has served as an arbitrator in more than 300 cases seated in Asia, Europe and North America under both ad hoc and institutional rules. Chambers Global ranked Moser in Chambers Global 2019 as a "Star individual" and one of the "Most in Demand Arbitrators" worldwide.

Dr. Noam Zamir is an Associate Professor of Law at Lyon Catholic University. His academic research is focused on public international law, investor-State arbitrations and international commercial arbitrations, and his work has been published widely in the areas of international arbitration, international humanitarian law and human rights law. Dr. Zamir is also an independent arbitrator and serves as a tribunal secretary in both commercial international commercial arbitrations and investment treaty arbitrations.

Japan

Hiroyuki Tezuka heads Nishimura & Asahi's international dispute resolution practice, and specializes in international commercial litigation, arbitration, and mediation. He is admitted as an attorney in Japan and in New York and has been involved in a number of international arbitrations as counsel, sole arbitrator, co-arbitrator, or chairman, including the ICC, JCAA, AAA-ICDR, VIAC, KCAB, and SIAC. Hiroyuki serves as a member of the International Court of Arbitration of the ICC, and since 2018, he has been a council member of the ICC Institute of World Business Law. From 2013 to 2016, he taught International Arbitration and International Dispute Resolution at the University of Tokyo, School of Law as visiting professor. Since 2013, he has been a member of the SIAC's Court of Arbitration.

Mihiro Koeda is an associate at Nishimura & Asahi's international dispute resolution practice team. He received his LL.B. from Hitotsubashi University, Tokyo, in 2013 and J.D. from the University of Tokyo, Tokyo, in 2015. He has been involved in multiple international arbitrations as counsel as well as tribunal secretary. He has published multiple articles pertaining to arbitration in Japan and East Asia. He also is a member of several organizations, including the Japan Association of Arbitrators (JAA), Dispute Resolution and Arbitration Committee of the IPBA, and the Chartered Institute of Arbitrators (CIArb).

Malaysia

Sharon Chong is a partner in Skrine's dispute resolution group whose portfolio includes aviation, international arbitration, joint venture and M&A disputes, commodity and oil and gas disputes and insolvency and restructuring. Sharon is the immediate past president of the Malaysian Institute of Arbitrators and is a member of YSIAC Committee and Maxwell Chambers Steering Committee. She is also a founding member and Co-Chair of the Malaysia Network of the International Women's Insolvency & Restructuring Confederation. She was recognized in *The Legal 500 Arbitration Power list 2022* for South East Asia and mentioned in the *Global Arbitration Review 100* as a "name to know."

Nimalan Devaraja is a partner in Skrine's dispute resolution group whose portfolio includes civil and commercial litigation, company law and shareholders' disputes, international arbitration, restructuring and insolvency and regulatory enforcement. Nimalan has been a member of the Kuala Lumpur Bar Committee since February 2021, holding the positions of Co-Chairperson for both the Civil Practice and Court Liasion Committee, and Technology Committee. Nimalan is also the co-author of the Malaysian Litigation Series—Disclosure (2021 edn) and is also a contributing author to the Malaysian Court Practice (Trial Courts) and to the Annotated Statutes of Malaysia (Limitation Act 1953 and Partnership Act 1961). Nimalan was listed as one of ALB Malaysia's Rising Stars for 2021.

Myanmar

Suegene Ang is a partner in the Commercial & Corporate Disputes Practice at WongPartnership, and was the Firm's resident partner in Myanmar from 2016 to 2020. Suegene's expertise in Myanmar has been recognized by *Chambers: Global* and *The Legal 500: Asia-Pacific* since 2017. She has been recognized as a Rising Star for her work in Myanmar in *IFLR1000—The Guide to the World's Leading Financial Law Firms* since 2019, and in 2020 and 2021, she was named the highest-rated lawyer to work with for General Business Law in Myanmar by *Asialaw*.

New Zealand

Dr. Janet Walker, CM is an independent arbitrator with chambers at Toronto Arbitration Chambers, Atkin Chambers in London, and Sydney Arbitration Chambers. She has served in commercial and treaty investment arbitrations as sole, presiding and co-arbitrator in ICC, ICDR, DIAC, HKIAC, LCIA PCA, SIAC administered and in ad hoc arbitrations in a variety of seats, covering a range of industries including construction, heavy equipment, M&A, shareholder, distribution, intellectual property, environmental, finance and employment. Janet is a Distinguished Research Professor of Law and former associate dean of Osgoode Hall Law School, York University.

Pakistan

Ali Almani is an advocate of the Supreme Court of Pakistan and a partner at Fazleghani Advocates. Almani completed his Bachelor's from Yale University, Connecticut, in 2004, J.D. from Harvard University, Massachusetts, and Master's in Law from the University of Cambridge, England, in 2008. He frequently represents clients before the Supreme Court and High Courts of Pakistan and in international arbitrations, including under the ICC, LCIA and DIAC rules. Almani's primary areas of practice include tax, commercial and regulatory disputes and constitutional law.

Aaminah Qadir is an advocate of the High Courts of Pakistan. She is the founder of She-her Pakistan, a public interest litigation firm and a former associate at Fazleghani Advocates. Qadir received her Bachelor's from Yale University, Connecticut, and Master's in Law in 2014.

Sameen Hayat is a junior associate. She joined Fazleghani Advocates in Pakistan in 2019. Hayat received her LL.B. with Honors from the University of Edinburgh, Scotland.

People's Republic of China

Fei Ning is the managing partner of the Beijing Hui Zhong Law Firm. He received his LL.B. from Nanjing Institute of Chemical Technology, China, in 1983, LL.M. from the University of International Business and Economics, China, in 1993 and graduated from the Graduate Program at the University of London, England, in 1998. Fei is the Vice Chairman of the Belt and Road Committee of the International Court of Arbitration of the International Chamber of Commerce (*ICC Court*). For many years he has been ranked a Band 1 lawyer in China at Chambers & Partner Asia Pacific and Global.

Ariel Ye is a senior partner of King & Wood Mallesons' Arbitration and dispute resolution practice group. She specializes in assisting clients with resolving complex business disputes through alternative dispute resolution methods, including domestic and international arbitration. Ms. Ye is a member of the SIAC Board of Directors and a member of the Advisory Board of International Council for Commercial Arbitration (*the ICCA*). She also served as Co-chair of the Asia Pacific Committee of the IBA Arbitration Commission.

Republic of India

Gopal Subramanium is a global lawyer, international arbitrator, and distinguished jurist. He is head of Chambers at the Chambers of Gopal Subramanium, a globally operating chambers based in New Delhi, India. For over 30 years, he has acted in numerous cases that have shaped legislative principles on privacy, human rights and freedom of speech internationally. Having trained under former Attorney General Soli Sorabjee, Subramanium was designated as a senior advocate suo-motu by the Supreme Court in 1993, one of the youngest in India's history to receive the designation, where he developed a reputation for his rigorous style. He is an Associate Member of 3 Verulam Buildings, an honorary Master of the Bench at the Honourable Society Gray's Inn and a Supplementary Judge at the Qatar Financial Centre Regulatory Tribunal.

Republic of Indonesia

Andreas Hartono is a senior partner at ASNP Law Offices (formerly Andreas, Sheila & Partners). He graduated from the Law Faculty of Tarumanagara University, Indonesia, in 1997 and from the Master of Laws Program in International Banking Law at the Boston University School of Law, Massachusetts, in 1999. In 2019, 2020, 2021, and 2022, Andreas Hartono was named one of Indonesia's A-List Top 100 Lawyers by the *Asia Business Law Journal*. His practice focuses on mergers and acquisitions, capital markets, energy and natural resources, shipping, project financing, restructuring and bankruptcy, employment, entertainment and media industry and arbitration and dispute resolution.

Republic of Korea

Mino Han is a partner at Peter & Kim's Seoul office. He has acted as counsel in various international arbitrations conducted under the auspices of the ICC, SIAC, HKIAC, KCAB or JCAA. Mino specializes in construction and engineering disputes. Mino qualified as a Korean lawyer in 2009 and was admitted as a solicitor in England and Wales in 2019. He received a Master of Laws in International Arbitration Law from Seoul National University, South Korea, in 2012 and an MSc in Construction Law and Dispute Resolution at King's College London, England, in 2018. Mino is the representative of the CIArb Korea Chapter. He is a Steering Committee member of KCAB Next and is on the committee of KOCIA (Korean Committee on International Arbitration). Mino is also on the panel of International Arbitrators at KCAB International. He is also a DIS (German Arbitration Institute) Council Member and the ICC YAAF Regional Representative for Korea.

Sameer Thakur is an associate at Peter & Kim's Seoul office. He is an Indian-qualified lawyer who acts for states and corporations in international disputes. He received a BA-LL.B. (hons.) from NALSAR University of Law, India. He has trained with some of the world's leading law firms in both common and civil law jurisdictions (India, Hong Kong, Germany and Korea) and is equally comfortable handling disputes arising from both legal systems. He currently serves as a member of the Editorial Board of the ICC Court of Arbitration's Indian Arbitration Newsletter as well as a member of the Steering Committee of the Y-IAMC.

Republic of the Philippines

Jorge Alfonso C. Melo is a partner of Zambrano Gruba Caganda and Advincula Law (ZGLaw) and a member of Wong Partnership Group. He graduated with Honors from the Ateneo de Manila University School of Law, Philippines, Juris Doctor program and was admitted to the Bar in 1998. As a law student, he was editor-in-chief of the *Ateneo Law Journal* and a Facilitator/Intern at the Ateneo Human Rights Center. Prior to entering law school, he finished his Bachelor of Commerce, majoring in Legal Management, at the Ateneo de Manila University. He specializes in court litigation, dispute resolution, arbitration, and special projects. In the area of litigation and arbitration, he has handled cases involving large government and asset privatization projects, large-scale tax litigation, asset recovery, infrastructure projects, public interest cases and large-scale fraud cases. He is currently a member of the faculty at the Ateneo de Manila University School of Law where he teaches civil procedure, mergers and acquisitions and other remedial law subjects.

Singapore

Dr. Michael Hwang S.C. currently practises as a barrister and arbitrator, with his main focus on international arbitration and a select advisory practice as counsel. Michael was educated at Oxford University where he was a college scholar (by competitive examination) and prize winner. He was called to the Singapore Bar in 1968, and was a partner at Allen & Gledhill, one of Singapore's largest law firms, for over 30 years. He served as a Judicial Commissioner (Contract Judge for a fixed term) of the Supreme Court of Singapore, and was in the pioneer cohort of Senior Counsel appointed by the Supreme Court of Singapore in 1997. In 2005, he was appointed the non-resident Deputy Chief Justice of the DIFC Courts, and from 2010, as a non-resident Chief Justice until his retirement in 2018. Michael is an accredited arbitrator of numerous international arbitration institutions, and his arbitrations and mediations have involved disputes in over 45 countries in the Asia Pacific region and beyond.

Yin Wai Chan is an associate at Michael Hwang Chambers LLC, Singapore. Yin Wai graduated with a Bachelor of Laws from King's College London, England, and was admitted as an advocate and solicitor of the Supreme Court of Singapore in 2020.

State of Qatar

Thomas Williams is a partner at Sultan Al-Abdulla & Partners. He graduated from Cambridge University, England, and was called to the Bar by Lincoln's Inn in 2002. Williams is an English-qualified barrister and leads the firm's arbitration practice. He is an experienced advocate in arbitrations under all the major institutional rules and in ad hoc arbitrations and has also appeared regularly as an advocate in the English High Court (including the Commercial Court), and the Court of Appeal.

Ahmed Durrani is a senior associate at Sultan Al-Abdulla & Partners. He holds a Bachelor of Law from City, University of London, London, where he graduated with Honors. His practice focuses on corporate and commercial advisory and dispute resolution work. Durrani is a member of the Honorable Society of Gray's Inn and a licensed advocate of the High Courts by Punjab Bar Council in Pakistan.

Umang Singh is a senior associate at Sultan Al-Abdulla & Partners. He holds an LL.B. from the Nalsar University of Law in India, where he graduated with Honors. Singh is a member of the Bar Council of Maharashtra and Goa, and Bombay Bar Association. His practice focuses on handling arbitrations and general corporate advisory work.

Taiwan

Nigel N.T. Li is a partner at Lee and Li, Attorneys-at-Law. Li graduated with an LL.B. from Soochow University, Taiwan, in 1977; an LL.M. from National Taiwan University, Taiwan, in 1980; and an LL.M. from Harvard University, Massachusetts, in 1983. His areas of expertise include dispute resolution and international arbitration, media law, human and civil rights, international litigation and constitutional law. Li is also an adjunct professor at the Graduate School of Law of Soochow University, Taiwan, and the Department of Political Science of National Taiwan University.

Joyce N. Chang is an attorney at Lee and Li, Attorneys-at-Law. Chang graduated from National Taiwan University, Taiwan, with an LL.B. in 2018. Her practice mainly focuses on international civil and commercial dispute resolution. Her experience includes assisting renowned local companies and multinational companies in civil disputes and government procurement and patent infringement cases.

Thailand

Pathorn Towongchuen is a partner in the dispute resolution practice group at Weerawong, Chinnavat & Partners Ltd. He is recognized as a leading lawyer by *The Legal 500*, *Asialaw Profiles* and *Benchmark Litigation*. He obtained an LL.B. (Honors) from Chulalongkorn University, Thailand, and an LL.M. from Northwestern University, School of Law, USA. Towongchuen is a Thai Barrister-at-Law.

Jedsarit Sahussarungsi is a senior associate in the dispute resolution practice group and the competition law group at Weerawong, Chinnavat & Partners Ltd. He obtained an LL.B. (Honors) from Thammasat University, Thailand, an LL.M. (Summa Cum Laude) from Université Toulouse 1 Capitole, France and an LL.M. (Merit) from University College London, UK. He specializes in domestic and international arbitration, cross-border litigation and antitrust matters. Sahussarungsi also advises clients on cases under arbitral rules, including the ICC, JAMS, SCAI, SIAC, TAI and UNCITRAL.

Napassorn Panitchewakul is an associate in the dispute resolution practice group at Weerawong, Chinnavat & Partners Ltd. She obtained an LL.B. (First Class with Honors) from Chulalongkorn University, Thailand, and an LL.M. from New York University School of Law, USA. Panitchewakul has a wide range of experience advising and representing public and private sector clients in different dispute resolution and business rehabilitation matters, particularly in relation to transportation, logistics, commercial law, labor law, breach of contract, fraud, consumer protection and anti-corruption. She is a Thai Barrister-at-Law.

United Arab Emirates

Dr. Hassan Arab is a partner and co-Head of Litigation at Al Tamimi & Company. He has a Ph.D. in Law from the University of Essex, England, a Bachelor's from Beirut University, Lebanon, and a Master's in International Business from the University of Wollongong, Australia. Dr. Arab's areas of practice include all forms of civil and commercial litigation, arbitration, ADR, recognition and enforcement of foreign judgments and arbitral awards.

Mosaab Th. Aly is a senior counsel at Al Tamimi & Company. Aly has a Diploma in Public Law from Tanta University, Egypt and an LL.B. from Cairo University, Egypt. He has extensive experience in dispute resolution practice and contentious matters, both in the form of litigation before UAE courts and in the form of domestic and international arbitration proceedings before different arbitral tribunals.

Vietnam

Do Khoi Nguyen is a key partner of YKVN's international arbitration practice. Nguyen received his J.D. from Gonzaga University, Washington. Nguyen is admitted as an attorney in both Washington State (2007) and Vietnam (2013). He has handled a broad range of disputes in construction, investment, oil and gas and professional liability. Nguyen regularly represents state-owned groups and entities, multinational enterprises and private companies. He is a sought-after speaker on Vietnam-related arbitration.

Pham Minh Thang is a YKVN partner and a member of YKVN's international arbitration practice. Thang received his Bachelor of Laws at Hanoi University, Vietnam (2007) and Master of Laws at Berkeley Law School, California, in 2015 and is dual-qualified in Vietnam and California. He has 15 years of experience combining both international arbitration and corporate practice. He has been involved in most major international arbitration cases handled by YKVN.

Summary of Contents

Table of Contents

Foreword

In *Hulley Enterprises Limited (Cyprus) v. The Russian Federation* (PCA Case No. AA 226), *Yukos Universal Limited (Isle of Man) v. The Russian Federation* (PCA Case No. AA 227) and *Veteran Petroleum Limited (Cyprus) v. The Russian Federation* (PCA Case No. AA 228), often referred to collectively as the Yukos Awards, the Tribunal awarded post-award interest which, as of October 2022, was reported[1] to be running at approximately USD 2.8 million per day. On this basis, in absolute terms, the post-award interest accrued has so far increased the value of the Yukos Awards from approximately USD 50 billion to USD 57 billion—an increase of a not insubstantial sum of USD 7 billion making the Yukos Awards not only the largest in terms of principal sum awarded but also the largest in respect of post-award interest. There can be no better example of the significance and potential value of an award for post-award interest. These, by far, outweigh the attention and time generally devoted to this issue in arbitral proceedings.

A publication dedicated to post-award interest and specifically one which takes a multi-jurisdictional, yet regional approach is not just timely, but long overdue. The focus on the Asia-Pacific and selected jurisdictions in the Middle East is apt given their economic importance and close economic relations—which, by all accounts, will only increase. While the jurisdictions covered include some of the largest economies in the world, the lineup of contributors is no less impressive with eminent practitioners from the region and beyond.

Each chapter provides an in-depth analysis of the law on post-award interest and the legal issues related thereto. As usual, the devil is in the details. Where parties are content either for the tribunal to award post-award interest at the statutory default rate in jurisdictions which provide for it or for post-award interest to accrue by statute without the award explicitly addressing this, the issue of post-award interest should be straightforward.

1. https://www.reuters.com/legal/government/yukos-shareholders-seek-enforce-50-bln-award-against-russia-london-court-2022-10-11/

However, where, for instance, questions of conflict of laws play a role, the issue of post-award interest may easily gain in complexity—no doubt invigorating counsel and tribunal alike. It is here, in their consideration of the various dimensions, that the authors' contributions truly stand out. Equally helpful are the contributors' insights into arbitral practice and how courts might approach matters of post-award interest in their jurisdiction. The structure of each chapter makes for easy navigation and permits the reader to quickly grasp the essential elements of how post-award interest is dealt with in each jurisdiction.

Parties and counsel involved in arbitral proceedings with a nexus to the jurisdictions covered in this book will find the insights provided valuable and unquestionable, and so will arbitral tribunals. From an academic perspective, this publication will be just as useful in shaping the future debate on the topic. Policymakers may also take inspiration from comparing the approach taken in other jurisdictions on matters of post-award interest when refining the legal framework in their home jurisdictions.

In short, this publication is warmly recommended.

Christopher Lau SC

Preface

The genesis of this book lies in two realizations that the General Editors had when speaking with some of the region's leading arbitration practitioners: first, that there were significant differences in the law governing post-award interest in international arbitration across jurisdictions, and second, that the question of post-award interest in the region (and arguably even outside of it) had not been given serious academic consideration despite its obvious importance to practitioners and academics.

Those realizations led to conversations that eventually led to this book.

Very quickly, it became evident to us that sufficient attention was being paid to the question of interest from the date of the alleged breach (or other trigger events) to the date of the award, that is, pre-award interest. Various formulaic approaches are taken towards ensuring that pre-award interest is accounted for in claims for compensation with submissions on damages often comprehensively setting out the applicable law, as well as the relevant interest rate for the eventual award to be determined by the Tribunal.

What is often overlooked is post-award interest—leading to significant negative consequences for the party seeking enforcement. It is important to remember that a party against whom an award has been made generally feels no particular sense of urgency to pay the sums due under the award. It may transpire (as it often does) that there are other more pressing financial debts that need to be paid first, such as loans, which have higher rates of interest attached to them. There is a lack of incentive for anyone but the most conscientious of award-debtors to make prompt payment to comply with the award in the absence of post-award interest. While we would always hope that all award-debtors will always be the most conscientious, as Oliver Wendell Holmes would say, the law must be considered from the perspective of the bad man, or in this case, a reluctant award-debtor.

Additionally, a failure to seek post-award interest deprives the award-creditor of a number of financial opportunities linked to the award sum in the period between the rendering of the award and the actual payment of such award. Post-award interest, then, can be said to serve a dual purpose: for the award-creditor, it provides a compensatory role, allowing it to recover its continuing financial losses and related lost opportunity costs until actual payment is made. For the award-debtor, it serves as a disincentive against late payment. With the importance of post-award interest being clear to the General Editors, they were surprised to note that there was no book with a multi-jurisdictional approach that could guide practitioners, arbitrators and academics on this issue.

From a distance, post-award interest can seem to deal with the simple question of what the applicable rate is. Unfortunately, that is not the case. To even arrive at that question, one must first navigate complicated questions of conflict of laws to determine what the applicable law is, as well as parse through the substantive law of the jurisdiction in question to determine what exactly one must be requesting or what one must award, as well as consider several procedural considerations that must be kept in mind.

In the current scenario, counsel often fails to make submissions on post-award interest, consciously, or unconsciously, relying instead on the pro-activeness (or lack thereof) of the Tribunal, who themselves might have their hands tied vis-à-vis the relevant legal framework.

This volume is a conscious attempt to fill this gap in the available literature and to generate further awareness on some of the more complicated questions surrounding the award of post-award interest.

This book aims to collate discussions on law and practice relating to post-award interest in the Asia-Pacific region, with a focus on *18* jurisdictions: Australia, Hong Kong, India, Indonesia, Japan, Malaysia, Myanmar, New Zealand, People's Republic of China, Philippines, Pakistan, Republic of Korea, Singapore, Thailand, Taiwan, Qatar, United Arab Emirates and Vietnam. The book is structured in a way that each chapter deals with one jurisdiction ensuring that the most relevant questions regarding post-award interest including the power to award post-award interest, its nature, the impact of the applicable law, any questions of public policy, the role of the national courts, could be examined at length in a manner that would be easy for users to access.

The focus of this project has been directed at jurisdictions in the Asia-Pacific region, for two reasons:

(1) owing to the very jurisdiction-specific nature of post-award interests, a global focus would require several additional volumes; and
(2) the rising percentage of arbitrations that have strong Asia-Pacific elements—ither through the applicable substantive law, or the choice of jurisdictions in the Asia-Pacific as the seat, as well as due to the high volume of users of international arbitration from the Asia-Pacific region merited an urgent intervention focusing on the region.

This book will hopefully contribute to the ongoing efforts to bring about consistency and predictability in the way Tribunals deal with damages in general, and post-award interest in particular, while also generating academic interest in the questions that arise from it. This is an ongoing effort and will benefit from continued input from all readers. We welcome all feedback.

Kevin Kim and John Bang[1]

1. This book would not be possible without the editorial support we received from Peter & Kim staff and from research assistants who provided assistance as and when necessary. In particular, we are grateful to Yongsun Kim and Michael van Muelken at Peter & Kim, as well as research assistants Himanshu Raghuvanshi, Umang Bhat Nair (both from Nalsar University of Law) and Mingyun Hwang (from Cornell Law School).

Acknowledgments

We are grateful to the late Alvin Yeo,[1] Michael Moser (Twenty Essex), Christopher Lau (Maxwell Chambers in Singapore and 3 Verulam Buildings in London), Michael Hwang (Michael Hwang Chambers), Ariel Ye (King & Wood Mallesons), Tay Yu Jin (Mayer Brown), Douglas Jones AO (Sydney Arbitration Chambers, Atkin Chambers and Toronto Arbitration Chambers), Janet Walker, CM (Toronto Arbitration Chambers, Atkin Chambers, and Sydney Arbitration Chambers), Hiroyuki Tezuka (Nishimura & Asahi), Fei Ning (Hui Zhong Law Firm), Chan Hock Keng (Wong Partnership) and Yoshimi Ohara (Nagashima Ohno & Tsunematsu) for their thoughtful collaboration from the very beginning of this project, when it was not much more than an idea.

Not only were the individuals listed above crucial in the development of the structure of the comparative approach this book adopts but they were also essential in identifying the right authors across jurisdictions. We are also thankful to Sameer Thakur for co-ordinating with all the authors and supporting the General Editors throughout the development of this book.

While it is one thing to determine that it would be helpful for readers across the world to understand how jurisdictions in the region treat questions regarding post-award interest—we were obviously not in a position to be writing about all of the jurisdictions we have covered ourselves. As such, we are very thankful to lawyers from all jurisdictions who shared our vision and worked with us to bring this idea to life by contributing chapters.

We are also grateful to the team at Kluwer International, led by Eleanor Taylor, without whose support and patience this project could never have been completed.

-Kevin Kim and John Bang

1. Alvin Yeo was a dear friend and an exceptional colleague to the General Editors over the last two decades. He brought his intelligence and good humor to all conversations regarding this book, as he did to all conversations he participated in. He is dearly missed.

Australia

Janet Walker, CM

INTRODUCTION

This chapter examines the power of an arbitrator to make an order for post-award interest in Australia. First, it is important to understand the sources of this power to be found in Australian legislation and elsewhere. As a federal system, the power to legislate in Australia is divided between the State and the Federal Governments. International arbitration in Australia is regulated by the Federal International Arbitration Act 1974 (Cth), and domestic arbitration is governed by the harmonised State Commercial Arbitration Acts. Both regimes grant the power to order post-award interest. Further, the International Arbitration Act 1974 (Cth), together with a mechanism adopted by the Federal Court of Australia, provides guidance in determining the meaning of a '*reasonable rate.*' Finally, international standards may also be of assistance in this determination.

This leads into discussions of the substantive and procedural issues raised by post-award interest in Australia. The chapter begins with the role of the terms of the contract governing non-payment and late payment. Then it considers the application of the procedural rules of the governing law and the narrow exception for the use of public policy to order post-award interest. Following this, it considers procedural issues, including those of interpretation and limitation periods.

Finally, the chapter turns to the courts' ability to enforce foreign court orders and to vary them in respect of orders of post-award interest. The Australian Common Law typically views orders in relation to the payment of post-award interest made in foreign jurisdictions as part of the judgment debt. Accordingly, these payments are usually enforceable within Australia. Additionally, consideration is given to the Federal Court of Australia's ability to vary the relevant dates for the purposes of calculating post-award interest. The discussion then turns to the significant decision of the Federal

Court of Australia in Energy Service Company (*ESCO*) *Corporation v. Bradken Resources* (*ESCO*),[1] which dealt with the application of differing interest rates.

I POWER TO GRANT POST-AWARD INTEREST

1. Does an Arbitral Tribunal Have the Power to Grant Post-award Interest under the National Law?

Unless otherwise agreed by the parties, the Australian International Arbitration Act 1974 (Cth) (*the IAA*) enables arbitrators to make an award for interest overall or as part of a principal claim at such a rate as the arbitrator determines reasonable. Typically, an agreement to exclude interest would be found in the parties' contract.[2]

The relevant provision of the IAA is section 26, which provides as follows:

> *26. Interest on debt under award*
> (1) This Section applies if:
> (a) an arbitral tribunal makes an award for the payment of an amount of money; and
> (b) under the award, the amount is to be paid by a particular day ("the due date").
> (2) The arbitral tribunal may direct that interest, including compound interest, is payable if the amount is not paid on or before the due date.
> (3) The arbitral tribunal may set a reasonable rate of interest.
> (4) The interest is payable:
> (a) from the day immediately following the due date; and
> (b) on so much of the amount as remains unpaid.
> (5) The direction is taken to form part of the award.

Similar provisions exist for domestic arbitrations in the Commercial Arbitration Acts. For example, the power to award post-award interest is provided in section 33F of the Commercial Arbitration Act 2010 in New South Wales (NSW):

> *33F Interest on debt under Award*
> (1) This Section applies if:
> (a) an arbitral tribunal makes an award for the payment of an amount of money, and
> (b) under the award, the amount is to be paid by a particular day ("the due date"), unless otherwise agreed by the parties.
> (2) The arbitral tribunal may direct that interest, including compound interest, is payable if the amount is not paid on or before the due date.
> (3) The arbitral tribunal may set a reasonable rate of interest.
> (4) The interest is payable:
> (a) from the day immediately following the due date, and
> (b) on so much of the money as remains unpaid.
> (5) The direction is taken to form part of the award.

---

1. [2011] 282 ALR 282.
2. Doug Jones, AO, Janet Walker, CM, *Commercial Arbitration in Australia under the Model* (3rd edn, Law Book Co 2022), at para. [9.840].

The institutional rules of the Australian Centre for International Commercial Arbitration do not address the power to award interest. Arbitrators have broad discretion to award interest, including compound interest, with or without a request from the parties. Unless the parties agree otherwise, there is no statutory constraint on the final remedy that an arbitral tribunal can award, and there are no specific statutory or other requirements for exercising or excluding this power. However, arbitral tribunals typically order pre-award interest *in* the award pursuant to a claim by a party for it, and, subject to the parties' agreement, arbitral tribunals typically permit the court to order post-award interest *on* the award if the award is not paid promptly.

2. Is the Power Exercisable Without a Request or Submission, or is Such a Submission Required?

Under the IAA, an arbitration agreement is deemed to provide the arbitral tribunal with the power to award interest as a court would have in deciding a case before it. There is no formal prohibition on awarding interest without a request or submission, although interest is typically a form of relief that is sought explicitly. In *Government Insurance Office (NSW) v. Atkinson-Leighton Joint Venture*,[3] a case concerning the power of an arbitral tribunal to award interest, the High Court endorsed the power at common law of an arbitral tribunal to exercise '*every right and discretionary remedy given to a court of law*'.[4]

3. Is the Power Classified as One Under the Substantive Applicable Law or the Procedural Law of the Arbitration?

Subject to the matter being provided for in the agreement between the parties, which would form part of the substantive issues to be addressed under the applicable law, the power in section 26 of the IAA is part of the procedural law of international commercial arbitrations seated in Australia.[5] It serves as an additional provision to the Model Law, which has the force of law in Australia.[6] The inclusion of this power among the remedial powers of the arbitral tribunal renders it procedural in nature.[7]

II CHOICE OF LAW

4. What Is the Law That Applies to Determining the Rate of Post-award Interest? Would This Be the Governing Law of the Dispute or the Law of the Seat?

According to the arbitration law in Australia, the arbitral tribunal may set '*a reasonable rate of interest*'.[8] Therefore, arbitrators have broad discretion to determine the

3. *Government Insurance Office (NSW) v. Atkinson-Leighton Joint Venture* [1981] 146 CLR 206, (Mason J) at pp. [246]-[247].
4. *Chandris v. Isbrandtsen-Moller* [1950] 84 Ll L Rep 347, (Tucker J) at p. [352].
5. Richard Garnett, 'The Legal Framework for International Arbitration in Australia: The Old and the New' in Luke Nottage and Richard Garnett (eds), International Arbitration in Australia (The Federation Press 2010) at pp. [38], [53].
6. *See* International Arbitration Act 1974 (Cth) section 16.
7. Doug Jones, AO, Janet Walker, CM, *Commercial Arbitration in Australia under the Model* (3rd edn, Law Book Co 2022) at para. [9.500].
8. International Arbitration Act 1974 (Cth) section 26(3).

entitlement and rate of post-award interest. Some parties may argue that the rate applied by Australian courts may serve as a reasonable analogue. Where the parties have prescribed the availability of interest and the rate of interest, these questions may both be considered matters of substance governed by the law that governs the parties' agreement. Where the parties have not provided this in their agreement, the availability and rate of interest are, in principle, governed by the law of the seat in Australia.

Section 52(2)(a) of the Federal Court of Australia Act 1976 (Cth) provides that the post-judgment period is payable at the rate prescribed by r. 39.06 of the Federal Court Rules:[9]

> (a) for the period from 1 January to 30 June in any year – the rate that is 6 per cent above the cash rate last published by the Reserve Bank of Australia before the period commenced; and
> (b) for the period from 1 July to 31 December in any year – the rate that is 6 per cent above the cash rate last published by the Reserve Bank of Australia before the period commenced.

For example, effective from 1 July 2022 to 31 December 2022, the Federal Court Interest on Judgments Practice Notice provides for a post-judgment interest rate of 6.85%.[10] Arbitral tribunals may also have regard to general commercial rates.

III DO THE COURTS TAKE INTO ACCOUNT INTERNATIONAL STANDARDS WHEN FACING CHALLENGES ON THE POST-AWARD INTEREST?

According to Allsop P in *Telephone Communication Limited (TCL) Air Conditioner (Zhongshan) Co Ltd v. Castel Electronics Pty Ltd TCL*, the IAA's adoption of the Model Law reflects '*Australia's acceptance of United Nations General Assembly's recommendation to give 'due consideration' to the Model Law in the interests of international uniformity*'.[11] Therefore, an Australian court may be persuaded to consider foreign precedents in adjusting a post-award interest if asked to do so.

IV SUBSTANTIVE LAW ISSUES

5. How are Contractual Provisions on Late or Non-payment of Interest Relevant to Post-award Interest? Will These Be Considered by the Arbitral Tribunal?

Pursuant to section 26 of the IAA, arbitral tribunals may consider the terms of the parties' contract on late payment or non-payment of interest in determining the availability of post-award interest and the rate of interest. The ability of the Federal

9. Federal Court of Australia, *Interest on Judgments Practice Note*, 18 September 2017, at para [3.2].
10. *Pre-judgment & Post-judgment Interest Rates*, Federal Court of Australia (January 2019), http://www.fedcourt.gov.au/forms-and-fees/interest-rates.
11. [2014] FCAFC 83, at p. [57].

Court to award a lower rate of interest if justice so requires[12] may also be relevant to the arbitral tribunal's determination.

6. How Do the Procedural Rules of the Substantive Law Apply?

Australia's choice of law rules are derived from the United Nations Commission on International Trade (UNCITRAL) Model Law. Article 28 of the Model Law, contained in Schedule 2 of the IAA, provides:

> (1) The arbitral tribunal shall decide the dispute in accordance with such rules of law as are chosen by the parties as applicable to the substance of the dispute. Any designation of the law or legal system of a given State shall be construed, unless otherwise expressed, as directly referring to the substantive law of that State and not to its conflict of laws rules.

Article 28(2) further provides that in the absence of an express or implied choice by the parties, the arbitral tribunal shall apply the conflict of law rules of the arbitral seat to determine the substantive law governing the dispute.

The procedural rules of the substantive law do not apply in determining interest if Australia is the seat.

7. Whether the Award of Interest Can Be Subjected to Public Policy Objections and if so, What Are They?

Section 19 of the IAA provides:

> Without limiting the generality of Articles 17I(1)(b)(ii), 34(2)(b)(ii) and 36(1)(b)(ii) of the Model Law, it is declared, for the avoidance of any doubt, that, for the purposes of those Articles, an interim measure or award is in conflict with, or is contrary to, the public policy of Australia if:
>
> (a) the making of the interim measure or award was induced or affected by fraud or corruption; or
> (b) a breach of the rules of natural justice occurred in connection with the making of the interim measure or award.

There is no explicit barrier to making a public policy objection to post-award interest, but Australian courts have generally adopted a restrictive interpretation of public policy objections. In *TCL*, the Full Federal Court held:[13]

> An international commercial arbitration award will not be set aside or denied recognition or enforcement under Arts 34 and 36 of the Model Law (or under Art V of the New York Convention) unless there is demonstrated real unfairness or real practical injustice in how the international litigation or dispute resolution was conducted or resolved, by reference to established principles of natural justice or procedural fairness. The demonstration of real unfairness or real practical injustice will generally be able to be expressed, and demonstrated, with tolerable clarity and

12. *See* the Note to r 39.06 which reads: Section 52(2) of the Act provides that interest is payable: '*if the Court, in a particular case, thinks that justice so requires – at such lower rate as the Court determines*': Federal Court Rules 2011 r 39.06.
13. *TCL Air Conditioner (Zhongshan) Co Ltd v. Castel Electronics Pty Ltd* [2014] FCAFC 83, at p. [55].

> expedition. It does not involve the contested evaluation of a fact-finding process or 'fact interpretation process' or the factual analysis of asserted 'reasoning failure,' as was argued here.

Erroneous legal reasoning or misapplication of law is not a violation of public policy; rather, Australia's public policy is to enforce arbitral awards '*wherever possible*'.[14] The parties' adoption of institutional rules which are putatively inconsistent has also been held to not overrule Model Law provisions with respect to public policy.[15]

According to the International Bar Association (IBA) Guide to Arbitration in Australia, '*the question of whether punitive or exemplary damages or interest can be awarded by an arbitrator is doubtful and has yet to come before the courts*'.[16]

V PROCEDURAL LAW ISSUES

8. What Are the Main Procedural Law Issues When Considering Post-award Interest? How Are the Arbitration Laws and Other Laws or Regulations of the Seat Relevant?

When Australia is the seat of the arbitration, the IAA applies. Parties should be aware of the general avenues of recourse open to them under the IAA.

Under Schedule 2, Article 33(1), which is based on the Model Law, a party may request a correction or interpretation of an award within 30 days of receipt of the award. This provides one means of recourse for an evident mistake or miscalculation of the interest.

In addition, a party may request the making of an additional award where the award has not addressed a claim of post-award interest made in the proceedings.[17]

A party may apply to set aside the award and/or request that the court remit the award to the arbitral tribunal under Schedule 2, Article 34 of the Act.

The limitation for an action to enforce an award is six years; or it is 12 years if the award is made under an arbitration agreement and the arbitration agreement is made by deed. The time runs from the date on which the cause of action accrued, which, in

14. *Uganda Telecom Pty Ltd v. Hi-Tech Telecom* [2011] 277 ALR 415, (Foster J) at p. [436]:

> The whole rationale of the Act, and thus the public policy of Australia, is to enforce such awards wherever possible in order to uphold contractual arrangements entered into in the course of international trade, in order to support certainty and finality in international dispute resolution and in order to meet the other objects specified in s 2D of the Act.

15. *Cargill International SA v. Peabody Australia Mining Ltd* [2010] 78 NSWLR 53, 3 (Ward J) at p. [534], which noted by way of example that '*insofar as Art 19 of the Model Law allows the parties to adopt a set of procedural rules different from those which would otherwise apply under the Model Law, it cannot be said that the Model Law and International Chamber of Commerce Rules are inconsistent and irreconcilable*'.
16. Doug Jones, *Arbitration Guide: Australia*, International Bar Association Arbitration Committee (March 2012) https://www.ibanet.org/MediaHandler?id=6A71C416-8AAC-4738-A0E1-8A06B5DD7E5E.
17. International Arbitration Act 1974 (Cth) sch 2, Article 33(3).

the case of enforcing an arbitral award, is the date on which default first happens in observance of the award.[18]

VI EFFECT OF ENFORCEMENT ORDERS ON INTEREST ON THE AWARD AT THE SEAT AND ELSEWHERE

In enforcement proceedings, Australian courts have generally respected arbitrators' decisions when determining interest. For example, in *Antclizo Shipping Corporation v. The Food Corporation of India,*[19] the plaintiff brought an application to enforce a foreign arbitral award under section 8 of the IAA. The award was made in London, and it required the defendant to pay various sums to the plaintiff, including post-award interest and costs. The Supreme Court of Western Australia entered judgment on the same terms as the award, including the post-award interest rate, which was determined by English law. Post-award interest was also ordered in the enforcement of the London Court of International Arbitration (*LCIA*) award in *Traxys Europe SA v. Balaji Coke Industry Pvt Ltd (No 2)*.[20] These authorities confirm that post-award interest is payable as part of the judgment debt and therefore constitutes a part of the award on which enforcement is sought.

VII POWERS OF THE COURT TO ORDER OR ADJUST POST-AWARD INTEREST

9. Does the Australian Court Have the Power to Order or Adjust the Post-award Interest, Assuming It is Either the Seat Court or the Enforcing Court?

Pursuant to section 51A of the Federal Court of Australia Act 1976 (Cth), the enforcing court has the power to award interest from the date of the award at such a rate as the court thinks fit.[21] Section 52 also permits interest on the judgment at a rate fixed by the Rules of Court or at such a lower rate as the court determines. An Australian court may also order partial enforcement, for example, severing interest from the remainder of the award.[22]

In *ESCO,*[23] the Federal Court of Australia was asked to consider the application of a different interest rate from that awarded by the arbitral tribunal. ESCO sought to have the arbitration award enforced in Australia under section 8(3) of the IAA after Bradken refused to pay costs under the award. The outcome of their enforcement proceedings

18. *See*, e.g., New South Wales Limitation Act 1969, section 20.
19. [1998] WASC 342 (6 November 1998).
20. [2012] FCA 276.
21. *See ESCO Corporation v. Bradken Resources* [2011] 282 ALR 282 at p. 284, in which the relief sought by ESCO included the payment of interest pursuant to section 51A(1) of the Federal Court of Australia Act 1976 (Cth).
22. *William Hare UAE LLC v. Aircraft Support Industries Pty Ltd* [2014] NSWSC 1403, at pp. [105]-[106] and [136]. In this case, the judge found that it was open to the court to sever a portion of the interest affected by the breach of the rules of natural justice.
23. *ESCO Corporation v. Bradken Resources* [2011] 282 ALR 282.

in the United States (US) was yet to be decided by the time of the Australian hearing. In the US District Court, the dispute as to interest centred on whether post-award interest should be ordered at the US federal rate of 0.19% per annum or the Oregon State rate of 9%.

In Australia, the parties were in dispute as to the relief to which ESCO was entitled and whether ESCO was entitled to post-judgment interest at Australian rates pursuant to section 51A of the Federal Court Act 1976 (Cth) (which were higher than the US federal rate). ESCO was prepared to stay or adjourn the Australian proceedings until the US proceedings were finished, but only if Bradken provided a bank guarantee for the award amount and additional sums of interest. The court granted the adjournment, ordering Bradken to provide security for the award, but not for the interest.

Hong Kong SAR, China

Michael J. Moser & Noam Zamir

INTRODUCTION

At the outset, it is important to briefly explain the legal system of Hong Kong. In accordance with the *one country, two systems* principle and its status as a Special Administrative Region (*SAR*), Hong Kong enjoys a certain degree of autonomy (except in defence and foreign affairs) and retains a separate legal system from that of Mainland China.

Hong Kong's legal system is based on the English Common Law. The legislation that regulates arbitration in Hong Kong is the Arbitration Ordinance (Cap 609) ('*the Arbitration Ordinance*'),[1] which governs all arbitrations seated in Hong Kong regardless of whether the arbitration agreement is entered into in Hong Kong.[2] It should be noted that the Arbitration Ordinance, which adopted the United Nations Commission on International Trade (UNCITRAL) Model Law (2006), contains a single regime applicable to both domestic and international arbitrations. However, in contrast to the UNCITRAL Model Law (2006), the Arbitration Ordinance deals explicitly with the authority of arbitral tribunals to award interest on money awarded by it.

The structure of this chapter is as follows. Section I and II of this chapter examine the extent of post-award interest that may be granted by an arbitral tribunal under the Arbitration Ordinance. Section III then addresses the consideration given by the Hong Kong courts to international standards when facing challenges related to post-award interest.

Section IV of this chapter discusses substantive law issues, including the application of contractual provisions to post-award interest and the use of public policy as grounds to refuse the recognition and enforcement of international awards. Section V of this chapter addresses the application of the Arbitration Ordinance to procedural law

1. The Arbitration Ordinance came into force on 1 Jun. 2011, and was subsequently amended in July and December 2013, July 2015 and 22 Jun. 2017.
2. *See* the Arbitration Ordinance (Cap 609), section 5.1.

issues. Section VI focuses on the enforcement of an award for interest by the Hong Kong courts (both in relation to a local arbitral award and a foreign arbitral award). Finally, section VII discusses the Hong Kong courts' lack of authority to order or adjust post-award interest.

I POWER TO GRANT POST-AWARD INTEREST

1. Does an Arbitral Tribunal Have the Power to Grant Post-award Interest under National law?

Yes. Under the Arbitration Ordinance, an arbitral tribunal can award any remedy or relief that could have been ordered in civil proceedings by the Hong Kong courts, including interest.[3]

Unless otherwise agreed by the parties, the arbitral tribunal may award simple or compound interest from the dates at rates it considers appropriate.[4] Interest may be awarded on any of the following:[5] (i) money awarded by the arbitral tribunal; (ii) money claimed in and outstanding at the commencement of the arbitral proceedings but paid before the award is made; or (iii) costs awarded or ordered by the tribunal.

Accordingly, in accordance with sections 79 and 80 of the Arbitration Ordinance, arbitral tribunals may and often do award both pre- and post-award interests usually accruing until the date of payment of the outstanding sums. In relation to post-award interest, arbitral tribunals may provide for a grace period to comply with the award and order that the post-award interest would run only after the grace period has ended.

The Arbitration Ordinance does not state which considerations and factors the arbitral tribunal must take into account when making a decision on post-award interest.

While arbitral tribunals frequently do not explain in detail their reasons and considerations for awarding post-award interest, arbitral tribunals would usually consider the contractual provisions (if any) concerning interest. These provisions may prescribe the interest rate and relevant currency.

Furthermore, in exercising their discretion, arbitral tribunals usually invite the parties to make submissions on their requested relief including their request for interest. Accordingly, the parties often make submissions on the applicable interest rate and the exact period that the interest rate should apply. In the absence of contractual provisions to the contrary, arbitral tribunals will often accept the request of the prevailing party for post-award interest. To the extent that the parties to the dispute have opposing submissions in relation to post-award interest (e.g., the start date, interest rate and simple versus compound interest rate), arbitral tribunals would usually consider the overall circumstances of the case including the conduct of the losing party.

3. *See* the Arbitration Ordinance (Cap 609), section 70.
4. *See* the Arbitration Ordinance (Cap 609), section 79.
5. *See* the Arbitration Ordinance (Cap 609), section 79(1).

2. Is the Power Exercisable Without a Request or Submission, or Are Such Submissions Required?

Sections 79 and 80 of the Arbitration Ordinance that deal with post-award interest do not state that the power of arbitral tribunals to grant interest is subject to the parties' request or submission.

Nevertheless, in general, it should be noted that arbitral tribunals have no authority to decide on matters that were not referred to or requested by the parties. Indeed, the Arbitration Ordinance stipulates that the award may be set aside by the court if '*the award deals with a dispute not contemplated by or not falling within the terms of the submission to arbitration, or contains decisions on matters beyond the scope of the submission to arbitration [...]*'.[6]

Therefore, as a matter of caution, most arbitral tribunals will only decide on the grant of post-award interest if one party requests such a decision and the opposing party has been provided with a reasonable opportunity to present its view in relation to post-award interest.

However, if the award is silent on the issue of post-award interest, section 80 of the Arbitration Ordinance explicitly states that post-award interest is payable on money and costs awarded by an arbitral tribunal at the judgment rate, which is 8% per annum as of 29 August 2022.[7]

Therefore, as a matter of good practice, if the parties have not made any submissions on the issue of interest, the arbitral tribunal should bring to the attention of the parties the effect of section 80 of the Arbitration Ordinance.

3. Is the Power Classified As One under the Substantive Applicable Law or the Procedural Law of the Arbitration?

The power to grant post-award interest is a matter of procedural law, which is specifically governed by the Arbitration Ordinance.[8] Nevertheless, as explained in the following section, arbitral tribunals may need to apply the substantive law of the contract when dealing with post-award interest to the extent that the contract regulates matters concerning post-award interest.

II CHOICE OF LAW

4. What is the Law That Applies to Determining What the Post-award Interest Should Be? Would This Be the Governing Law of the Dispute or the Law of the Seat?

As explained above, the power to grant post-award interest in arbitrations seated in Hong Kong is explicitly regulated by sections 79 and 80 of the Arbitration Ordinance.

6. *See* the Arbitration Ordinance (Cap 609), section 80.
7. *See Interest on Judgments and Interest Rate* issued under section 49(1) of the High Court Ordinance, Cap. 4 – https://www.judiciary.hk/en/court_services_facilities/interest_rate.html.
8. John Choong & Joseph Weeramantry (eds), The *Hong Kong Arbitration Ordinance: Commentary and Annotations* (Sweet and Maxwell 2015), at p. [452] (noting that '*[i]t is likely that in Hong Kong, the award on interest will be considered primary a matter of procedural law*').

While there are authorities that suggest that the entitlement to interest is a matter governed by the substantive law of the contract and the interest rate is a matter governed by procedural law,[9] we consider that the Arbitration Ordinance is the law that applies to determining what the post-award interest should be. In any case, in light of the arbitral tribunal's broad discretion to award post-award interest under the Arbitration Ordinance, we consider that absent contrary agreement between the parties, arbitral tribunals have wide discretion to select the appropriate law (whether it is the substantive law or procedural law) in determining what the post-award interest should be.[10]

Nevertheless, in general, if the contract has specific provisions in relation to interest such as the interest rate, the substantive law of the contract is the law that applies to determining what the post-award interest should be. This is in line with section 79(2) of the Arbitration Ordinance which provides that the arbitral tribunal's authority to award interest under the Arbitration Ordinance '*does not affect any other power of an arbitral tribunal to award damages*'.

III DO THE COURTS TAKE INTO ACCOUNT INTERNATIONAL STANDARDS WHEN FACING CHALLENGES ON THE POST-AWARD INTEREST?

In accordance with the 1958 New York Convention and international standards, the Hong Kong courts adopt a pro-enforcement approach to arbitration. We are not aware of any cases in which the Hong Kong courts have considered international standards when faced with a challenge of an award for post-award interest.

IV SUBSTANTIVE LAW ISSUES

5. How Are Contractual Provisions on Late or Non-payment Interest Relevant to Post-award Interest? Will These Be Considered By the Arbitral Tribunal?

Yes, arbitral tribunals will consider the contractual provisions (if any) that impose interest rates in respect of late/non-payment when awarding post-award interest.

6. How Do the Procedural Rules of the Substantive Law Apply?

If parties choose Hong Kong as the seat of arbitration, the procedural rules of the substantive law (if they are not Hong Kong law) will not be applicable. This is because

9. Lord Collins of Mapesbury (ed.), *Dicey, Morris & Collins on the Conflict of Laws* (15th edn, Sweet & Maxwell 2012), at para. [7-098]: '*the existence of a right to claim interest is properly classified as a substantive matter and thus should be referred to the lex causae of the relevant claim.*'.

10. John Choong, Joseph Weeramantry (eds), *The Hong Kong Arbitration Ordinance: Commentary and Annotations* (Sweet and Maxwell 2015), at p. [452] (noting that '*[i]t is likely that in Hong Kong, the award on interest will be considered primary a matter of procedural law […] Since the issue of whether the award of interest is a matter of substance or procedure is not clear cut and since different jurisdictions may come to different conclusions, the governing law of the contract, the law of the place of enforcement of the award and the possibility of an award being rendered unenforceable in certain countries on the ground of public policy, should also be considered.*').

all matters of arbitration procedure will be determined by the Arbitration Ordinance and the applicable institutional rules.

7. Whether the Award of Interest Can Be Subjected to Public Policy Objections and if So, What Are They?

The terms of the 1958 New York Convention have largely been incorporated into the Arbitration Ordinance.[11] Accordingly, '*public policy*' is one of the grounds for refusing recognition and enforcement of international arbitral awards. In practice, the courts in Hong Kong seldom refuse to recognise and enforce foreign awards.

Granting post-award interest is not contrary to Hong Kong's public interest. Nevertheless, pursuant to section 46 of the Arbitration Ordinance, arbitral tribunals must exercise their discretion to award interest in a fair and impartial way. The purpose of an award of interest is not to punish the paying party but to compensate the aggrieved party for being kept out of the use of its money.[12]

V PROCEDURAL LAW ISSUES

8. What Are the Main Procedural Law Issues When Considering Post-award Interest? How Are the Arbitration Laws and Other Laws or Regulations of the Seat Relevant?

As explained above, arbitral tribunals enjoy wide discretion in awarding post-award interest in accordance with the Arbitration Ordinance and in the absence of party agreement on the issue of interest. If the arbitral award is silent on the issue of post-award interest, section 80 of the Arbitration Ordinance will apply. Therefore, as explained above, arbitral tribunals should explain to the parties the effect of section 80 of the Arbitration Ordinance as a matter of good practice.

If a party presents a claim for post-award interest but the arbitral tribunal fails to address it, a party may, unless otherwise agreed by the parties, request that the arbitral tribunal make an additional award addressing the claim for post-award interest within 30 days of the date of the award. If the arbitral tribunal considers the request justified, it shall make the additional award within 60 days.[13]

Finally, it should be noted that if the arbitral tribunal makes '*any errors in computation, any clerical or typographical errors or any errors of similar nature,*' each of the parties to the arbitration may submit a request to the arbitral tribunal to correct the award within 30 days of receipt of the award (unless another period of time has been agreed upon by the parties).[14] In addition, the arbitral tribunal is entitled to correct any mistakes on its own initiative within 30 days of the date of the award.

11. *See* the Arbitration Ordinance (Cap 609), sections 87-91.
12. John Choong, Joseph Weeramantry (eds), *The Hong Kong Arbitration Ordinance: Commentary and Annotations* (Sweet and Maxwell 2015), at p. [443] (noting that '*[a]lthough the tribunal is giving a wide discretion, it has an overall duty to act fairly and impartially as between the parties, pursuant to section 46 [of the Arbitration Ordinance]. The purpose of the award is not to punish the paying party [...].*').
13. The Arbitration Ordinance (Cap 609), section 69.
14. The Arbitration Ordinance (Cap 609), section 69.

VI EFFECT OF ENFORCEMENT ORDERS ON INTEREST ON THE AWARD ON BOTH THE SEAT AND ELSEWHERE

This question relates to the effect of enforcement of an award for interest by the Hong Kong court (both in relation to a local arbitral award and a foreign arbitral award).

Awards with orders on post-award interest can be enforced in accordance with section 84 of the Arbitration Ordinance. The successful party in arbitration may apply to the court for leave to enter judgment on the same terms as the award.[15] Once judgment has been obtained, the successful party may pursue the same enforcement measures as it may do for any court judgment.

In addition, the court has the power to enforce an order or direction made by an arbitral tribunal (whether inside or outside Hong Kong) in the same manner as an order or direction of the court, but only with the leave of the court.[16]

VII POWERS OF THE COURT TO ORDER OR ADJUST POST-AWARD INTEREST

9. Does the Hong Kong Court Have the Power to Order or Adjust the Post-award Interest, Assuming It Is Either the Seat Court or the Enforcing Court?

In accordance with the 1958 New York Convention, the Arbitration Ordinance does not confer authority on the courts to review the merits of any awards. The enforcement orders, if granted, are strictly based on the awards. We are not aware of any precedent in which revisions were made by a Hong Kong court to the post-award interest awarded by an arbitral tribunal. Nevertheless, an aggrieved party may apply to the court to set aside the award of interest under one of the prescribed grounds pursuant to section 81 of the Arbitration Ordinance.

Finally, as noted above, a party may, unless otherwise agreed, request that the arbitral tribunal make an additional award as to interest claims presented in the arbitral proceedings but omitted from the award in accordance with section 69 of the Arbitration Ordinance.

15. *See* the Arbitration Ordinance (Cap 609), section 84(2).
16. *See* the Arbitration Ordinance (Cap 609), section 61(1).

Japan

Hiroyuki Tezuka & Mihiro Koeda

INTRODUCTION

In Japan, post-award interest is considered to be a matter of substantive law and there is no distinction between pre- and post-award interest. Under Japanese substantive law, interest is categorized as a claim incidental to the principal claim and accrues when parties to a contract agree to it or there is an applicable statutory basis.

It should be noted that the applicable statutory interest rate may differ as a result of the amendment to the Japanese Civil Code (*the Civil Code*) depending on when the interest starts accruing. While parties are generally free to agree on a specific interest rate, it can be annulled by Japanese courts if it is considered to be contrary to public policy under Japanese law.

An award on interest can be enforced in Japan if it is explicitly awarded or an enforcing party explicitly makes a claim for an enforcement order regarding the interest that is to apply automatically under the law of the relevant jurisdiction. If the interest awarded in arbitration is excessive and unreasonably high, Japanese courts may not enforce the interest as a whole or in part. This is because it would be violative of the public policy of Japan, even though Japanese courts generally interpret the concept of "*public policy*" in the Japanese Arbitration Act narrowly.

Section I of this chapter further discusses the substantive law behind awarding interest in Japan. Section II discusses the choice of law rules to be applied when awarding post-award interest in a Japan-seated arbitration. Section III then examines the likelihood of Japanese courts considering international standards in the context of post-award interest. Sections IV and V of this chapter explore the actual substantive and procedural issues regarding awarding post-award interest. These include circumstances when an agreement concerning interest would be annulled and whether an award of interest triggers provisions in the Arbitration Act that warrant setting aside or denying enforcement of an arbitral award.

Section VI analyzes the binding effect of an arbitral award under the Arbitration Act by discussing the recognition of foreign judgments by Japanese courts. Finally, Section VII of this chapter examines the general absence of authority of a Japanese court to order or adjust post-award interest.

I POWER TO GRANT POST-AWARD INTEREST

1. Does an Arbitral Tribunal Have the Power to Grant Post-award Interest under Japanese Law?

No, as a matter of procedural law. The Japanese Arbitration Act is based on the pre-2006 United Nations Commission on International Trade (UNCITRAL) Model Law on International Commercial Arbitration ("*the UNCITRAL Model Law*").[1] There is no provision expressly providing the tribunal with the power to order a party to pay post-award interest. Likewise, the Commercial Arbitration Rules 2021 of the Japan Commercial Arbitration Association (*the JCAA*)[2] do not address the issue of post-award interest. Therefore, any issue regarding post-award interest would be addressed as an issue of substantive law when the seat of arbitration is in Japan.

2. Is the Power Exercisable Without a Request or Submission, or Is Such a Submission Required?

Legal Bases of Interest Accruing

Interest on a monetary claim is generally regarded as a substantive entitlement in Japan. A claim for interest is considered an "*incidental claim*," i.e., a claim incidental to the principal claim. As such, for the purpose of calculating the filing fees in Japanese litigation, the amount of the claim for interest will not be included in the total amount of the claim, which is the basis for such filing fees. On the contrary, in arbitrations under the JCAA Commercial Arbitration Rules 2021, the administrative fee that a claimant shall pay at the time of submitting a Request for Arbitration will be calculated based on the amount of the claim plus the amount of interest accruing for a period of one year from the date of submitting the Request for Arbitration.[3]

Interest accrues where contractual parties have agreed to it in a "*contract of interest*,"[4] or where there is any applicable statutory basis under Japanese law. In the latter case, interest shall accrue even if the parties have not agreed to it. The two statutory provisions (i) and (ii) below are typical examples of such statutory basis:

1. At the time of this chapter, a discussion to amend the Japanese Arbitration Act is underway to reflect the 2006 UNCITRAL Model Law amendment in the act.
2. The JCAA provides three sets of arbitration rules: the Commercial Arbitration Rules; the Interactive Arbitration Rules and the Administrative Rules for UNCITRAL Arbitration. Unless specifically indicated otherwise in arbitration agreements, parties to a JCAA arbitration are deemed to have agreed on the Commercial Arbitration Rules (Articles 3.1 and 3.2 of the Commercial Arbitration Rules 2021).
3. Article 103.3 of the JCAA Commercial Arbitration Rules 2021.
4. The contract of interest does not need to be a separate contract. It is usually stipulated as one of the clauses included in a main contract in practice.

(i) Monetary loans between "*Merchants*"[5] and payments for a third party by a Merchant give rise to interest without an agreement on interest under the following provision:

Article 513 of the Japanese Commercial Code (Claim to Interest)
(1) If money is lent between Merchants, the lender may claim statutory interest.
(2) If a Merchant pays money on behalf of another person within the scope of the Merchant's business, the Merchant may claim statutory interest for the period beginning on the date of the payment.

In principle, monetary loans are not accompanied by interest unless parties agree otherwise under the Civil Code. On the contrary, as stated above, monetary loans between "*Merchants*" give rise to interest unless parties agree otherwise.

(ii) Once an obligor is in default of its monetary obligation, interest will accrue as delay interest:

Article 419 of the (amended) Japanese Civil Code (Special Provisions for Monetary Debt)
(1) The amount of the damages for failure to perform any monetary obligation shall be determined with reference to the statutory interest rate as of the time when the obligor became liable for the delay; provided, however, that in cases where the agreed interest rate exceeds the statutory interest rate, the agreed interest rate shall prevail.
(2) The obligee shall not be required to prove his/her damages with respect to the damages set forth in the preceding paragraph.
(3) The obligor may not raise the defense of force majeure with respect to the damages referred to in paragraph (1).

Interest incidental to a principal monetary obligation (e.g., arising from a contract for loan), accruing on and before the due date for performance, and delay interest that is incidental to any monetary obligation, accruing after the due date for performance, are theoretically different from each other. The former accrues by reason of a contract for interest or pursuant to statutory provisions, such as Article 513(1) of the Commercial Code, as the consideration for the benefit that the obligor gains from the principal. The latter accrues by statute as compensation for damages arising from the non-performance of a principal monetary obligation by an obligor.

Interest Rate

(i) Amendment of the statutory interest rate.

As stated in Section IV below, an amendment of the Japanese Civil Code and other related laws was promulgated on June 2, 2017, and came into force on April 1, 2020. As a result, interest that starts accruing prior to the effective date of the amendment,

5. Article 4 Commercial Code provides the definition of "*Merchants*" as follows: "*(1) The term 'Merchant' as used in this Code means a person in the business of conducting commercial transactions in its own name. (2) A person in the business of selling goods at a store or other similar facility or a person engaged in the mining business is deemed to be a Merchant even if that person is not in the business of conducting commercial transactions.*"

i.e., April 1, 2020, is governed by the relevant provisions of the pre-amendment laws, whereas interest that starts accruing on or after the effective date is governed by the amended laws.[6] Even if April 1, 2020, has passed after the accrual of certain interest, the interest rate for that particular interest remains unchanged.

(ii) Statutory interest rates under the pre-amendment laws:

(a) Article 404 of the Civil Code provides that "*unless the parties indicate otherwise with respect to a claim which bears interest, the rate of such interest shall be five percent per annum;*" and

(b) Article 514 of the Commercial Code provides that "*the statutory interest rate applicable to obligations arising from commercial transactions is six percent per annum.*"

It should be noted that Article 514 of the Commercial Code applies to damages claims based on tort, where the alleged tort liability is based on the failure to perform a contractual obligation arising from a commercial transaction.[7]

(iii) Statutory interest rate under the amended law.

The amended Civil Code adopts a floating interest rate system, under which the statutory interest rate will be reviewed every three years.[8] In order to avoid discrepancies between the statutory rate and the market rate but also to maintain foreseeability and stability, adjusted interest rates will be calculated automatically, taking into account the average contract interest rates on loans and discounts published by the Bank of Japan.[9]

The statutory interest rate under the amended law starts from 3% per annum.[10] As the higher statutory rate for commercial transactions under Article 514 of the Commercial Code was abolished by the amendment, the statutory rate of 3% per annum applies to all interest that starts accruing on or after April 1, 2020, unless otherwise agreed by parties.

Under the floating interest rate system, the statutory interest rate in force at the time when certain interest starts accruing will apply. Even if the statutory interest rate is adjusted while that interest continues accruing, the applicable statutory interest rate will not be altered.

(iv) Interest rates in post-award interest.

Japanese law does not make a distinction between the interest rate before the award and the interest rate thereafter.

Parties to a contract are free to agree on rates for contractual interest and delay interest separately. The former is considered as a contract of interest, as stated above,

6. Articles 404(1) and 419(1) amended Civil Code (amended).
7. Supreme Court Judgment [May 25, 1972] 671 *Hanrei Jiho* 83.
8. Article 404(3) Civil Code (amended).
9. Article 404(5) Civil Code.
10. Article 404(2) Civil Code (amended).

while the latter is considered as agreed liquidated damages.[11] When parties have agreed only on a contractual interest rate, the obligee can claim delay interest at the higher rate of (i) the statutory rate and (ii) the contractually agreed rate.[12]

Accordingly, where the substantive applicable law governing the parties' underlying claims is Japanese law, a party may claim a flat rate of interest before and after an award, according to the statutory interest rates. Alternatively, a party may claim a fluctuating rate of interest such as "*post-award interest*" or a higher rate of interest than the statutory rate, where the contractual parties have agreed to it.

(v) Exceptional statutory interest rate

In addition to the above, Japanese law also sets an exceptionally higher statutory interest rate of 14.6% per annum for the delay interest that accrues when a business operator fails to pay the wages of its workers in order to encourage the smooth performance of such payments, as follows:

> Article 6(1) of the Act on Ensuring Wage Payment
>
> "In cases where a business operator fails to pay all or part of the wages (excluding retirement allowance ...) of a worker by the date of the worker's separation from employment ..., the business operator must pay the worker delay interest on unpaid wages... at the rate specified by Cabinet Order up to an annual rate of 14.6 percent for the number of days from the day following the date of the worker's separation from employment until the actual payment date." [The Cabinet Order specifies the rate as 14.6 per cent.]

Although the purpose of this provision is similar to that of post-award interest, this provision grants the worker a substantial right to interest that does not have any connection with a judgment or award.

Period of Time for Accrual of Interest

Some jurisdictions grant parties statutory interest, among others, after the judgment or award under a procedural rule in order to ensure the prompt realization of the rights and duties of the parties and to facilitate the settlement of disputes. However, Japanese law does not make such distinction between the interest before and after the award.

As a general rule, contractual interest accrues from the date on which the parties executed the contract for interest incidental to the principal contract until the date on which the obligor is to perform its obligation, unless the parties agree otherwise.[13] The interest will continue accruing until the full payment of the principal monetary obligation or until the obligor is in default. The same applies to the interest accruing pursuant to Article 513 of the Commercial Code.

The date from which the delay interest accrues differs depending on the due date of the principal obligation, as follows:

11. Article 420(1) Civil Code.
12. Article 419(1) Civil Code.
13. Supreme Court Judgment [June 6, 1958] 12 *Minshu* (9) 1373.

(a) Obligation under a contract with no provision setting forth the due date.

As a general rule, the obligee can claim the principal at any time. Delay interest accrues from the date following the claim made by the obligee.[14] However, Japanese law provides an exception for contracts for loans with no provision setting forth the due date. The due date in such contracts for loan arrives following the elapse of a "*reasonable period*" after the time when the demand by the obligee is made to the obligor.[15] The length of the "*reasonable period*" is examined on a case-by-case basis. Delay interest hereunder accrues from the date following such due date.

(b) Obligation under a contract with a specified due date.

An obligee can claim the delay interest from the date following the due date.[16]

(c) Obligation under a contract with an unspecified due date.

An obligee can claim the delay interest from the date following the date on which the obligor receives a request for performance after the due date arrives or the date on which the obligor becomes aware of the arrival of the due date, whichever comes earlier.[17]

(d) Obligation arising from tort.

Although no due date is provided for such obligation, it is accepted, as an exception to item (a) above, that the delay interest accrues from the date on which the damage arose.[18]

Delay interest accrues until the obligor performs its obligation consistent with the purpose of this obligation sufficiently.

Simple Interest in Principle

Unlike some other jurisdictions, Japanese law does not restrict compound interest itself. However, compound interest would be restricted under the substantive law stated in Section IV, Question 7 below, if the obligation becomes too onerous for the obligor.

Statutory interest is provided as a simple interest in general. However, there is an exceptional provision, which grants an obligee the option to incorporate the interest into the principal only in a specified situation as follows:

14. Article 412(3) Civil Code.
15. Article 591(1) Civil Code. The Article provides that an obligee may demand the return payment, specifying the reasonable period. If the obligee does not specify any period or if the period specified by the obligee cannot be deemed to be reasonable, the due date will arrive following the elapse of the period that is objectively considered to be reasonable (Supreme Court Judgment [January 29, 1930] 9 *Dai-Minshu* 97).
16. Article 412(1) Civil Code.
17. Article 412(2) Civil Code (amended).
18. Supreme Court Judgment [September 4, 1962] 16 *Minshu* (9) 1834.

Article 405 of the Civil Code (Incorporation of Interest into Principal)

In cases where the payment of interest corresponding to one year or more is delayed, and if the obligor does not pay such interest notwithstanding the demand by the obligee, the obligee may incorporate such interest into the principal.

3. Is the Power Classified as One under the Substantive Applicable Law or the Procedural Law of the Arbitration?

As stated above, Japanese law provides interest as a substantive entitlement. Under Japanese law, interest accrues incidentally subject to the parties' agreement or certain provisions of substantive law. An obligee can claim interest from the time agreed by the parties or from the time provided under substantive law, until the obligor performs its obligation consistently with the purpose of such obligation sufficiently. The period of time for the accrual of interest is not related to the judgment or award. Japanese law provides for a flat interest rate unless the parties agree otherwise.

II CHOICE OF LAW

4. What is the Law That Applies to Determining What the Post-award Interest Should Be? Would This Be the Governing Law of the Dispute or the Law of the Seat?

As stated above, Japanese law does not provide for interest through procedural rules but essentially as a matter of substantive right that is incidental to the principal right. Thus, Japanese law considers the matters of interest as issues relating to the effect of a substantive right.

As interest is incidental to the principal obligation, it is categorized as one of the effects of the principal obligation; therefore, it is generally governed by the law applicable to the principal obligation.

Applicable Provisions in the Japanese Arbitration Act

The Japanese Arbitration Act provides as follows:

Article 36 of the Arbitration Act (Substantive Law to be Applied in Arbitral Award)

(1) The law with which the Arbitral Tribunal should comply in making an Arbitral Award shall be as provided by the agreement of the parties. In this case, if the laws and regulations of a given State have been designated, such designation shall be deemed as designating the laws and regulations of the State that shall be directly applied to the case and not the laws and regulations of the State providing the application of conflicting domestic and foreign laws and regulations, unless a contrary intention has been clearly indicated.

(2) If no agreement set forth in the preceding paragraph has been reached, the Arbitral Tribunal shall apply the laws and regulations of a State that has the closest relationship to the civil dispute referred to the arbitration procedure and which should be directly applied to the case.

(3) Notwithstanding the provisions of the preceding two paragraphs, if a clearly indicated request has been made by both of the parties, the Arbitral Tribunal shall decide ex aequo et bono.

> (4) The Arbitral Tribunal shall decide in accordance with the terms of the contract pertaining to the civil dispute that has been referred to the arbitral procedure, if such contract exists, and shall take into account the usages applicable to the relevant civil dispute, if any such usage exists.

As mentioned above, the Japanese Arbitration Act is based on the pre-2006 UNCITRAL Model Law. However, the Japanese Arbitration Act provides that the substantive law of the state that is most closely connected to the case applies directly to the dispute, as in the arbitration acts of Germany and Korea. This is different from the UNCITRAL Model Law, under which, the arbitral tribunal first chooses the appropriate conflict-of-laws principles and then applies the substantive law according to the determination reached by reference to such conflict-of-laws principles.

III DO THE COURTS TAKE INTO ACCOUNT INTERNATIONAL STANDARDS WHEN FACING CHALLENGES ON THE POST-AWARD INTEREST?

As the Japanese Arbitration Act is based on the UNCITRAL Model Law, Japanese courts are likely to take into consideration international standards (if any) on the interpretation of the UNCITRAL Model Law prevailing in UNCITRAL Model Law jurisdictions.

Japanese courts would thus interpret grounds to set aside or not enforce arbitral awards narrowly in accordance with the international standard among other pro-arbitration countries adopting the UNCITRAL Model Law.

The issue of post-award interest is considered to be a matter of substantive law in Japan, as mentioned above. Under the New York Convention and the Japanese Arbitration Act, which is based on the UNCITRAL Model Law, Japanese courts only examine whether arbitral awards are enforceable as they are or whether they should be set aside, and the courts do not alter the entitlements granted therein nor give additional entitlements.

From this perspective, Japanese courts likely do not consider international standards (if any) to alter or supplement the parties' entitlement to post-award interest.

In the context of enforcement or setting aside arbitral awards, Japanese courts may consider international standards (if any) in interpreting the New York Convention or the Japanese Arbitration Act to the extent appropriate.

IV SUBSTANTIVE LAW ISSUES

5. How Are Contractual Provisions on Late or Non-payment Interest Relevant to Post-award Interest? Will These Be Considered by the Arbitral Tribunal?

Japanese law does not make a distinction between the interest before the award and the interest thereafter. If the parties simply agree on an interest rate without specifying the scope of application, it will apply throughout the period when the interest accrues.

In accordance with the freedom of contract, parties to a contract are free to agree on an interest rate applicable to the post-award interest separately from the interest rate to apply beforehand.

6. How Do the Procedural Rules of the Substantive Law Apply?

As mentioned in Section I, Question 1 above, any issue regarding post-award interest would be addressed as an issue of substantive law when the seat of arbitration is in Japan. Procedural issues relating to the post-award interest are addressed in Section V below.

7. Whether the Award of Interest Can Be Subjected to Public Policy Objection, and if so, What Are They?

Given that the parties are generally free to agree on the interest, including on the interest rate and the timing of the interest accruing, setting post-award interest itself is not contrary to public policy under Japanese law. However, agreements concerning interest would be annulled in the following circumstances as a matter of Japanese substantive law:

(a) When a contract is deemed to be excessive profiteering or where a party has taken advantage of the other party's ignorance, lack of comprehension or financial difficulties, such contract shall be contrary to public policy[19] and be partly invalid, or wholly invalid in serious cases. Under Japanese law, however, the public policy objections would be granted only in exceptional cases.
(b) Regarding contracts for monetary loans, the Interest Rate Restriction Act sets forth the upper limits on the interest rates for interest before due date and for delayed interest separately. The maximum interest rate that can be agreed by parties differs depending on the amount of the principal monetary loan. If the amount of a principal monetary loan is Japanese Yen (JPY) one million or more, the maximum interest rate for interest before a due date is 15% per annum,[20] while 21.9% per annum for delayed interest.[21] If the principal loan has been provided by the creditor in its regular business, the upper limit of 20% per annum applies instead of 21.9% per annum, in terms of delay interest.[22] Even if parties agree on interest rates higher than the maximum interest rates, excess interest is deemed to be invalid.

In cases where the content of an arbitral award contradicts these rules and regulations above, the public policy considerations under the Arbitration Act that may be applied in the context of examining the grounds for setting aside or refusing enforcement of the arbitral award, as mentioned at the end of this chapter, may become an issue.

19. Article 90 Civil Code.
20. Article 1(iii) Interest Rate Restriction Act.
21. Article 4(1) Interest Rate Restriction Act.
22. Article 7(1) Interest Rate Restriction Act.

Amendment of the Civil Code

As a result of public discussions over recent years in Japan, the amendment of the Japanese Civil Code and other related laws was promulgated on June 2, 2017, which came into force on April 1, 2020. Although this amendment mainly focuses on reflecting the development of the case precedents in the law of obligations, it includes a notable statutory interest-rate change. As discussed above, the amendment has lowered the statutory interest rate to 3% and introduced a mechanism for reviewing the statutory interest rate, according to economic circumstances, every three years.

Since the amended Civil Code came into force, it has been important to stipulate interest rates in contracts due to the lower statutory interest rate. In addition to this, the amendment affects claims arising from tort or unjust enrichment, as the statutory interest rate would inevitably apply to them.

V PROCEDURAL LAW ISSUES

8. What Are the Main Procedural Law Issues When Considering Post-award Interest? How Are the Arbitration Laws and Other Laws or Regulations of the Seat Relevant?

As mentioned above, the Japanese Arbitration Act does not explicitly address the issue of interest. Given that interest is regarded as a substantive entitlement in Japan, issues regarding interest are subject to the following procedural rules:

(a) Article 44(1)(v) of the Arbitration Act sets forth the ground for setting aside an arbitral award where "the Arbitral Award contains a decision on matters beyond the scope of the Arbitration Agreement or of the petition presented in the arbitration procedure," which corresponds to Article 34(2)(a)(iii) of the UNCITRAL Model Law.

(b) Article 45(2)(v) of the Arbitration Act provides grounds for a Japanese court to deny enforcement of an arbitral award where "*the Arbitral Award contains a decision on matters beyond the scope of the Arbitration Agreement or of a petition in the arbitration procedure,*" which corresponds to Article 36(1)(a)(iii) of the UNCITRAL Model Law and Article V(1)(c) of the New York Convention.

According to the above provisions, an arbitral tribunal may be inclined not to award interest unless a party claims the same in order not to jeopardize the legitimacy of the award.

Therefore, a claimant would have to explicitly claim and establish the right to interest. For example, in a case where the principal claim is based on a contract with no provision setting forth the duration, the claimant may claim interest as of the day following the counterparty's receipt of the notice of Request for Arbitration. This is the usual approach under Japanese law as this is the date evident to the arbitral tribunal from which the claimant explicitly makes a claim and is a prerequisite for interest accruing in such a case as mentioned in Section I Question 2 above. Thus, an arbitral tribunal seated in Japan may not render an award including interest unless the claimant explicitly claims the same, even if the applicable substantive law is the law of a state that has procedural rules that enable the parties to enforce interest not based on the parties' explicit claims or wording of the award, since the procedural rules of the arbitration are governed by the law of the seat of arbitration.

As to the conduct of arbitral proceedings, the old arbitration law in Japan, based on nineteenth-century German law, had a provision that granted an arbitral tribunal a broad discretion to examine and decide any matters relating to the case without any allegations from the parties. That provision has been deleted from the Arbitration Act, which came into force in 2004, to afford the parties more autonomy and responsibility in the conduct of the arbitration proceedings.

The Arbitration Act also respects due process. It provides the following grounds for setting aside and not enforcing arbitral awards in order to prevent the parties from suffering as a result of unexpected decisions:

> Article 44 of the Arbitration Act (Setting Aside of Arbitral Award)
> "(1) If any of the following grounds exist, the parties may file a petition with the court to set aside the Arbitral Award: ...
> (iv) the petitioner was unable to defend itself properly in the arbitration procedure"
>
> Article 45 of the Arbitration Act (Recognition of Arbitral Award)
> "(2) The preceding paragraph [the provision empowering the court to recognize arbitral awards] shall not apply if any of the following gounds exist (regarding the grounds set forth in items (i) to (vii), limited to the case where any of the parties has proved the existence of the grounds): ...
> (iv) the party was unable to defend itself properly in the arbitration procedure"

Thus, under the Japanese Arbitration Act, an arbitral tribunal would neither be able to examine evidence that is not adduced by the parties, find facts contrary to those agreed by the parties nor find facts that are not alleged by either party, as such conducted by the arbitral tribunal may unjustifiably harm the parties' autonomy and the rights to be heard.

VI EFFECT OF ENFORCEMENT ORDERS ON INTEREST ON THE AWARD ON BOTH THE SEAT AND ELSEWHERE

Introduction for Legal Analysis

Regarding the recognition and enforcement of arbitral awards, the Arbitration Act provides as follows:

> Article 45 of the Arbitration Act (Recognition of Arbitral Award)
>
> *(1)* An Arbitral Award (irrespective of whether or not the place of arbitration is in Japan; hereinafter the same shall apply in this Chapter) shall have the same effect as a final and binding judgment; provided, however, that a civil execution based on said Arbitral Award requires an execution order under the provisions of the following Article.

As there are a relatively larger number of Japanese court precedents regarding the enforcement of foreign judgments compared to those regarding arbitral awards, court precedents on the enforcement of foreign judgments in Japan may be referred to as helpful guidance in analyzing the effect of enforcement of arbitral awards. Therefore, they are also discussed in detail below.

Legal Effect of "Enforcement" Orders By Japanese Courts

There is a notable judgment rendered by the Supreme Court, which dealt with the issue regarding the enforcement of interest incidental to a foreign judgment ("*the Mansei Kogyo Judgment*").[23] It states that "*to recognize the effect of the judgment of a foreign court in Japan is to recognize the effect that the very same judgment has in the relevant jurisdiction.*"

What if Post-award Interest is Not Explicitly Stated in the Award?

It is evident from the aforementioned statement that if an arbitral award explicitly mentioning post-award interest is recognized in an enforcement order, the claimant may enforce it as a whole in the same way as the court decision in Japan.

If post-award interest is not expressly ordered in the foreign arbitral award on its face but is to apply automatically under the law in the relevant jurisdiction, the claimant would be able to obtain an enforcement order to enforce the award including the interest, as was held in the Mansei Kogyo Judgment. The Supreme Court held in the judgment that "*according to the law of the State of California, the interest in question is to accrue in connection with the sum of money ordered to be paid by the judgment and is to be enforceable as such. Therefore, the original judgment...should be affirmed in that it granted the enforcement of part of the Foreign Judgment, which ordered the payment of the interest in question....*" Although the court did not specify the statutory provision that is the legal basis for post-award interest accruing, the above conclusion would not change regardless of whether its legal basis is a substantive or procedural rule. If the legal basis requires that the interest applies despite the parties' allegations, a Japanese court would interpret from the purpose of the relevant applicable rules that the award simply omitted the wording of the interest because it is not necessary for it to be explicitly stated.

It should be noted, however, that the party cannot execute an enforcement of interest that is incidental to but not explicitly stated in the award, unless it explicitly makes a claim for an enforcement order including the interest to the enforcing court. The interest needs to be explicitly granted in the execution order, as the executive agency under Japanese law does not have the power to execute any enforcement beyond the wording of the execution order.

23. Supreme Court Judgment [July 11, 1997] 51 *Minshu* (6) 2530. There is another Supreme Court Judgment on the same date, arising from the same judgment of the court of prior instance, by which the Supreme Court held that punitive damages rendered by a foreign court are contrary to public policy in Japan and thus not enforceable (Supreme Court Judgment [July 11, 1997] 51 *Minshu* (6) 2573).

VII POWERS OF THE COURT TO ORDER OR ADJUST POST-AWARD INTEREST

9. Does the Japanese Court Have the Power to Order or Adjust Post-award Interest, Assuming It is Either the Seat Court or the Enforcing Court?

The enforcing court in Japan in principle does not have the power to order post-award interest that was not awarded in the arbitral award. Provided, however, that as discussed in Section VI above, it may order post-award interest that is not expressly stated in the arbitral award but the claimant is entitled to claim under the law applicable to the award, so long as the claimant asks for such post-award interest to be included in the enforcement order as stated above.

There are no provisions that empower the enforcing court to adjust post-award interest rendered in an arbitral award. Although the enforcing court cannot adjust post-award interest, it may achieve the same purpose to some extent by specifying the portion in which the court partly does not recognize the award in the enforcement order, on the grounds that the portion of the award ordering payment of the interest is contrary to public policy under the Japanese Arbitration Act. The relevant provision of the Arbitration Act is as follows:

> Article 45 of the Arbitration Act (Recognition of Arbitral Award)
> (2) The preceding paragraph [the provision empowering the court to recognize arbitral awards] shall not apply if any of the following grounds exist (regarding the grounds set forth in items (i) to (vii), limited to the case where any of the parties has proved the existence of the grounds): ...
> (ix) the content of the Arbitral Award is contrary to public policy in Japan.

Potential Risk of Post-award Interest Not Being Recognized

Similar to courts in other pro-arbitration countries, Japanese courts generally interpret the concept of "public policy" in the Arbitration Act narrowly. For example, a judgment or an arbitral award ordering punitive damages would be considered to violate public policy in Japan.[24] Except for this typical example, however, no concrete criteria have been established, and the decisions of the courts do not seem to always follow the same trend. It seems that the courts generally consider whether the arbitral award is contrary to a fundamental policy under Japanese law by considering the relevant circumstances in the particular case.

24. Supreme Court Judgment [July 11, 1997] 51 *Minshu* (6) 2573.

Malaysia

Sharon Chong & Nimalan Devaraja

INTRODUCTION

In Malaysia, the legislature has vested the arbitral tribunals with statutory power to award both pre- and post-award interests pursuant to section 33(6) of the Malaysian Arbitration Act, 2005 (*the Act*). This wide power extends to the determination of whether the interest awarded should be simple or compound, the rate of interest and the time period for which the interest should accrue, so long as the time period does not extend beyond the date of payment. This power is given to arbitral tribunals sitting in both domestic and international arbitrations.

The power to grant interest on an award rests solely within the discretion of the arbitral tribunal, save for any agreement between the parties. Parties have the freedom to contractually agree on matters relating to the payment of interest and the various relevant factors (such as interest rate), and the arbitral tribunal is bound to follow it. Similarly, parties may also agree on the extent of the arbitral tribunal's powers to award interest and may even expressly exclude it, thereby limiting the arbitral tribunal's discretion.

The ambit of intervention by the courts is minimal. The courts would generally be reluctant to reverse, vary or adjust interest ordered by the arbitral tribunal. Given that the Malaysian Courts are empowered to award interest in cases before them, it is highly unlikely that the courts would interfere with interest orders in arbitral awards on the grounds of public policy. The only exception may be where the decision is found to be contrary to the parties' agreement under the contract.

In cases where the arbitral tribunal does not expressly make a ruling on interest, the default position in Malaysia is that post-award interest would apply at the same rate as a judgment debt (which is 5% per annum presently). It must be mentioned here that there is no requirement for a request or application for interest to be made by the parties to an arbitral tribunal before it can exercise its power to award the same.

Section I of this chapter begins with an explanation of an arbitral tribunal's express statutory authority to order post-award interest under the Act and the implications of this power. Sections II and III discuss the consideration of post-award interest by Malaysian Courts as a matter of procedural law and the likelihood of adopting international standards when applicable.

Sections IV and V of this chapter discuss substantive and procedural issues associated with granting interest in an arbitral award in greater detail. Regarding substantive law issues, this includes the aforementioned freedom of arbitral tribunals to award interest. Procedural issues focus mainly on the limitations of correcting or applying for an additional arbitral award, applying for an additional award when an arbitral tribunal fails to address interest in the arbitral award and the time limitation for setting aside an arbitral award in Malaysia.

Section VI briefly explains the effect of enforcement orders on the interest of arbitral awards in Malaysia. Section VII of this chapter discusses the likely absence of an enforcement court's authority to adjust post-award interest while Section VIII and final part once again explains the considerable authority of the enforcement court to determine the interest rate it considers appropriate… .

I POWER TO GRANT POST-AWARD INTEREST

1. Does an Arbitral Tribunal Have The Power to Grant Post-award Interest under Malaysian Law?

In arbitration, it is accepted that the successful party is entitled to have included in the arbitral award an amount in respect of interest on the principal sum awarded in his favour. This is enshrined in section 33(6) of the Act.

At the outset, it should be made clear that section 33(6) of the Act applies to both domestic and international arbitrations seated in Malaysia. *'Domestic arbitration'* is defined to mean any arbitration which is not international arbitration. *'International arbitration'*[1] is in turn defined as an arbitration where (i) one of the parties to an arbitration agreement, at the time of the conclusion of that agreement, has its place of business in any State other than Malaysia; (ii) either the seat of arbitration or the place where a substantial part of the obligations of the commercial or other relationship is to be performed or the place with which the subject matter of the dispute is most closely connected, is situated in any State other than Malaysia in which the parties have their places of business; or (iii) the parties have expressly agreed that the subject matter of the arbitration agreement relates to more than one State.

Pursuant to section 33(6) of the Act, the arbitral tribunal is, unless otherwise agreed by the parties, vested with the power to award simple or compound interest

1. This definition was adopted from Article 1(3) of the UNCITRAL Model Law on International Commercial Arbitration.

from such date, at such rate as the arbitral tribunal considers appropriate of the whole or any part of:

(i) Any sum awarded by the arbitral tribunal in the arbitral proceedings.
(ii) Any sum in issue in the arbitral proceedings but is paid before the date of the award.
(iii) Costs awarded or ordered by the arbitral tribunal in the arbitral proceedings.

This provision was inserted into the Act through an amendment,[2] which came into force on 8 May 2018. Following the amendment, the Act expressly confers the power on the arbitral tribunal to grant interest for '*any period*' ending no later than the date of payment. This means that an arbitral tribunal now has the statutory power to grant both pre- and post-award interest. These provisions are analogous to the relevant statutory provisions in Singapore and Hong Kong.

This amendment was introduced to address the Federal Court's decision in *Far East Holdings Bhd & Anor v. Majlis Ugama Islam Dan Adat Resam Melayu Pahang and other appeals* ('*Far East Holdings Bhd*')[3] where it was held that '*[u]nless otherwise provided in the arbitration agreement, an arbitrator could only award post-award interest*'. The Federal Court's decision had departed from the previous decisions held by the Malaysian Courts in, among others, *Leong Kum Whay v. QBE Insurance (M) Sdn Bhd* (Court of Appeal)[4] and *Raja Lope & Tan Co v. Malayan Flour Mills Bhd* (High Court)[5] (both decided under the now-repealed Arbitration Act 1952) which held that the arbitral tribunal possesses the same powers as those of a court to award pre-award interest.

In that case, the Federal Court held that the (pre-amended) Arbitration Act 2005 (applicable at that time) did not contemplate granting pre-award interest unless provided in the arbitration agreement, and, thus, it could not be awarded by the arbitral tribunal as there was no indication that the parties had agreed on pre-award interest in the arbitration agreement. *Far East Holdings Bhd* was followed by the High Court in *Tasja Sdn Bhd v. Kementerian Kesihatan Malaysia*,[6] where it was held that, by virtue of the doctrine of *stare decisis*, the High Court was bound by the Federal Court decision and the arbitrator did not have the power to grant pre-award interest.

At present, there are no pronouncements by the courts on the factors or elements which the arbitral tribunals must take into account when deciding whether to award interest. In the absence of parties' agreement, the matter is at the full discretion of the arbitral tribunal. However, it should be noted that when deciding to grant pre-award interest and/or post-award interest beyond the interest rate of a judgment debt (as

2. Arbitration (Amendment) (No. 2) Act 2018.
3. [2018] 1 MLJ 1 at p. [187].
4. [2006] 1 CLJ 1.
5. [2000] 6 CLJ 194.
6. [2018] 8 CLJ 652; [2018] 10 MLJ 277.

provided for under section 33(8) of the Act discussed below), the arbitral tribunal should provide their reasons for doing so in the arbitral award.[7]

Further, section 33(8) of the Act states that when an award directs a sum to be paid, that sum shall, unless the award otherwise directs, carry interest from the date of the award and at the same rate as a judgment debt.[8] This, therefore, has the effect of ensuring that all arbitral awards would carry post-award interest unless otherwise ordered.

Lastly, as there is presently no guidance from the Malaysian Courts as to the threshold to be met to exclude the applicability of section 33(6) of the Act to an arbitral dispute, the authors suggest that clear and express wording stating the parties' intention to exclude the applicability of section 33(6) and/or (8) of the Act from the arbitral dispute be used in the arbitration agreement. Alternatively, the parties' intention may also be ascertained through their agreement to adopt certain institutional arbitration, pursuant to section 2(2)(c) of the Act.

2. Is the Power Exercisable Without a Request or Submission, or Is Such a Submission Required?

Section 33(6) of the Act which gives an arbitral tribunal the power to grant post-award interest does not expressly require a request or submission to be made as a condition to the exercise of that power. In fact, the newly inserted section 33(8) of the Act provides that all sums directed to be paid in an award shall carry post-award interest (unless the award otherwise directs) from the date of the award, at the same interest rate as a judgment debt.

On this point, it is worth noting that the Federal Court in *Far East Holdings Bhd* had upheld the setting aside of, among other things, post-award interest awarded by the arbitrator (under the now-repealed section 42 of the Act '*reference on the question of law*') on the ground that post-award interest was not pleaded in the case. The Federal Court also opined that '*it would not seem fair that the discretion to award interest should be exercised in favour of post-award interest*'.[9]

In light of the wording in section 33(8) of the Act, it is arguable that post-award interest is no longer required to be specifically pleaded. The arbitral tribunal has the discretion to award post-award interest (whether simple or compound) and at any rate, as the arbitral tribunal considers appropriate.[10] However, if it does not exercise this discretion, any sum awarded would automatically carry post-award interest at the same rate as a judgment debt unless directed otherwise by the arbitral tribunal.

---

7. *JY Creative Sdn Bhd v. Meacs Construction Sdn Bhd and Another Case* [2022] 1 LNS 945, where Lim Chong Fong J in dealing, among others, with a complaint that an arbitrator had failed to provide reasons for allowing pre-award interest, opined that '*the court will use its best endeavours to comprehend the award contextually and purposively and not be overzealous to condemn the award*'.
8. As determined under section 11 of the Civil Law Act 1956 and Order 42 Rule 12 of the Rules of Court 2012.
9. Federal Court decision of *Far East Holdings Bhd & Anor v. Majlis Ugama Islam Dan Adat Resam Melayu Pahang and other appeals* [2018] 1 MLJ 1, ('*Far East Holdings*') at p. [187].
10. Pursuant to section 33(6) of the Act.

As such, even if post-award interest is not pleaded by the parties or considered by the arbitral tribunal in the arbitration proceedings, the sums awarded would nonetheless carry post-award interest at the same rate as a judgment debt. However, a claim for pre-award interest should be expressly pleaded for by the parties.

3. Is the Power Classified As One under the Substantive Applicable Law or the Procedural Law of the Arbitration?

While there has been no definitive pronouncement on this question by the Malaysian Courts, it is suggested by the authors that the power of the arbitral tribunal to award post-award interest is to be regarded as a matter governed by the procedural law of the arbitration (i.e., the law of the arbitration), subject to contrary agreement, as it is that law which is generally regarded as having the closest connection to the question of the arbitral tribunal's powers.[11]

However, this must be contrasted with the rights of parties to contractual interest, which will be governed by the applicable substantive law.

II CHOICE OF LAW

4. What Is the Law That Applies to Determine What the Post-award Interest Should Be? Would This Be the Governing Law of the Dispute or the Law of the Seat?

As set out under Question 3 above, while there has been no definitive pronouncement on this question by the Malaysian Courts, it appears that the Malaysian Courts have considered the issue of post-award interest under the procedural law of the arbitration.

III DO THE COURTS TAKE INTO ACCOUNT INTERNATIONAL STANDARDS WHEN FACING CHALLENGES ON THE POST-AWARD INTEREST?

There are no pronouncements or deliberations by the Malaysian Courts on this issue. However, the Malaysian Courts will likely consider and adopt international standards if the Malaysian Courts draw guidance from persuasive authorities pronounced in Model Law countries, where applicable. In *Far East Holdings*, the Federal Court considered the positions in other countries, such as the United Kingdom, Singapore, Australia, New Zealand and Canada, but concluded that they were not applicable in that case.

11. Gary Born, *International Commercial Arbitration* (2nd edn, Kluwer Law International 2014) at §23.09[B]; and *Lesotho Highlands Development Authority v. Impregilo SpA and others* [2005] 3 All ER 789, where the House of Lords held that the arbitral tribunal had the power to award pre-award interest under the law of the seat of the arbitration.

IV SUBSTANTIVE LAW ISSUES

5. How Are Contractual Provisions on Late or Non-payment of Interest Relevant to Post-award Interest? Will These Be Considered By the Arbitral Tribunal?

Parties have the freedom to agree contractually on late or non-payment of interest. Parties can also reach an agreement on the applicable rate of interest, application of simple or compound interest, etc. Where the underlying contract between the parties includes provisions concerning contractual interest, the arbitral tribunal must give effect to that agreement.[12] The applicability of the contractual provisions on late or non-payment of interest will be governed by the substantive law of the contract.

Further, parties are also at liberty to agree on not only the extent of the arbitral tribunal's powers to grant post-award interest but the rate of interest as well. Considering that section 33(6) of the Act contains the phrase '*unless otherwise agreed by the parties*', the arbitral tribunal will arguably not have the discretion to award interest if parties agree to exclude the power of the tribunal to grant interest. Similarly, the parties are also at liberty to agree on the interest rate.

6. How Do the Procedural Rules of the Substantive Law Apply?

As explained under Questions 3 and 4 above, the power to grant post-award interest is best regarded as a matter for the procedural law of the arbitration, i.e., the arbitration agreement. Hence, it may be unlikely for the procedural rules of the substantive law of the contract to be applicable in determining whether the arbitral tribunal has the power to order pre-award or post-award interest.

7. Whether the Award of Interest Can Be Subjected to Public Policy Objections and if So, What Are They?

There has been no pronouncement or deliberation by the Malaysian Courts on this issue. However, it is unlikely that the grant of interest in awards would be successfully challenged on the grounds of public policy in Malaysia, as the Malaysian Courts are themselves empowered to award interest in cases before them. This is in addition to the fact that arbitral tribunals are empowered under the Act to make awards of interest.

In Malaysia, two sets of laws co-exist: the common law and Syariah law. Further, Malaysia has a dual court structure. The Syariah Court has limited jurisdiction only over Muslims in matters of family law and religious observances. While the award of interest is prohibited under Syariah law, it is not prohibited by Malaysia's common law legal system.

Arbitration matters clearly fall within the jurisdiction of the common law courts, and any arbitration-related court proceedings must be filed at the High Court in Malaya or the High Court in Sabah and Sarawak. Therefore, any challenge against the award of interest in Malaysia on the public policy ground would likely fail.

12. Sundra Rajoo, *UNCITRAL Model Law & Arbitration Rules, The Arbitration Act 2005* (1st edn, Sweet & Maxwell 2007) and the *Asian International Arbitration Centre (AIAC) Arbitration Rules 2018* (1st edn, Sweet & Maxwell 2019) at p. [33.77].

In cases on registration of foreign judgments for gambling debts (where under Malaysian law, gaming or wagering agreements are null and void),[13] the Malaysian Courts have drawn a distinction between a case where a party commences legal proceedings in Malaysia based on a cause of action that is founded on a gaming debt and one that involves the registration and enforcement of foreign judgments obtained with respect to a gaming debt.

The High Court in *Resorts World At Sentosa Pte Ltd v. Lim Soo Kok* (affirmed on appeal by the Court of Appeal)[14] held that where a gaming transaction is lawful in the foreign country from where the judgment originates, the registration of the foreign judgment is not against the public policy of Malaysia. The High Court further observed that the judgment creditor was not filing a civil suit to enforce the gaming debt. Instead, the judgment creditor was availing itself to the right of reciprocity of registering a valid and lawful judgment of a foreign court as expressly provided under Reciprocal Enforcement of Judgement Act (REJA), which should be allowed. Similarly, the High Court in *Wynn Resorts (Macau) S.A. v. Poh Yang Hong* [2019] 1 LNS)2323 (affirmed on appeal by the Court of Appeal), held that credit agreements entered to enable a party to gamble at a casino is equally not contrary to Malaysian public policy. The Learned High Court Judge also opined that as Malaysia allows for legalised betting, gaming and gambling activities to take place and collects tax revenue from the same, it cannot be said that legal action for recovery of amounts outstanding under gaming credit facilities is against the public policy of Malaysia.

V PROCEDURAL LAW ISSUES

8. What Are the Main Procedural Law Issues When Considering Post-award Interest? How Are the Arbitration Laws and Other Laws or Regulations of the Seat Relevant?

The procedural law applicable when considering post-award interest is the Act. Where Malaysia is the seat of the arbitration, parties should familiarise themselves with the general avenues of recourse open to them under the Act.

First, section 35 of the Act allows a party to request the arbitral tribunal to correct any error in computation, any clerical or typographical error or other error of similar nature in the award, or to give an interpretation of a specific point or part of the award. Any party seeking to avail the benefits of section 35 must make a request to the arbitral tribunal within 30 days of the receipt of the award[15] and must notify the other party of the same. In case a party requests the tribunal to provide an interpretation of a specific point or part of the award, the agreement of the other party must be procured. The

13. Section 26 of the Civil Law Act 1956 and section 31 of the Contracts Act 1950.
14. [2017] 1 CLJ 363.
15. Under section 35(3) of the Act, the arbitral tribunal has the power to extend the period within which it makes a correction where it thinks it is necessary. In the English High Court case of *Xstrata Coal Queensland Pty Ltd v. Benxi Iron & Steel (Group) International Economic & Trading Co Ltd* [2016] EWHC 2022 (Comm), it was held that a court may even grant a retroactive extension of time to enable arbitral tribunal to correct an ambiguity in the award. In this case, the said extension of time was given six years after the date of the award publication.

arbitral tribunal may also correct any computational, clerical or typographical errors on its own initiative within 30 days of the date of the award.

However, the power conferred by section 35 of the Act is rigidly limited to mere clerical mistakes or errors arising from any accidental slip or omission.[16] Therefore, if the error in the award is an error in the expression of the arbitral tribunal's thoughts, the award can be corrected as a clerical error.

However, if it is an error in the arbitral tribunal's thinking itself, it cannot be corrected.[17] The issue of whether the absence of post-award interest can be corrected under section 35 of the Act depends upon the explanation of the arbitral tribunal for its non-inclusion. An example where a failure to award interest was considered a suitable oversight to fall within the rule is the English Court of Appeal case of *Pancommerce SA v. Veecheema BV*.[18] However, the Court of Appeal for British Columbia in *McKechnie v. McKechnie*[19] did not allow a correction under this rule when the tribunal had awarded compound interest, though it meant to award simple interest, on the basis that the determination in the initial instance to use compound interest did not run afoul of the applicable Act. Therefore, the arbitrator could not change the arbitral award subsequently at a party's instruction.

Second, if the arbitral tribunal fails to deal with the issue of interest in its award, despite it being claimed for, a party may (unless otherwise agreed by the parties) request the arbitral tribunal under section 35(4) of the Act[20] to make an additional award as to claims presented in the arbitral proceedings but omitted from the award. If the arbitral tribunal considers the request to be justified, it shall make an additional award within 60 days from the receipt of such a request. However, the tribunal may extend the time period from the default 60 days in case it felt necessary.[21] However, if a party did not claim interest and the tribunal made an award without granting interest, it will not be open to the arbitrators to make an additional award, as they become

16. The High Court case of *Firmpower Sdn Bhd v. Philip Tuite* [2012] MLJU 103.
17. The English High Court case of *CNH Global NV v. PGN Logistics Ltd* [2009] EWHC 977, (Comm) at p. [26] where Burton J held that '*[t]he error must be an error affecting the expression the arbitrator's thought, not an error in the thought process itself*'.
18. [1983] 2 Lloyd's Rep 304, CA. While ultimately disallowing the application for interest on the ground of delay, Sir John Donaldson M.R. held that the successful party should have, upon realising there was no reference to interest in the arbitral award, immediately written to the tribunal and invited them to exercise their powers to correct an error in the award arising from an accidental omission of the same given that the counter-party had no objection to the claim for interest and/or applied within the statutory timeframe to remit the award back to the tribunal to consider the same.
19. [2005] BCCA 570 (Can LII) at p. [50], CA.
20. The English High Court case of *Van Der Zijden Wildhandel (PJ) NV v. Tucker and Cross (No 2)* [1976] 1 Lloyd's Rep 341. Here, Kerr J remitted the award back to the tribunal on the basis that the arbitrator had erred in not granting the claim for interest having found that: (i) the tribunal had all the material before him for the purposes of making an award which includes interest; (ii) there was an absence of any objection to such an award by the counter-party; and (iii) '*in commercial arbitration the arbitrator should ordinarily include interest in an award for damages*'. Kerr J went on to hold that the tribunal had failed to act judicially in not dealing with the question of interest thereby amounting to technical misconduct.
21. Section 35(6) of the Act.

functus officio as soon as their award is made unless the matter of interest has been expressly held over for a further award.[22]

Third, a party may apply to set aside the award under section 37 of the Act.[23] The application to set aside the award must be made within 90 days from the date on which the party making the application received the award or from the date on which that request had been disposed of by the arbitral tribunal if a request had been made under section 35. The grounds for setting aside are the limited grounds set out in section 37 of the Act, which are adopted from the United Nations Commission on International Trade (UNCITRAL Model Law on International Commercial Arbitration.

It is apposite to note that in cases where post-award interest is not awarded by the tribunal, the court itself cannot grant post-award interest when giving permission to enforce the award.[24] This is because the order is confined to the enforcement of the obligation of the parties to honour the award.

Parties can also rely on the applicable institutional arbitration rules (if any). In relation to the powers of the arbitral tribunal to award interest, Rule 13.5(m) of the Asian International Arbitration Centre's Arbitration Rules 2021 provides that the arbitral tribunal may, unless otherwise agreed by the parties, award interest on terms which are the same as that set out in section 33(6) of the Act.

VI EFFECT OF ENFORCEMENT ORDERS ON INTEREST ON THE AWARD ON BOTH THE SEAT AND ELSEWHERE

It is clear that any sum awarded in an award shall, unless the award otherwise directs, carry interest as from the date of the award and at the same rate as a judgment debt.[25]

Unless there is ground(s) for refusing recognition or enforcement of an arbitral award under section 39 of the Act, the award will be recognised and enforced.

VII POWERS OF THE COURT TO ORDER OR ADJUST POST-AWARD INTEREST

9. Does the Malaysian Court Have the Power to Order or Adjust Post-award Interest, Assuming It is Either the Seat Court or the Enforcing Court?

22. The Singapore Court of Appeal case of *LW Infrastructure Pte Ltd v. Lim Chin San Contractors Pte Ltd* [2013] 1 SLR 125 where it was held that the final award was to be construed as an award where only post-award interest was ordered, thereby rendering the additional award of pre-award interest an illegal variation of the final award.
23. The High Court case of *Sebor (Sarawak) Marketing & Services Sdn Bhd v. SA Shee (Sarawak) Sdn Bhd* [2000] 6 MLJ 1. In this case, the court found that it was implicit in the claim of the applicant that the interest claimed run right to the date of the award and thereafter. Further, since there was no objection as to the award of interest, the court held that post-award interest should be awarded unless there is a valid reason for it.
24. The English High Court case of *Walker v. Rome* [2000] 1 Lloyd's Rep 116; The English High Court case of *Pirtek v. Deanswood* [2005] 2 Lloyd's Rep728; The High Court case of *Associated Cover Sdn Bhd v. Mcis Zurich Insurance Berhad* [2010] 1 LNS 1580.
25. Section 33(8) of the Act.

Generally, an unsuccessful party may challenge an award by applying to set it aside under section 37 of the Act, or it may resist enforcement of the award under section 39 of the Act. However, save for these powers and exceptional cases, it is unlikely that the court has a free-standing power to order or adjust post-award interest where the issue has been determined by the tribunal. The award of interest is within the tribunal's discretion, and it is unlikely that the exercise of this discretion would be interfered with by the Malaysian Courts, unless the decision is found to be contrary to the parties' agreement under the contract. This is in line with the general principle of non-intervention and the pro-arbitration approach adopted by the Malaysian Courts.

VIII WHAT ARE THE INTEREST RATES AWARDED IN MALAYSIA?

Under section 33(6) of the Act, the arbitral tribunal has the discretion to apply any rate of interest that it considers appropriate. In exercising that discretion, the tribunal would usually invite parties to the arbitration to make submissions setting out their respective positions on the rate of interest to be applied.

In respect of post-award interest, where an award directs a sum to be paid and the award does not provide for the time period for applicability of interest or the rate of interest, section 33(8) of the Act provides that the sum shall carry interest as from the date of the award and at the same rate as a judgment debt. The judgment rate is currently set at 5% per annum pursuant to the Chief Justice Practice Direction No. 1 of 2012.

Myanmar

Suegene Ang

INTRODUCTION

Under the Myanmar Arbitration Law (2016) ("*Arbitration Law*"), arbitral tribunals in Myanmar-seated arbitrations are afforded discretion on matters concerning post-award interest.

This chapter discusses the power of an arbitrator to grant an award for post-award interest in Myanmar. Section I first examines the statutes and procedural rules pertaining to this area. Section II then focuses on the applicable law when granting an award of post-award interest. When the seat of arbitration is in Myanmar, the applicable law is that chosen by the parties. Section III discusses the extent to which Myanmar's arbitration laws have been brought in line with international norms after adopting its Arbitration Law.

Sections IV and V of this chapter discuss the substantive and procedural issues surrounding the grant of post-award interest, including the role Myanmar as the seat plays when determining the applicable law.

Finally, Sections VI and VII of this chapter briefly explain the overall enforceability of and powers of a court to order or adjust post-award interest.

I POWER TO GRANT POST-AWARD INTEREST

1 Does an Arbitral Tribunal Have the Power to Grant Post-award Interest Under Myanmar's Law?

Yes, under section 51 of the Arbitration Law, arbitral tribunals have the power to award post-award interest. Section 51 of the Arbitration Law provides: "*[w]here an award directs a sum to be paid, that sum shall, unless the award otherwise directs, carry interest as from the date of the award and at the same rate as a judgment debt made by the court.*"

Section 34 of the Myanmar Code of Civil Procedure (*the CPC*) provides:

> (1) Where and in so far as a decree is for the payment of money, the Court may, in the decree, order interest at such rate as the Court deems reasonable to be paid on the principal sum adjudged, from the date of the suit to the date of the decree, in addition to any interest adjudged on such principal sum for any period prior to the institution of the suit, with further interest at such rate as the Court deems reasonable on the aggregate sum so adjudged from the date of the decree to the date of payment or to such earlier date as the Court thinks fit.
>
> (2) Where such a decree is silent with respect to the payment of further interest on such aggregate sum as aforesaid from the date of the decree to the date of payment or other earlier date, the Court shall be deemed to have refused such interest, and a separate suit therefor shall not lie.

Section 173 of the Myanmar courts Manual (*the CM*) provides:

> The Court rate of interest allowed to decree-holders under section 34 of the Code of Civil Procedure should ordinarily be fixed at nine percent or at such lesser rate as may be expressed or implied in the contract.

In determining post-judgment interest to be awarded for money judgments, the Myanmar court determines the appropriate interest rate to be ordered from the date of the court's decree to the date of repayment of the judgment sum, bearing in mind the principles of equity and justice. In a case involving the sale of mortgaged property by the mortgagee bank upon the mortgagor's default on the terms of the mortgage, the Yangon High Court awarded post-judgment interest from the date of the preliminary decree to the date of full payment by the defendant at 6% per annum.[1]

Therefore, applying section 43 of CPC, the court (and accordingly, a tribunal) has the discretion to determine the appropriate interest rate for post-judgment or post-award interest, which should be no more than 9% per annum.

2. Is the Power Exercisable Without a Request or Submission, or Is Such a Submission Required?

Section 51 of the Arbitration Law provides that post-award will be granted unless the award otherwise directs. That said, the claimant is required to specify the relief or remedy sought in its statement of claim under section 26(a) of the Arbitration Law. In the context of litigation before a Myanmar court, the CPC also stipulates that a plaintiff shall state "*the precise amount claimed*" where the plaintiff seeks the recovery of money.[2]

As a matter of prudence and in view of common arbitration practice, it is advisable for a claimant (or a respondent with a counterclaim) to specify post-award interest (and for the party to state and include reasons for the appropriate interest rate to be applied) as part of the relief or remedy sought in the arbitration.

1. The Yangon High Court case of *Manager, Myanmar Economic Bank, Pathein v. U Sein Mya 2*, 2000, 178.
2. Clause 2 of Order VII of CPC.

3. Is the Power Classified as One under the Substantive Applicable Law or the Procedural Law of the Arbitration?

The Myanmar courts do not appear to have determined this issue. Where Myanmar is the seat of the arbitration, the provisions of the Arbitration Law[3] and section 51 of the Arbitration Law, which expressly provides for awards to carry post-award interest (unless the award otherwise directs), apply.

II CHOICE OF LAW

4. What Is the Law That Applies to Determine What the Post-award Interest Should Be? Would This Be the Governing Law of the Dispute or the Law of the Seat?

Under the Arbitration Law, the applicable law is Myanmar law[4] for domestic arbitration where Myanmar is the arbitral seat, and the arbitral tribunal has the power to determine what the post-award interest should be under section 51 of the Arbitration Law with reference to the CPC and CM.

In international arbitration, where Myanmar is the arbitral seat, the arbitral tribunal shall decide the dispute in accordance with the law chosen by the parties.[5]

The Arbitration Law further provides that "*in all cases, the arbitral tribunal shall decide in accordance with the terms of the contract and shall take into account the usages of the trade applicable to the transaction.*"[6]

If the governing law of the dispute and/or the contract provide a different position as to post-award interest, it would be open to the parties to make the relevant submissions, under the governing law of the dispute and/or with reference to the terms of the contract between the parties.

Based on the wording of section 51 of the Arbitration Law, it would appear to be in the tribunal's power to make directions "*other*" than that the award shall carry post-award interest at the same rate as a judgment debt made by the court.

III DO THE COURTS TAKE INTO ACCOUNT INTERNATIONAL STANDARDS WHEN FACING CHALLENGES ON THE POST-AWARD INTEREST?

In 2013, Myanmar acceded to the New York Convention on the Recognition and Enforcement of Arbitral Awards 1958,[7] and Myanmar's parliament enacted its Arbitration Law[8] in January 2016, repealing the previous Myanmar Arbitration Act 1944. The

3. Section 2(a) of the Arbitration Law.
4. Section 32(a) of the Arbitration Law.
5. Section 32(a)(2)(aa) of the Arbitration Law.
6. Section 32(c) of the Arbitration Law.
7. Myanmar acceded to the New York Convention on April 16, 2013 (http://www.newyorkconvention.org/countries).
8. The Pyidaungsu Hluttaw Law No. 5/2016, the 10th Waning Day of Nadaw, 1377 M.E. (January 5, 2016).

Arbitration Law covers both domestic and international arbitration and enforcement of both domestic and foreign awards in Myanmar.

The Arbitration Law is based closely on the United Nations Commission on International Trade (UNCITRAL) Model Law[9] and incorporates many of its provisions.[10] While the Arbitration Law brings Myanmar's laws in line with international norms and best practices,[11] the attitude of Myanmar courts toward the interpretation and application of the legislation has yet to be determined. In view of the lack of reported decisions and legal precedents in Myanmar, it is hoped that in interpreting the provisions of the Arbitration Law, the Myanmar courts will take into account and have reference to international standards and best practices.

IV SUBSTANTIVE LAW ISSUES

5. How Are Contractual Provisions on Late or Non-payment of Interest Relevant to Post-award Interest? Will These Be Considered By the Arbitral Tribunal?

Under the Arbitration Law, the arbitral tribunal is required to determine the dispute "*in accordance with the terms of the contract,*"[12] such that if or where there are contractual provisions relating to late or non-payment, they will be duly considered by the tribunal.

6. How do the Procedural Rules of the Substantive Law Apply?

Subject to the provisions of the Arbitration Law, parties are free to agree on the rules of procedure to be followed by the arbitral tribunal.[13] If the parties fail to agree on the applicable procedural rules, the arbitral tribunal has the power to conduct the arbitration in such manner as it considers appropriate.[14]

Where parties choose Myanmar as the seat, the procedural rules of the substantive law (if other than Myanmar law) would not generally apply,[15] and Myanmar law will be the procedural law/rules for the arbitration.[16]

So, for example, the choice of law rules (being procedural rules) of the substantive applicable law would not normally be applicable, as "*any designation of the law or*

9. Robert San Pe, *The way forward on resolving commercial disputes*, Frontier Myanmar (September 2, 2016),http://frontiermyanmar.net/en/robert-san-pe-the-way-forward-on-resolving-commer cial-disputes.
10. John Hancock, Ola Nicolai Borge, Jo Delaney, Leng Sun Chan SC, Gary Seib and Philipp Hanusch, *Myanmar enacts new Arbitration Law,* Global Arbitration News (March 22, 2016), https://globalarbitrationnews.com/myanmar-enacts-new-arbitration-law-2016-03-11/.
11. Christopher Chuah & Goh Wanjing, *Myanmar, The Asia-Pacific Arbitration Review 2017*, Global Arbitration Review, https://globalarbitrationreview.com/insight/the-asia-pacific-arbitration-review-2017/1036997/myanmar.
12. Section 32(c) of the Arbitration Law.
13. Section 22 (a) of the Arbitration Law.
14. Section 22(b) of the Arbitration Law.
15. Section 2(b) of the Arbitration Law.
16. Christopher Chuah, Goh Wanjing, *Myanmar, The Asia-Pacific Arbitration Review 2017*, Global Arbitration Review, https://globalarbitrationreview.com/insight/the-asia-pacific-arbitration-review-2017/1036997/myanmar.

legal state of a given State shall be construed, unless otherwise agreed by the parties, as directly referring to the substantive law of that State and not its conflict of laws rules."[17]

7. Whether the Award of Interest Can Be Subjected to Public Policy Objections and if So, What Are They?

As seen by the CPC and the CM, it is not against Myanmar's public policy to award post-judgment or post-award interest. However, it would be against Myanmar's public policy to enforce a clause or award interest that is viewed as being penal in nature. On this, section 74 of the Myanmar Contract Act (1872) provides that penalties are not enforceable and may be reduced to "*reasonable compensation.*"

Under Myanmar substantive law, the court will consider whether a contractually agreed enhanced rate of interest may be a penalty with regard to the specific circumstances of the case[18] and the principles of justice, equity and good conscience.[19]

V PROCEDURAL LAW ISSUES

8. What Are the Main Procedural Law Issues When Considering Post-award Interest? How Are the Arbitration Laws and Other Laws or Regulations of the Seat Relevant?

Where Myanmar is the seat of the arbitration, the provisions of the Arbitration Law apply[20] and Myanmar law will be the procedural law/rules for the arbitration. Section 51 of the Arbitration Law, which expressly provides for awards to carry post-award interest (unless the award otherwise directs), applies.

Where the seat is outside Myanmar, the arbitration laws and the other laws or regulations of the seat are relevant.

If the arbitral tribunal makes an error in computation, any clerical or typographical error or any error of similar nature in an award, a party may request the arbitral tribunal to correct the error(s) within 30 days from the date of the award with notice to the other party.[21] The arbitral tribunal may correct such errors upon the consideration of such request or at its own initiative.[22]

If the arbitral tribunal omits to address a claim presented in the arbitral proceedings in the award, a party may request the arbitral tribunal to make an additional award within 30 days of the date of the award with notice to the other party (unless another period of time has been agreed upon by the parties).[23] If the arbitral tribunal considers the request justified, it shall make the additional award within 60 days from the receipt of such request.[24]

17. Section 32(a)(2)(bb) of the Arbitration Law.
18. *P.C. Pal v. K.A.L.R. Firm and Another,* 1 Rangoon, 460.
19. Section 13 (3) of Burma Law Act (1898).
20. Section 32(a)(2)(aa) and (bb) of the Arbitration Law.
21. Section 37(a) of the Arbitration Law.
22. Section 37(b) of the Arbitration Law.
23. Section 37(e) of the Arbitration Law.
24. Section 37(f) of the Arbitration Law.

VI EFFECT OF ENFORCEMENT ORDERS ON INTEREST ON THE AWARD ON BOTH THE SEAT AND ELSEWHERE

Unless otherwise agreed by the parties, the award made by the arbitral tribunal pursuant to the arbitration agreement shall be final and binding on the parties and persons claiming under them respectively.[25]

Enforcement applications may be commenced in a competent district court that has the jurisdiction to determine the arbitration dispute as if it had been the subject of a civil suit.[26]

In respect of applications for the enforcement of arbitral awards, there is a lack of local jurisprudence and reported cases in Myanmar.[27]

VII POWERS OF THE COURT TO ORDER OR ADJUST POST-AWARD INTEREST

9. Does a Myanmar Court Have the Power to Order or Adjust the Post-award Interest Awarded by the Tribunal, Assuming It Is the Seat Court or the Enforcing Court?

Domestic arbitration awards can be challenged by way of a setting aside application under the grounds specified in the Arbitration Law,[28] or by way of an appeal on an issue of law arising from the award.[29] Upon an appeal, the Myanmar courts have the powers to approve the award, amend or vary the award, return the decision to the arbitral tribunal to review and reconsider the whole or any part of the award and/or to set aside the whole or any part of the award.[30]

In respect of foreign arbitral awards, the Arbitration Law provides that a foreign arbitral award shall be enforced in the same manner as if it were a decree of the court unless an application to set aside the award under the grounds specified in the Arbitration Law is successful/allowed.[31] As such, it appears that as an enforcing court, the Myanmar court does not have the power to amend or adjust the award.

25. Section 38 of the Arbitration Law.
26. Notification No. 643 of 2018 issued by the Supreme Court of the Union (July 31, 2018), at para [42], [43] and [45].
27. Minn Naing Oo, Kang Yanyi, Ei Ei Khin, *Myanmar, The International Arbitration Review* (13th edn, June 2022). https://thelawreviews.co.uk/title/the-international-arbitration-review; The publishing company is Law Business Research.
28. Section 41 of the Arbitration Law.
29. Section 42 of the Arbitration Law.
30. Section 43(b) of the Arbitration Law.
31. Section 46(a) of the Arbitration Law.

New Zealand

Janet Walker, CM

INTRODUCTION

This chapter examines the power of an arbitrator to make an order for post-award interest in New Zealand. Section I sets out the national law and institutional rules that regulate this area. In New Zealand, international and domestic arbitration are both governed by the Arbitration Act 1996 (*the Act*), which grants an arbitrator the power to make an order for post-award interest. In addition, the New Zealand Dispute Resolution Centre's rules explicitly provide for post-award interest. Furthermore, as a result of the basis on which interest is awarded, it may be regarded part of the procedural law.

Section II of this chapter considers instances where the arbitration agreement does not prohibit interest from accruing on an arbitral award. In such cases, interest is calculated in accordance with the rules applicable to a judgment debt, as provided in the national legislation.

Section III of this chapter considers the acceptance in New Zealand of international standards for post-award interest. As a Model Law jurisdiction for over 20 years, international decisions have often influenced the approach taken by New Zealand courts.

Sections IV and V of this chapter then consider substantive and procedural law issues raised by post-award interest. In *Parts & Services Ltd v. Brooks*,[1] the High Court of New Zealand held that some circumstances may require the tribunal to depart from contractual terms in calculating interest. The implications of this decision and the importance of contractual terms of interest are explored, followed by a consideration of the public policy objection provided by the Act and the narrow scope for this exception recommended in the High Court's decision in *Ironsands Investments Ltd & Anor v. Toward Industries Ltd & Anor* ('*Ironsand*').[2]

1. [Nov. 25, 2005] Rotorua CIV 2005-463-431, (Cooper J).
2. [Jul. 8, 2011] Auckland CIV-2010-404-4879, (Courtney J).

Section VI of the chapter turns to the enforcement of foreign court orders, and Section VII discusses the power of the enforcing court to vary post-award interest. In New Zealand, foreign court orders and awards are usually enforced. However, the limited circumstances in which an award may be varied are considered in the High Court's decision in *Rosser v. Global Construction Services Ltd.*[3]

I POWER TO GRANT POST-AWARD INTEREST

1. Does an Arbitral Tribunal Have the Power to Grant Post-Award Interest Under New Zealand's Law?

Unless otherwise agreed by the parties, an arbitral tribunal may award interest on the whole or part of any sum awarded to a party. Typically, an agreement to exclude interest would be found in the parties' contract.[4]

The Act, which applies to all domestic and international arbitrations seated in New Zealand, provides:

> 12 Powers of an arbitral tribunal in deciding disputes
> (1) An arbitration agreement, unless otherwise agreed by the parties, is deemed to provide that an arbitral tribunal–
> ...
> (b) may award interest on the whole or any part of any sum which—
> (i) is awarded to any party, for the whole or any part of the period up to the day on which the sum awarded (including all interest) is paid in full; or
> (ii) is in issue in the arbitral proceedings but is paid before the date of the award, for the whole or any part of the period up to the date of payment.

As noted in the International Bar Association (IBA) Guide to Arbitration in New Zealand, '*there is no prohibition under the Act on the awarding of compound interest. Since the High Court has the power to award compound interest in particular situations, it follows that arbitrators in a New Zealand arbitration also have this power,*'[5] as they have all the powers of the court under section 12(1) of the Act.

Moreover, the New Zealand Dispute Resolution Centre's (NZDRC) Arbitration Rules provide for post-award interest in Article 34.6:

> Unless otherwise agreed by the Parties, the Arbitral Tribunal may award simple or compound interest from such dates, at such rates and with such rests, as the Arbitral Tribunal considers meet the justice of the case, on the whole, or any part of:

3. [10 Aug. 2004] Auckland CIV 2004-404-2564, (Randerson J). *See* further discussion in Section VII below.
4. Doug Jones, AO, Janet Walker, CM, *Commercial Arbitration in Australia under the Model Law* (3rd edn, Law Book Co 2022) at para. [9.840].
5. Daniel Kalderimis, *Arbitration Guide: New Zealand*, International Bar Association Arbitration Committee (February 2018) https://www.ibanet.org/MediaHandler?id=278729D0-AAA9-4D8B-A7D8-A27F2E3F711D.

(a) any sum which the Arbitral Tribunal determines any Party is liable to pay any other Party, for the whole or any part of the period from the date on which the cause of action arose up to the date of the Award; and/or
(b) any amount claimed in the Arbitration and outstanding at the commencement of the Arbitration proceedings but paid before the Award is made, for the whole or any part of the period from the date on which the cause of action arose up to the date of payment.

2. Is the Power Exercisable Without a Request or Submission, or Is Such a Submission Required?

Under the Act, an arbitration agreement is deemed to provide the arbitral tribunal with the power to award interest as a court would have in deciding a case before it. There is no formal prohibition on awarding interest without a request or submission, although interest is typically a form of relief that is sought explicitly.

3. Is the Power Classified as One under the Substantive Applicable Law or the Procedural Law of the Arbitration?

Subject to the matter being provided for in the agreement between the parties, which would form part of the substantive issues to be addressed under the applicable law, the inclusion of this power among the remedial powers of the tribunal renders it part of the procedural law of the arbitration,[6] particularly as the arbitration law of New Zealand is closely based on the Model Law.

II CHOICE OF LAW

4. What is the Law That Applies to Determine the Rate of Post-award Interest? Would This Be the Governing Law of the Dispute or the Law of the Seat?

Article 31(5) of Schedule 1 of the Act provides '*unless the arbitration agreement or the award provide otherwise, a sum directed to be paid by an award carries interest as from the date of the award and at the same rate as a judgment debt*'. Accordingly, where the question is not answered by the parties' agreement, the tribunal is free to determine the availability and rate of interest, which will likely be regarded as a matter for the law of the seat as in many common law jurisdictions.

The rate of judgment debt in New Zealand is governed by the Interest on Money Claims Act 2016 for cases which commenced on or after 1 January 2018. Section 12 of the same provides:

Calculation of interest awarded under Section 10
(1) Interest awarded under Section 10 for a period is to be calculated at the relevant interest rate or interest rates on a daily basis using the Internet site calculator in accordance with Sections 14 and 15, except if this Act expressly provides otherwise.

6. Nigel Blackaby, Constantine Partasides KC, Alan Redfern, Martin Hunter, *Redfern and Hunter on International Arbitration* (6th edn, Oxford University Press 2015), at para. [9.73].

(2) For the purposes of Subsection (1), interest accrued over any particular year is to be added to the principal in the subsequent year.
(3) In this Section, interest rate, for any given day ('day A'), means the base rate plus the premium expressed as a daily effective rate, where—
  (a) base rate means—
    (i) the average of the 6 observations for the retail 6-month term deposit rate most recently published by the Reserve Bank of New Zealand before day A; or
    (ii) if some other indicator interest rate is prescribed as the base rate that applies for the purposes of this Section from a specified date, the prescribed rate, if day A is after the specified date; and
  (b) premium means—
    (i) 0.15 per cent; or
    (ii) if some other percentage is prescribed as the premium that applies for the purposes of this Section from a specified date, the prescribed premium if day A is after the specified date.

III DO THE COURTS TAKE INTO ACCOUNT INTERNATIONAL STANDARDS WHEN FACING CHALLENGES ON THE POST-AWARD INTEREST?

New Zealand has adopted international standards in arbitration by enacting a statute based on the Model Law in 1996. Judgments interpreting the Model Law have referred to international decisions, including decisions from the United Kingdom Court of Appeal, the Supreme Court of India, and the United States Court of Appeals for the Second Circuit.[7] Therefore, New Zealand courts are likely to consider international standards in disputes involving post-award interest.

IV SUBSTANTIVE LAW ISSUES

5. How are Contractual Provisions on Late or Non-payment of Interest Relevant to Post-Award Interest? Will These Be Considered By the Arbitral Tribunal?

Contractual provisions may be considered in the award of post-award interest by arbitral tribunals and by courts in the enforcement of an award. For example, in *Parts & Services Ltd v. Brooks*,[8] the High Court set aside an award on the ground that there had been a breach of natural justice, as the tribunal reduced the rate of interest to less than that provided for in the contract without prior notice to the parties.

7. *See*, e.g., *Almatal Corporation Ltd v. Maruha (NZ) Corporation Ltd* [2004] 2 NZLR 614 (CA), which referred to international decisions on the threshold to establish a conflict with public policy; *Ironsands Investments Ltd & Anor v. Toward Industries Ltd & Anor*, [8 Jul. 2011] HC Auckland CIV-2010-404-4879, (Courtney J) at pp. [9]-[11].
8. [November 25, 2005] Rotorua CIV 2005-463-431, (Cooper J).

Section 22 of the Interest on Money Claims Act 2016 also provides:

> 22 Award of interest if contract makes relevant provision
> (1) This Section and Section 23 apply to a period for which a contract provides for the award of interest, or provides that no interest is payable, on any amount payable under, or for the breach of, the contract.
> (2) A court may award interest for a period to which this Section applies in accordance with the rights and obligations of the parties specified in the contract.
> ...
> (5) A court may not award interest under Part 1 or Section 24 for a period to which this Section applies if it would be inconsistent with the provisions of the contract to do so.

6. How Do the Procedural Rules of the Substantive Law Apply?

New Zealand's choice of law provisions are based on the United Nations Commission on International Trade (UNCITRAL) Model Law. According to the Model Law Article 28(1), incorporated in Article 28(1) of Schedule 1 of the Act:

> (1) The arbitral tribunal shall decide the dispute in accordance with such rules of law as are chosen by the parties as applicable to the substance of the dispute. Any designation of the law or legal system of a given State shall be construed, unless otherwise expressed, as directly referring to the substantive law of that State and not to its conflict of laws rules.

Therefore, where the law of the seat is New Zealand, the procedural rules of the governing law of the arbitration are not applied to the determination of interest. Instead, the power of arbitral tribunals to award interest is provided in the Act.

7. Whether the Award of Interest Can Be Subjected to Public Policy Objections, and if So, What Are They?

The Act differs from the Model Law in providing expressly, in Article 34(6) of Schedule 1, for the application of the public policy exception in New Zealand:

> For the avoidance of doubt, and without limiting the generality of paragraph (2)(b)(ii), it is hereby declared that an award is in conflict with the public policy of New Zealand if—
>
> (a) the making of the award was induced or affected by fraud or corruption; or
> (b) a breach of the rules of natural justice occurred—
> (i) during the arbitral proceedings; or
> (ii) in connection with the making of the award.

Although a violation of public policy is a ground for setting aside an award, it is a narrow ground of recourse, the threshold for which has not yet been settled by the courts. In the case of *Ironsands*,[9] the High Court endorsed a '*high threshold*' for what constitutes a conflict with New Zealand's public policy. Courtney J suggested that it is

9. *Ironsands Investments Ltd & Anor v. Toward Industries Ltd & Anor* [8 Jul. 2011] HC Auckland CIV-2010-404-4879, (Courtney J).

necessary to '*show some element of illegality or that the enforcement of the award would be clearly injurious to the public good or wholly offensive to the ordinary, reasonable and fully informed member of the public*'.[10]

V PROCEDURAL LAW ISSUES

8. What Are the Main Procedural Law Issues When Considering Post-Award Interest? How Are the Arbitration Laws and Other Laws or Regulations of the Seat Relevant?

New Zealand has been a Model Law jurisdiction for over 20 years and has developed a jurisprudence largely consistent with other Model Law jurisdictions. An award may be set aside under Article 34 of Schedule 1 of the Act. Grounds for a court to deny enforcement of an arbitral award include where the award contains a decision on matters beyond the scope of the arbitration agreement.

Under Article 33(1) of Schedule 1, which is based on the Model Law, a party may request a correction or interpretation of an award within 30 days of receipt of the award. Therefore, the parties have an avenue of recourse should there be an evident mistake or miscalculation of the interest.

Where an award has not addressed a claim of post-award interest made in the proceedings, a party may also request the making of an additional award.[11]

It is also notable that New Zealand makes one reservation to the New York Convention – that of reciprocity:

> (a) This State will apply the Convention only to recognition and enforcement of awards made in the territory of another contracting State.

VI EFFECT OF ENFORCEMENT ORDERS ON INTEREST ON THE AWARD AT THE SEAT AND ELSEWHERE

New Zealand's enforcement regime is based on the Model Law. Therefore, the effect of enforcement orders is typically to uphold the money award and interest contained in the award. Setting aside an award in part or in full is generally difficult. In an early case, prior to the adoption of the Act, the New Zealand Court of Appeal stated in *Money v. Ven-Lu-Ree Ltd*[12] that:

> Reasons given by an arbitrator or umpire should be read fairly and as a whole. Awards should not be vitiated by fine points; the modern approach is in favour of upholding awards where that can fairly be done, rather than setting them aside in their entirety.

10. *Ironsands Investments Ltd & Anor v. Toward Industries Ltd & Anor* [8 July, 2011] HC Auckland CIV-2010-404-4879, (Courtney J).
11. Ch 1, Article 33(3), Arbitration Act, 1996.
12. [1988] 2 NZLR 414 (CA), 417.

VII POWERS OF THE COURT TO ORDER OR ADJUST POST-AWARD INTEREST

9. Does a New Zealand Court Have the Power to Order or Adjust the Post-award Interest Awarded By the Tribunal, as the Court at the Seat or an Enforcing Court?

An award may be enforced by application to the High Court or District Court. The value of the award, including interest, may be enforced in its original currency. The power of the court to order interest was formerly restricted by the statutory maximum interest rate. Section 87 of the Judicature Act 1908 enforced a maximum interest rate on damages, which would also apply in arbitral proceedings.[13] However, this provision was repealed on 1 January 2018.

In *Rosser v. Global Construction Services Ltd*,[14] the arbitrator awarded costs of NZD 28,864 in respect of an award of NZD 23,298 plus interest. The High Court stated:[15]

> This court will not lightly interfere with costs awards made by an arbitrator unless it is plainly shown that the award was unreasonable in all the circumstances. This court will not interfere merely because it would have arrived at a different conclusion. If the award accords with principle and if it is one which would reasonably be made by an arbitrator in all the circumstances, this court will not interfere.

Based on the court's approach to the award of costs in arbitration, the court has the power to adjust the interest awarded but, typically, will not do so.

13. *Angus Group Ltd v. Lincoln Industries Ltd* [1990] 3 NZLR 82.
14. *Rosser v. Global Construction Services Ltd*, [10 Aug. 2004] High Court Auckland CIV 2004-404-2564, (Randerson J).
15. *Rosser v. Global Construction Services Ltd*, [10 Aug. 2004] High Court Auckland CIV 2004-404-2564, (Randerson J).

Pakistan

Ali Almani, Aaminah Qadir & Sameen Hayat

INTRODUCTION

This chapter examines the power of an arbitral tribunal to grant post-award interest in Pakistan. The chapter is divided into the following seven sections:

(i) Section I examines the legal principles governing the power of an arbitral tribunal to grant post-award interest, in particular, the implied bar imposed by section 29 of the Arbitration Act 1940 on the grant of post-decree interest by an arbitral tribunal.

(ii) Section II analyzes whether it is the substantive law of the contract or the procedural law of the seat that applies to the determination of post-award interest.

(iii) Section III examines whether courts in Pakistan accept and apply international standards to determine post-award interest. While there is no reported judgment addressing this issue in Pakistan, there does not appear to be any statutory or other restriction on courts from accepting and applying international standards when determining post-award interest.

(iv) Section IV addresses specific issues of substantive law relating to post-award interest and in particular whether post-award interest can be set aside for public policy reasons.

(v) Section V addresses specific issues of procedural law relating to post-award interest.

(vi) Section VI examines how arbitration awards, including those for post-award interest, are enforced in Pakistan.

(vii) Finally, section VII explains the power of Pakistani courts to adjust post-award interest.

I POWER TO GRANT POST-AWARD INTEREST

1. Does an Arbitral Tribunal Have the Power to Grant Post-award Interest Under Pakistani Law?

The conduct of arbitration proceedings in Pakistan is governed by the Arbitration Act of 1940 ("*the 1940 Act*").[1] Section 13 of the 1940 Act sets out the general powers of arbitrators. These include the powers to:

(i) administer oath to parties and witnesses;
(ii) state a special case for the opinion of the court on any question of law or issue an award in the form of a special case for the opinion of the court;
(iii) make the award conditional, or, in the alternative;
(iv) correct any clerical mistakes in an award; and
(v) administer to any party to the arbitration such interrogatories as may be necessary.

There is no provision in the 1940 Act that deals with an arbitrator's power to grant interest. Section 29 of the 1940 Act,[2] however, empowers a court to allow interest from the date of the decree while issuing a decree on an award filed before it.[3] In light of this provision and the principle of party autonomy, which has been consistently upheld by the courts in Pakistan, there has been considerable judicial debate as to whether arbitrators can (i) grant post-award interest; and, if so, (ii) under what circumstances. The dominant view of the courts has been that post-award interest can be awarded by arbitrators in the following situations where:

1. There are two other statutes, which also relate to arbitration. The first is the Recognition and Enforcement (of Arbitration Proceedings and Foreign Arbitral Awards) Act 2011, which incorporates the Convention on the Recognition and Enforcement of Foreign Arbitral Awards 1958 into the law of Pakistan. The second is the Arbitration (International Investment Disputes) Act 2011, which incorporates the International Convention on the Settlement of Investment Disputes between States and Nationals of other States into the law of Pakistan. Neither of these Acts, however, relates to the conduct of arbitration proceedings and powers of arbitrators in Pakistan and is, therefore, not relevant to the present discussion. Apart from these, there are a number of statutes, such as the Cooperative Societies Act 1925, the Electricity Act 1910 and the Trusts Act 1882, among others, which provide for statutory arbitration. In accordance with section 46 of the 1940 Act, however, the 1940 Act is applicable to all statutory arbitrations except in so far as any of its provisions is in conflict with a provision of the other enactment or any rules made thereunder.
2. "*Interest on awards. Where and insofar as an award is for the payment of money the Court may in the decree order interest, from the date of the decree at such rate as the Court deems reasonable, to be paid on the principal sum as adjudged by the award and confirmed by the decree.*"
3. To enforce an award in Pakistan, it has to be filed in court and a judgment and decree obtained from the court in terms of the award. Once an award has been filed, a court may, on an application from an aggrieved party—(i) modify the award (section 15 of the 1940 Act); (ii) remit the award to the arbitrator(s) for reconsideration (section 16 of the 1940 Act) or (iii) set aside the award (section 30 of the 1940 Act). Once the time for making an application to set aside the award has expired (30 days from the date of filing the award in accordance with Article 158 of the Limitation Act of 1908) or an application, having been made, is refused, in accordance with section 17 of the 1940 Act, the court shall announce judgment and decree on the award. The award is, thereafter, to be enforced in the same manner as a decree of the court as set out in the Civil Procedure Code of 1908.

(i) the issue is specifically raised in reference to arbitration;
(ii) it is provided for in the agreement between the parties; and
(iii) it is just and equitable to do so.

Each of these situations is analyzed separately below.

Reference to Arbitration

In *Ghulam Abbas v. Trustees of Port of Karachi*,[4] the Supreme Court of Pakistan ("*Supreme Court*")[5] issued a landmark judgment on the powers of arbitrators to award interest. The case arose out of a contract for construction. The contract, which was awarded to the appellant, contained an arbitration clause. A disagreement arose between the parties as to the amount of work carried out by the contractor and the compensation due to him. The appellant contractor initiated arbitration. The arbitrator issued an award on July 14, 1975, in favor of the appellant. The award included future interest up to the date of payment. The respondent filed objections to the award before a single judge of the High Court who affirmed the award. Aggrieved by the decision of the single judge, the respondent filed an appeal before a two-member bench of the High Court. The two-member bench modified the award and reduced the amount awarded to the appellant. One of the grounds which prevailed before the two-member bench was that the issue of future interest should have been left to the court in accordance with section 29 of the 1940 Act.

The appellant challenged this decision before the Supreme Court. One of the issues before the Supreme Court was whether the arbitrator was competent to award interest, and if so, under what circumstances. The Supreme Court observed that the High Court had misunderstood the real importance of section 29. According to the Supreme Court, an arbitrator could "*under no circumstances award interest for the period beyond the passing of the decree by the court on the award for the simple reason that the statutory provisions contained in Section 29 of the Arbitration Act take over and it is the court within whose discretion lies the power to order interest from the date of the decree at such rate as the court deemed reasonable....*"[6] The Supreme Court held that where post-decree interest was awarded by an arbitrator, a court could adopt that interest and incorporate it in the decree while issuing it.[7] If the court decided to do so,

4. Pakistan Law Digest (*PLD*) [1987] Supreme Court (*SC*) 393.
5. Under the Constitution of the Islamic Republic of Pakistan 1973 ("*the Constitution*"), the Federation of Pakistan consists of four provinces and the Islamabad Capital Territory ("*the ICT*") (Article 1 of the Constitution). Each of the provinces and the ICT has a High Court, which stands at the apex of the judicial hierarchy of that province or the ICT (Article 175). The judgments of the High Courts are binding on all subordinate courts in the province or ICT (Article 201). The High Courts also exercise supervisory jurisdiction over all subordinate courts in the provinces and ICT (Article 203). Judgments of the High Courts can be appealed to the Supreme Court of Pakistan (though matters can also be directly brought to the Supreme Court under specified circumstances) (Articles 184 and 185). The Supreme Court is the apex court of Pakistan. Its judgments are binding on all courts, including the High Courts, in Pakistan (Article 189).
6. PLD [1987] SC 393, at p. [412], para. [22].
7. The Supreme Court relied on and approved the Lahore High Court's judgment in *Sheikh Mahboob Alam v. Shaikh Mumtaz Ahmad*, PLD [1956] Lahore ("*Lah*") 276, in this regard. This judgment is discussed subsequently.

the award of post-decree interest by the arbitrator would be saved under section 29 of the 1940 Act.

Regarding post-award but pre-decree interest, the Supreme Court observed that while section 29 prohibits an arbitrator from granting post-decree interest, it "*does not contemplate or create any embargo on the power of the Arbitrator to award interest in adjudicating upon the reference before him.*"[8]

The Supreme Court noted that in his statement of claim, the appellant had only claimed interest up to October 3, 1973. Interest beyond October 3, 1973, was not the subject matter of reference for adjudication before the arbitrator. The Supreme Court, therefore, disallowed the interest that was granted from the date of award until the date of the decree in that case on the ground that this issue was not referred to the arbitrator. The court found that the arbitrator exceeded his authority by awarding future interest from the date of award until the date of the decree.

This judgment clearly implies that if the appellant had sought post-award interest in the statement of claim and this issue had been specifically framed by the arbitrator and made a part of the reference, the arbitrator could then have awarded such interest (up to the date of decree). The Supreme Court, therefore, impliedly upheld the power of an arbitrator to award interest between the date of award and the date of the decree if this issue was specifically referred to him.

This is, however, subject to an important caveat. The Supreme Court observed that post-award interest cannot be allowed in the specific case of damages for breach of contract in the absence of an express or implied contract to pay interest or of usage of trade to that effect. In expressing this view, the Supreme Court affirmed its earlier judgment in *A.Z. Company v. S. Maula Buksh Muhammad Bashir* ("*A.Z. Company*").[9]

Agreement Between the Parties

In *A.Z. Company*, the appellant entered into three separate contracts with the respondent for purchase of bales of cotton but failed to take delivery. The contracts provided for arbitration, which was invoked by the respondent. The arbitrators issued an award in favor of the respondent, including future interest from the date of award until the date of payment. The award was filed before a single judge of the High Court, who dismissed the appellant's objections and issued a decree on the award. The appellant challenged the decree before a two-member bench of the High Court. This challenge was rejected. The appellant, therefore, approached the Supreme Court. One of the main objections raised before the Supreme Court was that the arbitrators had erred in awarding interest.

The contracts were governed by the by-laws of the Karachi Cotton Association Limited. Since the by-laws included a specific provision stating that if a dispute was referred to arbitration, interest could be granted after the date of award, the Supreme Court held that the arbitrators "*acted within their power in granting future interest on the damages awarded by them.*"[10] This judgment, therefore, confirms that arbitrators

8. PLD [1987] SC 393 at p. [407], para. [16].
9. PLD [1965] SC 505.
10. PLD [1965] SC 516.

can award such interest until the date of the decree where the parties expressly or impliedly agree that interest may be awarded from the date of the award. Such an agreement does not have to be stipulated directly in the contract itself but may be part of the law governing the contract (as it was in this case) or the rules governing the arbitration.

It is interesting to note that in this case, the court upheld the award of future interest from the date of award onwards without making any distinction between the period from the date of award to the date of decree and the period after the date of the decree. This creates room to argue that where a contract expressly or impliedly provides for an award of future interest, such interest may also be awarded for the post-decree period. A similar view was expressed by a two-member bench of the Lahore High Court in *Sheikh Mahboob Alam v. Sheikh Mumtaz Ahmed.*[11] There the court held that "*while we do not agree that Section 29 altogether bars a decision as to post-decree interest by the arbitrator, we would accept that he cannot award such interest unless the award of interest was included in the reference.*"[12] The court, therefore, concluded "*that in the absence of any specific reference to an arbitrator on a question as to what interest is to be paid subsequent to the passing of the decree, the arbitrator does not possess any authority to award post-decree interest. His jurisdiction is limited by the terms of his reference.*"[13] The court found that in that case, however, the reference to the arbitrator included the award of post-decree interest and, therefore, upheld the grant of interest.

This judgment arose out of a challenge to the earlier judgment of a single judge of the Lahore High Court. The single judge dismissed the appellant's objection that the arbitrator had no power to grant post-decree interest on the ground that, even assuming that the arbitrator had no such power since the district judge had incorporated this portion of the interest in his decree, it must be deemed to have been adopted by him in the exercise of his own powers under section 29. Interestingly, the judgment of the single judge on this point was cited with approval by the Supreme Court in *Ghulam Abbas* (*supra*). The Supreme Court did not consider the judgment of the two-member bench in the appeal. Instead, it categorically stated that an arbitrator could not grant post-decree interest under any circumstances.

The Supreme Court has not had the occasion to revisit this issue in these terms.[14] At present, therefore, the prevailing judicial view appears to be that arbitrators cannot award post-decree interest under any circumstances.[15]

---

11. PLD [1960] Lah 601.
12. PLD [1960] Lah 608.
13. PLD [1960] Lah 608 and 609. *See also Hassan Brothers & Company v. Maqbool Cotton Ginning & Pressing Factory*, PLD 1986 Karachi ("*Kar*") 21 holding that an arbitrator cannot award interest beyond the date of decree unless a specific reference is made to him.
14. *See Dawood Cotton Mills Ltd. v. K.F. Development Corporation Ltd.* [2006] Supreme Court Monthly Review ("*SCMR*") 1555 where the issue before the Supreme Court was whether the High Court could have itself awarded interest for the period prior to the date of decree. While holding that the High Court had no power to award such interest since its power was circumscribed by section 29, the Supreme Court observed that "*[i]t is the grant of interest from the date of decree which falls within the exclusive domain of the Court proceedings … .*" Since the issue of post-decree interest was not before the Supreme Court, this observation is obiter dicta,

Just and Equitable

In *Federation of Pakistan v. Al-Farooq Builders*,[16] the High Court of Sindh considered whether an arbitrator's award of interest up to the date of award was justified. The dispute arose out of a construction contract and was referred to arbitration. The arbitrator was found to be in favor of the respondent. He had awarded interest from the date the respondent had issued a dispute notice to the appellant till the date of the award along with an amount due for work done. The award was filed before a single judge of the High Court of Sindh, who dismissed the appellant's objections and issued a decree on the award. The appellant challenged this decree before a two-member bench of the High Court of Sindh. After a thorough review of the jurisprudence on this issue, including extensive references to the Supreme Court's judgment in *Ghulam Abbas*, the court held that the arbitrator was in fact justified in equity to award interest on the amount found due and outstanding against the appellant but only from the date of the award. According to the court, "*on equitable consideration, his [the arbitrator's] authority to award interest from the date of award can undoubtedly be recognized.*"[17] The court, therefore, modified the decree by upholding the grant of interest but only from the date of award until the date of the decree. This issue was also considered by the Lahore High Court in *Water and Power Development Authority v. Ice Pak International Consulting Engineers of Pakistan*[18] and *Ibrahim Fibres Ltd. v. Hameed Masood*.[19] In both cases, the court held that an arbitrator can grant future interest on equitable grounds but must justify the reasons for doing so.

When granting post-award interest, arbitrators are limited by the court's power to award interest under section 29 of the 1940 Act. This provision impliedly bars arbitrators from granting interest after the date of the decree. As such, while arbitrators can grant post-award interest, they cannot grant post-decree interest, which is the exclusive prerogative of the courts.

Conclusion

In light of the foregoing, the following principles relating to the grant of post-award interest have been established in Pakistan:

---

but suggests that the view expressed in *Ghulam Abbas* is generally viewed as the law of the land on this issue. The High Courts have repeatedly held that arbitrators have no power to award post-decree interest. *See Muhammad Saleem Butt v. Trading Corporation of Pakistan*, [1986] Civil Law Cases ("*CLC*") 254 at p. [262], para. [H].

15. *See also A. Qutubuddin Khan v. Chec Millwala Dredging Co. (Pvt.) Ltd.* [2014] SCMR 1268 at p. [1288], para. [30]. This case was decided by a three-member bench of the Supreme Court. While the issue of award of interest by the arbitrator was raised, the majority did not address the issue and remanded the matter. In his dissenting judgment, however, Justice Khilji Arif Hussain discussed this issue in detail and reiterated the view taken by the Supreme Court in *Ghulam Abbas* that the arbitrator could, under no circumstances, award interest for the period after the passing of the decree.
16. 2001 Monthly Law Digest ("*MLD*") 99.
17. [2001] Monthly Law Digest 111.
18. [2003] Yearly Law Review ("*YLR*") 2494 at p. [2507], para. [L].
19. [2006] YLR 1523 at p. [1535], para. [E] and p. [1536], para. [E].

(i) There is no statutory power granted to arbitrators under the 1940 Act to grant post-award interest.
(ii) Arbitrators can, however, award such interest where:
  (a) It is specifically claimed before them (i.e., it forms part of the subject matter of the reference to arbitration).
  (b) It is provided for in the agreement between the parties (whether that is directly in agreement itself, in the law governing the arbitration or the rules under which the arbitration is conducted). Or
  (c) It is just and equitable to do so (this provides considerable flexibility to arbitrators to mold relief according to the circumstances of a case).
(iii) Arbitrators cannot, under any circumstances, award post-decree interest.

2. Is the Power Exercisable Without a Request or Submission, or Is Such a Submission Required?

Arbitrators can only grant post-award interest when (i) the issue is specifically raised in reference to the arbitrator(s); (ii) it is provided for in the agreement between the parties or (iii) it is just and equitable to do so.[20]

3. Is the Power Classified as One under the Substantive Applicable Law or the Procedural Law of the Arbitration?

This issue is addressed in detail in the section below.

II CHOICE OF LAW

4. What is the Law That Applies to Determine What the Post-award Interest Should Be? Would This Be the Governing Law of the Dispute or the Law of the Seat?

There is no reported judgment in Pakistan that directly addresses this issue (i.e., whether the basis for granting interest is the substantive law applicable to the dispute or the law of the seat). As such, to address this issue, we need to examine the general principles set out by courts in Pakistan regarding the award of interest. The three primary judgments in this regard are *Ghulam Abbas* and *A.Z. Company* (discussed

20. *See* Cf. *M.A. Aleem & Sons (Pvt.) Ltd. v. Pakistan Telecommunication Employees Trust* [2012] CLC 236, decided by a single judge of the Islamabad High Court, where on the basis of the counsel's concession that, according to law, the arbitrator could only award interest up to the date of award and not beyond that. The court modified the award and deleted the interest allowed beyond the date of the award. This judgment is based on an incorrect appreciation of the law; and *Province of Sindh v. Waseem Construction Company,* [1991] CLC 66 decided by a two-member bench of the High Court of Sindh. After extensively quoting from the Supreme Court's judgment in *Ghulam Abbas*, the Court held that "*[a]n arbitrator is not authorized to grant interest beyond the date of the award but if it was granted and has been made rule of the Court then in view of the observation of the Supreme Court it shall be deemed to have been adopted by the Court under Section 29.*" This holding is based on an incorrect appreciation of the Supreme Court's judgment in *Ghulam Abbas*. The correct view is that arbitrators have the power to award interest from the date of award until the date of decree but not post-decree.

above), and the Supreme Court's judgment in *Hitachi Corporation v. Rupali Polyester* ("*Hitachi*").[21]

In *Ghulam Abbas*, the Supreme Court held that the power to award interest for the period prior to the date of the suit or reference to arbitration is a matter of substantive law. According to the Supreme Court, interest for this period could be granted on the basis of the following:

(i) Agreement, express or implied between the parties.
(ii) Mercantile usage.
(iii) Statutory provisions. Or
(iv) Equitable grounds in proper cases.[22]

The Supreme Court contrasted this with the power to award interest during the pendency of a suit and after the date of the decree which, according to it, is a statutory power in the domain of procedural law.[23] It then went on to discuss interest pendente lite (i.e., during the pendency of the arbitration). Citing its judgment in *A.Z. Company*, the Supreme Court observed that interest cannot be allowed for the period prior to the date of the award except for the grounds already mentioned, i.e., the same grounds on which interest for the period prior to suit or reference to the arbitration can be granted.

In *A.Z. Company*, the Supreme Court disallowed interest that had been awarded for the period prior to the award on the ground that the by-laws of the Karachi Cotton Association Ltd. governing the contracts only provided for post-award interest, even though it noted that the appellant had kept the respondent out of money for an unreasonable time by adopting delaying tactics. The Supreme Court observed that the issue of interest before the date of the award may have been overlooked by the Association while framing the by-laws, and, therefore, it was for the Association to decide whether to amend the by-laws to address the present situation.

Since the contracts at issue in this case were governed by the by-laws, these observations suggest that the Supreme Court was proceeding on the assumption that interest pendente lite is a matter of substantive law. This is confirmed by various decisions of the High Court(s) holding that interest pendente lite can only be awarded if (i) the parties have agreed to it;[24] (ii) it is provided by a statute[25] or (iii) the issue is referred to the arbitrator.[26]

From these decisions, it can be concluded that interest for the period prior to the date of decree in Pakistan (that is, interest prior to the reference to arbitration, pendente lite and post-award) is treated as a matter of substantive law.

21. [1998] SCMR 1618.
22. PLD [1987] SC 393 at p. [407], para. [18].
23. PLD [1987] SC 393 at p. [407], para. [18]. In this regard, the Supreme Court referred to section 34 of the Civil Procedure Code 1908, which empowers a court to grant interest for the period from the date of the suit to the date of the decree and from the date of decree to the date of payment.
24. *See F.J. Rambarts (Pakistan) Ltd. v. Pakistan Steel Mills Corporation* [1987] CLC 2198 at p. [2204], para. [H].
25. *See F.J. Rambarts (Pakistan) Ltd. v. Pakistan Steel Mills Corporation* [1987] CLC 2198 at p. [2204], para. [H].
26. *See Millat Tractors Ltd. v. Millat Tractor House,* [1999] YLR 295, at p. [300], para. [A].

The leading case in Pakistan on conflict of laws in arbitration is the Supreme Court's judgment in the case of *Hitachi*.[27] In that case, the law governing the contract was the law of Pakistan. The seat of the arbitration was London. The arbitration was subject to the Rules of the International Chamber of Commerce (*the ICC*). A dispute arose as to whether the law of Pakistan was to govern the removal of arbitrators or whether such removal was to be governed by the law of the seat—the law of England. The court held that while the law of Pakistan, being the substantive law, would govern the merits of the dispute, procedural matters would be governed by the ICC Rules and the curial law of England.[28] As the removal of arbitrators is a matter of procedure, the court found that the ICC Rules and English law would govern the issue of the removal of arbitrators. The Supreme Court, however, noted that questions relating to the validity and scope of the arbitration agreement, the validity of the notice of arbitration, the constitution of the tribunal and the formal validity of the award, among others, would all be governed by the substantive law of the arbitration agreement.[29]

While the 1940 Act is applicable when the seat of arbitration is Pakistan, it is silent on the powers of arbitrators to grant interest except impliedly barring them from granting post-decree interest. As stated by the Supreme Court in *Hitachi*, the substantive law of the contract will govern the merits of the dispute. Since interest prior to the date of the decree is a matter of substantive law, interest for this period would be awarded in accordance with the substantive law of the contract in the absence of anything contrary to the law of Pakistan.

III DO THE COURTS TAKE INTO ACCOUNT INTERNATIONAL STANDARDS WHEN FACING CHALLENGES ON THE POST-AWARD INTEREST?

While there is no reported judgment where Pakistani courts have taken international standards into account when granting post-award interest, there is no restriction on the courts from taking such standards into account. In appropriate circumstances, therefore, a court may take such standards into account. This conforms with an increasing trend in Pakistani courts, including the Supreme Court, to adopt and seek guidance from international jurisprudence, particularly in commercial matters.[30]

27. [1998] SCMR 1618.
28. The court went further and observed that, even if it were assumed that in procedural matters the courts in Pakistan and England had concurrent jurisdiction because the applicable substantive law was the law of Pakistan, the former would be reluctant to press into service the concurrent discretionary jurisdiction. [1998] SCMR 1618.
29. [1998] SCMR 1684.
30. *See Orient Power Company (Private) Limited v Sui Northern Gas Pipelines Limited* [2021] SCMR 1728 at p. [1744], para. [34] until p. [1747], para. [D] and p. [1749], para. [G] until p. [1756], para. [W]; and *Universal Insurance Company and another v Karim Gul and another* [2021] CLD 1189 at p. [1194], para. [8].

IV SUBSTANTIVE LAW ISSUES

5. How Are Contractual Provisions on Late or Non-payment of Interest Relevant to Post-award Interest? Will These Be Considered By the Arbitral Tribunal?

This issue has already been discussed in detail under Question 1 above. The superior courts have consistently held that the arbitrators can grant post-award interest where the agreement between the parties provides for payment of such interest.

6. How Do the Procedural Rules of the Substantive Law Apply?

There is no reported judgment in Pakistan that has directly considered this point, i.e., whether and to what extent Pakistani law permits the procedural rules of the substantive law (where that law is not Pakistani law) to be applied by a tribunal seated in Pakistan determining interest. The question must, therefore, be addressed in light of (i) the general principles regarding the award of interest by arbitrators set out by the Supreme Court in *Ghulam Abbas* and *A.Z. Company*; (ii) the extent to which the "*procedural*" rules of the chosen substantive law are deemed part and parcel of the substantive law itself and (iii) the extent to which such "*procedural*" rules apply to arbitrations.[31]

Given that the 1940 Act is applicable to all arbitrations seated in Pakistan,[32] interest cannot be awarded in an arbitration seated in Pakistan even if the procedural rules of the substantive law (other than the law of Pakistan) applicable to a dispute allow an arbitrator to award post-decree interest.

7. Whether the Award of Interest Can Be Subjected to Public Policy Objections, and if So, What Are They?

Whether an award violates public policy is a highly fact-specific inquiry. There are, however, two aspects of Pakistani law that may raise public policy concerns on the grant of post-award interest. *First*, Pakistani law prohibits excessive compensation of a penal nature. *Second*, the grant of interest is a contentious issue in Pakistan, as charging or awarding interest has been held to be contrary to the tenets of Islam. Each of these issues is discussed in detail below.

Prohibition on Penalty

The execution and interpretation of contracts in Pakistan is governed by the Contract Act of 1872 ("*the Contract Act*"). Section 74 of the Contract Act relates to compensation for a breach of contract where a penalty has been stipulated in the contract. The relevant part of the provision provides:

> Compensation for breach of contract where penalty stipulated for.

31. For instance, in Pakistan, courts are empowered to award interest under section 34 of the Civil Procedure Code 1908. The superior courts have consistently held that the provisions of the Civil Procedure Code are not applicable to the conduct of arbitrations. Arbitrators, therefore, do not exercise the powers conferred on courts under the Civil Procedure Code 1908.
32. *See* footnote #46 below for a discussion on the applicability of the 1940 Act to arbitrations seated outside Pakistan but in which the substantive law of Pakistan is applicable to the dispute.

> When a contract has been broken, if a sum is named in the contract as the amount to be paid in case of such breach, or if the contract contains any other stipulation by way of penalty, the party complaining of the breach is entitled, whether or not actual damage or loss is proved to have been caused thereby, to receive from the party who has broken the contract reasonable compensation not exceeding the amount so named or, as the case may be, the penalty stipulated for.
>
> Explanation - A stipulation for increased interest from the date of default may be a stipulation by way of penalty.
>
> ...
>
> A gives B a bond for the repayment of Rupees 1,000 with interest at 12 per cent at the end of six months, with a stipulation that in case of default, interest shall be payable at the rate of 75 per cent from the date of default. This is a stipulation by way of penalty, and B is only entitled to recover from such, compensation as the Court considers reasonable.

Section 74 states that a party is only entitled to receive "*reasonable*" compensation for any breach—even if a specific penalty has been stipulated in the contract. The illustration quoted above highlights that if a contract contains a provision for the award of interest that is punitive or penal in nature, a party will not be entitled to recover the amount stipulated but will be limited to recovering a reasonable amount by way of interest. The superior courts have consistently held that reasonable compensation is a question of fact to be decided by an independent and impartial forum. The burden of proof is on the party claiming compensation.[33] Further, the amount must not exceed the amount mentioned in the contract, i.e., the amount stipulated in the contract caps the amount that the aggrieved party can receive.[34]

The effect of penalty clauses, in the context of interest, was considered by the High Court of Sindh in *National Development Finance Corporation v. Moona Liza Fruit Juices*.[35] In this case, a bank sought to claim additional interest from the customer based on a default provision in the credit agreement. The bank failed to produce any evidence to justify the additional interest, or the loss suffered by it due to the breach of contract. In these circumstances, the court found that this default provision amounted to a penalty clause and that reasonable compensation could not be awarded without adducing evidence. Since section 74 provides that reasonable compensation must be granted regardless of loss being proved, a token amount of INR. 1,000 was awarded as additional interest in this case.

33. *See National Development Finance Corporation v. Moona Liza Fruit Juices* [1999] YLR 500 at p. [504], para. [B]; *Habib Bank Limited v. Super Rice Limited* [1999] YLR 926 at p. [929], para. [B]; *National Bank of Pakistan v. West Pakistan Tanks Terminal* 2000 CLC 896 at p. [900], para. [D]; *Agriculture Development Bank of Pakistan v. Jasarat Hussain* [2002] CLD 94 at p. [96], para. [B]; and *Investment Corporation of Pakistan v. Sheikhapura Textile Mills* [2004] CLD 1396 at p. [1407], para. [C].
34. *See Province of West Pakistan v. Mistri Patel & Co. & another* PLD [1969] SC 80; *Syed Sibti Raza & another v. Habib Bank Ltd.* PLD [1971] SC 743 at p. [749]; *Ghee Corporation of Pakistan Ltd. v. Kuouk Oil Mills & Grains (Pvt) Ltd.* [1999] Monthly Law Digest 2617 at p. [2621], para. [5] and *A.J. Corporation v. Fauji Fertilizer Bin Qasim* [2013] CLD 636 at p. [641], para. [11].
35. [1999] YLR 500 at p. [505], para. [D]. *See also Agricultural Development Bank of Pakistan v. Jasarat Hussain* [2002] CLD 94 at p. [96], para. [B]; *Saudi-Pak Industrial and Agricultural Investment Company (Pvt.) Limited v. Allied Bank of Pakistan* [2003] CLD 596 at p. [603], para. [A] and *Harappa Textile Mills Limited v. B.A.S.F. Pakistan (Private) Limited* [2007] YLR 109 at p. [110], para. [A] and p. [11].

As such, courts in Pakistan may not enforce an award granting post-award interest that is punitive or penal in nature. Only post-award interest that provides reasonable compensation in accordance with the circumstances of a case is likely to be enforced.

Potential Invalidity of Interest

In *Dr. Mahmood-ur-Rahman Faisal and others v. Secretary of Law*, the Federal Shariat Court[36] held that certain provisions relating to interest in various laws[37] were repugnant to the injunctions of Islam and directed that these be deleted.[38] This judgment and other subsequent judgments of the Shariat Court were challenged before the Shariat Appellate Bench of the Supreme Court. In 1999, the Shariat Appellate Bench dismissed the appeals.[39] A review was filed against the judgment of the Shariat Appellate Bench.[40] Thereafter, in *United Bank v. Farooq Brothers*,[41] the Shariat Appellate Bench set its earlier judgment aside and remanded the case back to the Shariat Court for reconsideration on the grounds that it had not considered all the issues before it.

Subsequently, in the remand proceedings, titled *Farooq Ali v. UBL*, the Shariat Court held that "*furthermore, all the prevailing forms of interest, either in the banking transactions or in private transactions fall within the definition of Riba. We hereby declare that the prohibition of Riba is complete and absolute in all its forms and manifestations according to the Injunctions of Islam in accordance with the Holy Quran and Sunnah.*"[42] As a result, the Shariat Court concluded definitively that there was an absolute prohibition on interest in Islam. The government was directed to, therefore, delete the word "*interest*" wherever it appeared in the impugned provisions of law.[43] Appeals have been filed against this judgment before the Shariat Appellate Bench of the

36. Article 203C of the Constitution establishes a Federal Shariat Court. Under Article 203D, the Shariat Court has the power to examine and decide, on its own motion or a petition by any citizen or the government, whether any law or provision of law is repugnant to the injunctions of Islam as laid out in the Holy Quran or Sunnah of the Holy Prophet. In accordance with Article 203F, an appeal from any decision of the Shariat Court lies to the Supreme Court. The bench of the Supreme Court which hears appeals from judgments of the Shariat Court is known as the Shariat Appellate Bench. If an appeal has been filed against a judgment of the Shariat Court, the judgment does not take effect until the appeal is decided. If no appeal is filed, then the judgment takes effect on the expiry of the period for filing an appeal.
37. These laws included, among others, the Interest Act 1839, the Negotiable Instruments Act 1881, the Land Acquisition Act 1894, the Civil Procedure Code 1908, the State Bank of Pakistan 1956 and Banking Companies Ordinance 1962.
38. PLD 1992 Federal Shariat Court ("*FSC*") 1.
39. *Dr. M. Aslam Khaki v. Muhammad Hashim and others* PLD [2000] SC 225.
40. Under Article 188 of the Constitution, the Supreme Court has the power to review any judgments issued by it.
41. PLD [2002] SC 800.
42. Unreported judgment, dated April 28, 2022, in Shariat Petition No. 30-L of 1991 & 81 connected matters, p. [288], paras. [155] and [156]. This judgment is accessible at the Shariat Court's website at: https://www.federalshariatcourt.gov.pk/Judgments/S-P%2030-L1991%20Riba%20Case-28.04.2022.pdf.
43. Unreported judgment, dated April 28, 2022, in Shariat Petition No. 30-L of 1991 & 81 connected matters, p. [291], para. [159]. This judgment is accessible at the Shariat Court's website at:https://www.federalshariatcourt.gov.pk/Judgments/S-P%2030-L1991%20Riba%20Case-28.04.2022.pdf.

Supreme Court and no decision has been passed. The enforcement of this judgment depends on the decision in appeal. In accordance with Article 203D(2) of the Constitution, a judgment of the Shariat Court shall not take effect until the appeal is decided. At present, therefore, this judgment is not in effect.

In light of the aforementioned history of litigation on this issue, parties often raise a defense (both in arbitral and court proceedings) that interest is contrary to the injunctions of Islam and is thus not payable. The Supreme Court has, however, held in *Najm Koreshi v. Chase Manhattan Bank*[44] that judicial decrees ordering the payment of interest are enforceable. This may, however, change if the Shariat Appellate Bench of the Supreme Court upholds the Shariat Court's judgment in *Farooq Brothers v. UBL.*

V PROCEDURAL LAW ISSUES

8. What Are the Main Procedural Law Issues When Considering Post-award Interest? How Are the Arbitration Laws and Other Laws or Regulations of the Seat Relevant?

The main procedural law issues concern section 29 of the 1940 Act which impliedly bars arbitrators from granting post-decree interest. Arbitrators' powers are thus limited to granting interest up until the date of the decree. This has been discussed in detail under Question 1 above.

VI EFFECT OF ENFORCEMENT ORDERS ON INTEREST ON THE AWARD ON BOTH THE SEAT AND ELSEWHERE

There are three separate statutes in Pakistan which deal with enforcement of the award. An award granting post-award interest is enforced in the same manner as any other arbitration award. None of the statutes make any distinction between an arbitration award that does not grant post-award interest and an award (or part thereof) which grants such interest.

The first statute is the 1940 Act. This applies to all domestic awards, that is, awards where the seat of the arbitration is Pakistan.[45] Under the 1940 Act, a party

44. [2015] SCMR 1461.
45. The question of whether an award, where the seat is foreign but the substantive law is the law of Pakistan, is a domestic award under the 1940 Act or a foreign award for the purposes of the Recognition and Enforcement (Arbitration Agreements and Foreign Awards) Act 2011 (discussed subsequently) has yet to be authoritatively decided by the superior courts. In the case of an award issued in an International Chamber of Commerce arbitration where the seat of the arbitration was Singapore but the contract was governed by the law of Pakistan, the appellant (Taisei Corporation) sought enforcement of the award under the 2011 Act before the High Court of Sindh. The respondent (A.M. Corporation Company) filed an application under the 1940 Act before the Civil Judge Lahore challenging the award. In *Taisei Corporation v. A.M. Corporation Company* [2018] MLD 2058, the High Court of Sindh held that the award was a foreign award. In *Taisei Corporation v. A.M. Corporation Company* PLD [2012] Lahore 455, the High Court of Lahore held that the award was a domestic award. Appeals from both judgments are now pending before the Supreme Court of Pakistan. This issue, therefore, remains a grey area pending a ruling by the Supreme Court of Pakistan. In light of the definition of "*foreign award*" in the 2011 Act as any award issued in a contracting State the High Court of Sindh's judgment

seeking enforcement of an award must file the award in court. After notice of filing of the award in court is served on the opposing party, it may file an application objecting to the enforcement of the award within thirty days.[46] On the basis of such an application, the court may modify the award (section 15), remit it for reconsideration (section 16) or set it aside (section 30). The grounds for each are, however, limited.

For instance, under section 15, an award can only be modified where the award (i) is on a matter that was not referred to arbitration and such matter can be separated from the rest of the award without affecting the decision; (ii) is in the incorrect form or contains an obvious error, which can be amended without affecting the decision or (iii) contain a clerical mistake or error. Similarly, under section 16, an award can be remitted for reconsideration (i) where the award has not decided any matter that was referred to arbitration or has decided a matter which was not referred to arbitration and such part cannot be separated from the rest of the award without affecting the decision; (ii) where the award is so indefinite that it cannot be executed or (iii) where an objection to the legality of the award is apparent on its face. Finally, under section 30, the court can set aside the award where (i) an arbitrator has misconducted himself or the proceedings; (ii) the arbitration proceedings have been superseded by order of the court or where proceedings on the same subject have been commenced in court or (iii) it has been improperly procured or is otherwise invalid.

Once the time for filing an application has expired or an application, having been made, is refused, the court shall announce judgment and decree on the award. No appeal results from such a decree except on the ground that the decree exceeds or is not in accordance with the award.

A decree passed by the court is then executed in the manner provided in the Code of Civil Procedure 1908 ("*Code*"). The provisions for enforcement of decrees are contained in sections 36 to 74 of the Code and Order XXI of the First Schedule to the Code. The court has vast powers to ensure execution of decrees, including the power

appears to be the correct view. Pending an authoritative pronouncement by the Supreme Court, this view of the High Court of Sindh has been followed in recent judgments, i.e., the High Courts have held that awards, (and arbitration agreements) where the seat is outside Pakistan but the substantive law applicable is the law of Pakistan are foreign arbitration awards (and foreign arbitration agreements) to which the 2011 Act, and not the 1940 Act, is applicable. For instance, in *Orient Power Company (Private) Limited v. Sui Southern Gas Pipelines Limited* PLD [2019] Lahore 607, Lahore High Court held that an award issued under an arbitration agreement provided for London as the seat of arbitration and the substantive law as the law of Pakistan was a foreign arbitral award. This judgment was upheld by the Supreme Court. The Supreme Court did not, however, discuss this aspect of the judgment, presumably because, as observed by the Lahore High Court, petitioner eventually conceded that the award was a foreign arbitral award governed by the 2011 Act. Similarly, in *Karachi Development Limited Company v. IM Technologies Pakistan (Private) Limited and another* [2017] CLCN 157, the validity of an arbitration agreement providing for Singapore as the seat of arbitration and governed by the law of Pakistan was challenged before the High Court of Sindh. The High Court held that the validity of the agreement would be governed by the Act 2011 and not the 1940 Act.

46. As provided in Article 158 of the Limitation Act 1908. In accordance with section 37 of the 1940 Act, all provisions of the Limitation Act 1908 apply to arbitrations in the same manner as they do to court proceedings.

to order arrest and detention of persons,[47] attachment and seizure of property[48] and sale of property.[49]

The second statute is the Recognition and Enforcement (Arbitration Agreements and Foreign Awards) Act 2011 ("*the 2011 Act*"). The 2011 Act was enacted to implement the Convention on the Recognition and Enforcement of Foreign Arbitral Awards 1958 ("*New York Convention*"). It applies to all foreign arbitral awards made after July 14, 2005. Foreign arbitral awards are defined in section 2(e) of the 2011 Act as "*a foreign arbitral award made in a Contracting State and such other State as may be notified by the Federal Government.*" In accordance with section 6 of the 2011 Act, a foreign arbitral award is to be enforced in the same manner as a judgment or order of a court in Pakistan. Once an application for enforcement of an award is filed before the court, it may pass a decree thereon. A court can, however, refuse to enforce an award (i.e., pass a decree thereon) on the limited grounds set out in Article V of the New York Convention.

Courts in Pakistan favor the enforcement of foreign arbitral awards. Unless the award-debtor can establish that the award falls foul of any of the conditions prescribed in Article V of the New York Convention, the court will enforce the award.[50] In making this determination, the court will construe these conditions narrowly and will conduct a summary trial in the absence of any exceptional circumstances.[51]

A decree passed on such an award is then executed in the same manner as a decree under the Code.

The third statute is the Arbitration (International Investment Disputes) Act 2011 ("*the ICSID Act 2011*"). This Act implements the International Convention for the Settlement of Investment Disputes 1964 ("*the ICSID Convention*"). This Act deals exclusively with the registration and enforcement of ICSID awards and does not relate to other types of arbitrations and awards.

VII POWERS OF THE COURT TO ORDER OR ADJUST POST-AWARD INTEREST

9. Does the Pakistani Court Have the Power to Order or Adjust Post-award Interest, Assuming It is Either the Seat Court or the Enforcing Court?

In so far as domestic awards are concerned (i.e., where the seat of the arbitration is in Pakistan), courts have the power to order or adjust post-award interest granted in an

47. Sections 55 to 59 of the Code and Order XXI, Rules 37 to 40 of the Code.
48. Sections 60 to 64 of the Code and Order XXI, Rules 41 to 57 of the Code.
49. Sections 65 to 67 of the Code and Order XXI, Rules 64 to 96 of the Code.
50. *See Orient Power Company (Private) Limited v. Sui Northern Gas Pipelines Limited* [2021] SCMR 1728 at p. [1769], para. [112] where the Supreme Court while upholding the enforcement of a foreign arbitral award affirmed that "*[a] restrictive interpretation on challenge to enforcement of an award would therefore, ensure finality of award at its last stage, giving greater certainty to parties after having gone through rigorous arbitrations. The New York Convention itself advocates for a "pro-enforcement bias" and we are mindful of the same.*"
51. *See Dhanya Agro-Industrial (Pvt.) Ltd. v. Quetta Textile Mills Ltd.* [2019] CLD 160 at p. [163], para. [A]; *Louis Dreyfus Commodities Suisse S.A. v. Acro Textile Mills Ltd.* PLD [2018] Lahore 597 at p. [627], para. [38] and *Abdullah v. CNAN Group SPA*, PLD [2014] Karachi 349 at p. [356], para. [C].

award. As discussed in section I, in accordance with section 29 of the 1940 Act, only the court has the power to grant post-decree interest. A court may, however, adopt such interest if it is granted in the award. Regarding interest prior to this period, a court may adjust or set aside the interest granted or remit the matter to the arbitrators to reconsider for any of the grounds provided in sections 15, 16 and 30 of the 1940 Act.

For instance, in the *Ghulam Abbas*[52] case, the Supreme Court disallowed the interest that was granted from the date of award until the date of the decree on the ground that this issue was not referred to the arbitrator. In *Maqbool Associated Limited v. Sind Sugar Corporation Limited,*[53] the High Court of Sindh disallowed the interest granted in the award for the period prior to the date of reference to arbitration on the ground that the plaintiff's claim did not fall within any of the four categories of cases set out by the Supreme Court in *Ghulam Abbas* in which such interest could be granted. It, therefore, held that there was an error on the face of the award.[54]

Similarly, in *Federation of Pakistan v. Al-Farooq Builders,*[55] the High Court of Sindh considered whether an arbitrator's award of interest up to the date of award was justified. The court held that the arbitrator was justified in equity to award interest on the amount found due and outstanding against the appellant but only from the date of the award. The court, therefore, modified the decree by upholding the grant of interest but only from the date of award till the date of the decree. Likewise, in *Tracon Services (Pvt.) Limited v. Sui Southern Gas Company Limited,*[56] the High Court of Sindh modified the award to the extent that it granted interest pendente lite, as there was no provision in the agreement allowing for the grant of such interest. According to the High Court, this was an error or infirmity which rendered the award invalid on its face.

In so far as foreign arbitral awards are concerned, as discussed in section VII above, these are enforced under the 2011 Act. Under this Act, a court can only refuse to enforce an award on the limited grounds set out in Article V of the New York Convention. It is only if the award of interest falls foul of any of these grounds that a Pakistani court will refuse to enforce the award (including any post-award interest granted therein). For instance, if the interest granted is penal or punitive in nature, a court may refuse to enforce it on the grounds that it is contrary to public policy.

52. PLD [1987] SC 393.
53. [1990] CLC 55.
54. [1990] CLC 68.
55. [2001] MLD 99.
56. PLD [2009] Karachi 54 at p. [57], para. [A].

People's Republic of China

Fei Ning & Ariel Ye

INTRODUCTION

Traditionally, China is a civil law jurisdiction where statutes are essential references for judges or arbitrators adjudicating disputes. The sources of law in China, according to the order of rank, are the Constitution, legislation, administrative regulations, provincial, local regulations, autonomous regulations, separate regulations of national autonomous areas and departmental or local governmental rules. In addition, the Supreme Court of the People's Republic of China (PRC) (*the SPC*) is empowered to issue judicial interpretations on the application of law.[1]

With respect to arbitration, the Arbitration Law of the PRC ("*the Arbitration Law*") (effective as of September 1, 1995), the Civil Procedure Law of the PRC (the latest version effective as of January 1, 2022) and the relevant judicial interpretations issued by the SPC govern arbitration proceedings in China if the *lex arbitri* is Chinese law.

The Arbitration Law plays an important role. It applies as a supplement to the procedural rules agreed upon by the parties and operates in many other respects to which the parties cannot derogate from by agreement including, for example, the minimal requirements for validity of an arbitration agreement, qualifications of arbitrators, matters pertaining to establishment of arbitration institutions in China and judicial supervision over arbitration. Arbitrators are not bound to invoke the judicial interpretations to decide disputes, but they may opt to make a reference to judicial interpretations to strengthen their reasoning.

Under the Arbitration Law, arbitral tribunals in China-seated arbitrations are afforded broad power to decide on matters in dispute. In general, arbitral tribunals are decision-makers, provided that they settle disputes according to facts and applicable

1. For a detailed account of the sources of law in China, *see* the Legislation Law of the People's Republic of China adopted by the People's Congress on March 15, 2000, revised on March 15, 2015.

law. Article 54 of the Arbitration Law states that an arbitral award must state the arbitration claims, the matters in dispute, the grounds upon which an award is given, the results of the award, the allocation of the arbitration fees and the date of the award. No specific guidance is given as to how an arbitral tribunal awards interest. At the same time, no specific restriction is imposed upon its authority to do so.

In China, the issue of interest is deemed a substantive issue, usually dealt with by the applicable substantive law, and an arbitral tribunal may award it, simple or compound, pre- or post-award at the request of one or both parties. An award of interest is final and binding as to the matters determined, and it may also be challenged or enforced in the same manner as any other award issued by an arbitral tribunal.

This chapter will discuss several issues relating to interest in arbitration, taking China as an example. In sequence, it covers the arbitral tribunal's power to award post-award interest (Part one), choice of law (Part two), substantive issues (Part four), procedural law issues (Part five) and enforcement (Parts three, six and seven).

I POWER TO GRANT POST-AWARD INTEREST

1. Does an Arbitral Tribunal Have the Power to Grant Post-award Interest under National Law?

In PRC,[2] the Arbitration Law and its relevant judicial interpretations[3] are silent on whether an arbitral tribunal has the power to grant post-award interest. Thus, PRC law does not explicitly prohibit an arbitral tribunal from granting post-award interest under the applicable substantive law to the subject matters or procedural law to the arbitration proceedings.

It is generally understood that a wide range of remedies is available to arbitrators. Remedies granted by arbitral tribunals frequently include declaratory relief, specific performance, damages or monetary compensation and interest. When an arbitral tribunal decides upon disputes, the issue of interest normally falls within the scope of substantive law, which may be awarded only at the request of one or both parties.

2. There are four different legal regimes in the People's Republic of China (*PRC*), i.e., mainland China, the Hong Kong Special Administrative Region, the Macau Special Administrative Region and the Taiwan Province. In this chapter, the authors only discuss how the law applies to mainland China (excluding Hong Kong, Macau and Taiwan).
3. The Arbitration Law of People's Republic of China became effective on September 1, 1995, and was followed by the following judicial interpretations: the Interpretation of the Supreme People's Court concerning Some Issues on Application of the Arbitration Law of the PRC ("*2006 Interpretation*"), effective as of September 8, 2006; Provisions of the Supreme People's Court on Several Issues Concerning the Hearing of Cases Involving the Judicial Review of Arbitration ("*Hearing Provisions*"), effective as of January 1, 2018; Provisions of the Supreme People's Court on Issues concerning the Reporting and Examination of Cases Involving the Judicial Review of Arbitration ("*Reporting Provisions*"), effective as of January 1, 2018; Provisions of the Supreme People's Court on Several Issues Concerning the Handling of Cases of Enforcement of Arbitration Awards by People's Courts ("*Enforcement Provisions*"), effective as of March 1, 2018 and several official replies issued by the Supreme People's Court to address questions that arose from specific cases.

An arbitral tribunal risks exceeding its mandate or authority by awarding interest on its own initiative. The award may be set aside or considered incapable of being enforced without a request for interest by any of the parties.

Unless otherwise agreed by the parties, arbitral tribunals seated in PRC usually award simple interest on principal claims. Compound interest may be awarded based on parties' express agreement in the underlying transaction.

As a matter of substantive law, PRC law allows judges or arbitral tribunals to award interest at the request of the requesting party (not necessarily all parties to the dispute). Interest is regarded as a sort of compensation for loss, and the aggrieved party may claim for loss of interest in lieu of liquidated damage if the disputing parties have failed to agree on liquidated damage previously. For example, Article 24 of the Judicial Interpretation on Application of Law in Trial of Dispute over the Sale and Purchase Contract issued by the Supreme People's Court[4] provides:

> Where the sale and purchase contract does not contain the provisions on the liquidated damages for overdue payment or methods for calculation of such liquidated damages, and buyer claims for compensation for the loss caused by overdue payment on the ground of the breaches by the buyer, the people's court may calculate such loss on the basis of the RMB lending rate of the People's Bank of China applicable to such claim kind of loans in such claim period and by reference to the standards of penalty interest rate for overdue payment.

Article 24 clearly grants the power to award liquidated damages (with a similar function as interest) on overdue payment to a judicial institution. There is no specific period for such interest prescribed under Article 24.

According to the commentary of the senior justices from the Supreme People's Court,[5] the SPC intentionally left open the question of what the appropriate date for calculating the interest should be, as different situations arise when deciding the date from when interest should accrue. Any unambiguous definition of the term of the interest in Article 24 will lead to unfair results. It is for this reason that judicial institutions have the discretion to determine the closing date on a case-by-case basis.

The judicial interpretations issued by the SPC are frequently used as helpful references in arbitration. Similar to the judicial practice, it is reasonable to expect an arbitral tribunal seated in China to follow the established judicial practice in granting interest and drawing the inference that there is no general barrier for an arbitral tribunal to grant a post-award interest in PRC.

An arbitral tribunal's award of interest, including pre- and post-award interest, is considered similar to the general interest accruing on debt. The parties to the arbitration must comply with the arbitral award within the designated time limit or, if unable to, in a timely manner. Delay or non-compliance with the arbitral award may cause the defaulting party to undergo an additional financial burden known as

4. Fa Shi [2012] No. 8, adopted at the 1545th meeting of the Judicial Committee of the Supreme People's Court on March 31, 2012.
5. Songxiaoming, Zhang Yongjian, Wang Chuang, *Understanding and Application of the Interpretation on Application of Law in Trial of Dispute over the Sale and Purchase Contract* (15 edn, Remin Sifa 2012) at pp. [27]-[41].

"*doubled interest on debt.*" The doubled interest on debt is usually imposed by the enforcing court of law during the enforcement proceedings, not by an arbitral tribunal. Put in another way, general interest on debt is of a compensatory nature, but the doubled interest on debt is of a penalty nature: the defaulting party is obliged to pay twice the amount of general interest on debt because of its non-compliance with or delay in executing the judgment or award. Obviously, the power to impose doubled interest on debt is exclusively reserved for the enforcing court of law. An arbitral tribunal has no power to rule on the doubled interest on debt.

The practice of double interest on debt is created by Article 253 of *the Civil Procedure Law of the PRC* and its relevant interpretations, as discussed below. Article 253 concerns the calculation of the interest in enforcement proceedings and provides that:

> If a judgement debtor subject to execution fails to perform its obligations to pay within the time limit specified in a judgement, ruling or other legal document, it shall pay the doubled amount of interest on the debt for the period during which the performance is deferred.

The foregoing Article 253 is further elaborated by Article 1 of the *Interpretation of the Supreme People's Court on Several Issues Concerning the Application of Law in the Calculation of Interest on Debts During the Delay in the Performance of Execution Procedures*[6] as follows:

> According to the provisions in Article 253 of the Civil Procedure Law of the People's Republic of China, after doubled, the interest on the debts during the delay in the performance shall include the *general interest on debt and the doubled interest on debt during the delay in the performance.* (Emphasis added)
>
> The general interest on debt during the delay in the performance shall be calculated by methods determined by effective legal instruments; for interest that is not determined by the effective legal instruments, it will not be calculated.
>
> The formula of calculating the doubled interest in delay shall be as follows: the doubled interest in delay = the outstanding pecuniary debts determined by the effective legal instruments other than the general interest on debt × 0.175‰/day × the period of delay in the performance.

This provision essentially provides that a judgment debtor's delay of compliance with any effective legal instrument (i.e., a judgment or an arbitral award) will result in a penalty interest by doubling the amount for such a delay.

The interest after "*being doubled*" is comprised of two parts. The first is known as the "*general interest on debt,*" calculated by methods determined by the effective legal instrument. If no such interest is awarded in the legal instrument, then no "*general interest on debt*" will be available for the judgment creditor. The second is the "*doubled interest on debt*" in delay execution, calculated at the daily interest rate of 0.175% since the date of the delay in complying with the effective legal instrument.

After being doubled, these two parts of interest are designed to exist in parallel and serve different functions. The general interest on debt is designed to cover the

6. Fa Shi [2014] No. 8, adopted at the 1619th meeting of the Judicial Committee of the Supreme People's Court on June 9, 2014, coming into force on August 1, 2014.

actual loss suffered by judgment creditors, while the doubled interest on debt is designed to penalize the judgment debtors for their failure to comply with any legally binding instrument.

From the composition of the interest under Article 253, it can be inferred that a PRC enforcement court will generally respect what is awarded by the effective legal instruments, including the method of calculating post-award interest.

However, it is still unclear how Article 253 would work if the interest awarded in the arbitral awards also contains penalty interest. In general, an award of interest should be compensatory or restitutionary rather than penal in nature. If a general interest on debt states that it contains penal interest, it is better to clarify that the parties use the term "penal" and that it is meant to be within a general interest on debt as a caution.

Statistical figures regarding the award of such interest in arbitrations are unavailable, as arbitral awards are generally covered by confidentiality requirements, and not all the PRC courts' decisions on enforcement of arbitral awards are publicly available.

Among the few reported cases, awards of post-award interest are rare. One of the possible reasons for this is the fee charge mechanism of the PRC arbitration institutions. In PRC, arbitration fees are charged and calculated according to the amount claimed. Therefore, the amount awarded by the tribunal must be fixed to calculate the arbitration fee. Claimants are more likely to claim the interest up to the date when the arbitral awards are issued to advance fewer amounts of arbitration fees, rather than up to the date of actual execution.

Due to the lack of precedents and statistics, it is difficult to provide a clear answer as to how a PRC enforcement court would act if the interest awarded by the arbitral award contains a penalty element. Most arbitral tribunals would likely refrain from awarding penalty interest because of easily triggered public policy scrutiny by the enforcing court.

Additionally, Article 253 for the doubled interest on debt mentioned above is a provision designed for enforcement in the civil procedural law, which means it is irrelevant to the conduct of arbitration proceedings or the making of arbitral awards. Hence, arbitral tribunals cannot rely on Article 253 directly to impose doubled interest on debt in arbitral awards. Yet, in practice, some arbitral tribunals in PRC occasionally refer to doubled interest on debt under Article 253 in arbitration awards.

So doing in the arbitral awards, in the opinion of the authors, is more of a note or warning to the debtors rather than a substantive ruling. The tribunal might want to warn the debtor that if the effective arbitral award is not timely performed, the debtors may face doubled interest on debt mandatorily imposed by the PRC enforcing courts in subsequent enforcement procedures. However, the authors discourage doing so because the arbitral tribunal may go beyond its authority and bring enforcement risks if challenged by the debtor.

2. Is the Power Exercisable Without a Request or Submission, or Is Such a Submission Required?

The general presumption under PRC law and arbitral practice is that arbitral tribunals must issue arbitral awards based on applicants' requests or submissions. An arbitral tribunal should not award interest without the request of an applicant as the award will fall outside the scope of the arbitration.

This general position is confirmed by Article 13 of the Provisions of the Supreme People's Court on Several Issues Concerning the Handling of Cases by People's Courts to Enforce Arbitration Awards, effective on March 1, 2018. Article 13 specifies that, if a tribunal's arbitral award goes beyond the scope of the arbitral requests, the matters decided in the award would be considered as exceeding the scope of the arbitration agreement or going beyond the arbitral authority of the arbitration institution. This would constitute a ground for refusal of enforcement of the award.

3. Is the Power Classified as One under the Substantive Applicable Law or the Procedural Law of the Arbitration?

No PRC law specifies a tribunal's power and scope to award interest. Additionally, there is little scholarly commentary dealing with such a classification. Therefore, no certain answer exists to this question under PRC law.

However, the issue of interest is largely treated by PRC law as a substantive law question. The most important one is the Civil Code of the PRC,[7] in which there are twelve articles (Articles 389, 561, 579, 589, 667, 670, 671, 674, 676, 677, 680 and 691) addressing various types of interest, including ordinary interest, security interest, loan interest, overdue payment interest, usurious loan interest and suretyship interest. The Arbitration Law of the PRC has no express provision on interest. Nevertheless, it points out that the mission of an arbitral tribunal is to resolve commercial "*disputes*" which are arbitrable, including any dispute pertaining to interest.[8]

For the general interest on debt awarded by arbitral tribunals, unless the arbitral rules or *lex arbitri* specifically allows arbitral tribunals to award post-award interest, their power is based on the substantive laws of the subject matter. However, for the doubled interest on debt in delay execution cited in Article 253 above, this power is clearly conferred to PRC enforcement courts by the Civil Procedure Law of the PRC. Therefore, it is a power of courts under procedural law.

II CHOICE OF LAW

For the general interest on debt granted in arbitral awards, the choice of law will be subject to the substantive laws applicable to the subject matter.

Regarding doubled interest on debt in delay execution mentioned above, the choice of law is considered as falling under mandatory procedural law as it is provided by Article 253 of the Civil Procedure Law of the PRC.

7. Adopted at the Third Session of the Thirteenth National People's Congress on May 28, 2020, and entered into force on January 1, 2021.
8. *See* Article 1 Arbitration Law, which declares that "*This Law is formulated in order to ensure the impartial and prompt arbitration of economic disputes.*"

III DO THE COURTS TAKE INTO ACCOUNT INTERNATIONAL STANDARDS WHEN FACING CHALLENGES ON THE POST-AWARD INTEREST?

None exists to the knowledge of the authors.

IV SUBSTANTIVE LAW ISSUES

4. How Are Contractual Provisions on Late or Non-payment of Interest Relevant to Post-award Interest? Will These Be Considered By the Arbitral Tribunal?

If PRC law is applicable as substantive law, the contractual provisions of late or non-payment interest will be considered by the arbitral tribunal if a request on interest is pleaded by applicants. Such interest is considered a loss suffered by the innocent party and shall be decided by the contractual agreement or applicable substantive laws.

That being said, the contractual provisions on late or non-payment interest are not irrelevant to post-award interest if the requesting parties invoke these provisions to support their reliefs sought.

A case that the authors participated in serves as a good example. The arbitral tribunal awarded interest on overdue payment up to the date of the submission of the application for arbitration at the rate provided by the contractual provision. The arbitral tribunal particularly addressed in the award its awareness of the contractual provision on late or non-payment interest that could accumulate to the actual payment date. However, as the applicant's request only covered the period up to the submission of application for arbitration, the tribunal could only award the interest up to the date requested by the applicant.

The arbitral tribunal in the above case relied on the contractual provision to award interest. The tribunal also indicated that, if a request had been made by the applicant to cover the post-award interest, it would have supported such a request by relying on the contractual provision as well.

It must be emphasized that while arbitral tribunals in PRC are restrained from issuing awards beyond the scope of the applicants' requests, there are other occasions where the authors observed some tribunals awarding interest beyond the claimants' requests. Considering the basic rule of confidentiality of arbitration, the authors are unable to conclude how often tribunals in PRC will award interests beyond the applicants' requests, but the authors believe that it must be less common than usual to avoid potential challenges to arbitral awards.

5. How do the Procedural Rules of the Substantive Law Apply?

In terms of doubled interest on debt, arbitral tribunals are not provided with the same power granted to the enforcing courts by the PRC Civil Procedure law. Therefore, there is little room for the procedural rules of the substantive law to apply.

In terms of general interest on debt, arbitral tribunals may apply the relevant conflict of law rules contained in the applicable arbitration rules, supplemented by relevant rules of *lex arbitri*, to determine which substantive law shall be applied to awarding interest. A good example is paragraph 2 of Article 51 of the Arbitration Rules of the Shenzhen Court of International Arbitration (SCIA), which provides:

> Where the parties have agreed on the law as it applies to the merits of their dispute, the parties' agreement shall prevail. In the absence of such an agreement or where such agreement is in conflict with a mandatory provision of the law of the place of arbitration, the arbitral tribunal shall determine which law is applicable.[9]

V PROCEDURAL LAW ISSUES

6. What Are the Main Procedural Law Issues When Considering Post-award Interest? How Are the Arbitration Laws and Other Laws or Regulations of the Seat Relevant?

Miscalculation

According to Article 4 of the Provisions of the Supreme People's Court on Several Issues Concerning the Handling of Cases by People's Courts to Enforce Arbitration Awards,[10] if there is a miscalculation of the interest in an arbitral award, the court may invite the arbitral tribunal to clarify and correct the mistake. If the arbitral tribunal fails to clarify or correct the mistake and the court is still unsure about the amount to be enforced after reading the arbitral documentation, the court is entitled to reject the application for enforcement for that part of the award.[11]

Non-enforcement

If the law of the seat of arbitration has any specific restrictions on an arbitral tribunal's power to make a monetary award for any period after the date of the issuance of the arbitration award, the enforcement of post-award interest may be denied by the PRC enforcement courts for different reasons. These include an award falling outside the arbitral tribunal's jurisdiction or containing procedural mistakes. However, there is no precedent for such non-enforcement cases available in the PRC law database.[12]

9. Article 51.2 SCIA Arbitration Rules (effective from February 21, 2019, with amendments as adopted in 2020 effective from October 1, 2020).
10. Provisions of the Supreme People's Court on Several Issues Concerning the Handling of Cases by People's Courts to Enforce Arbitration Awards, effective as of March 1, 2018.
11. Full text of Article 4 reads: "*If there are errors in words or calculations in the main body of the arbitral award or in the arbitration mediation document, or matters that have been identified by the arbitral tribunal but are omitted from the main body of the award, which can be corrected or explained, the people's court shall notify the arbitral tribunal in writing to make corrections or explanations, or borrow arbitration case file from the arbitration institution to find out and ascertain the issues. If the arbitral tribunal neither makes corrections nor explains, and the people's court has reviewed the arbitration case file and the enforcement content is still unclear and cannot be enforced, it may rule to reject the enforcement application.*"
12. The latest day of searching https://wenshu.court.gov.cn (中国裁判文书网): 25 August 2022.

Doubled Interest on Debt

If the seat of the arbitration is in PRC, according to the Arbitration Law of the PRC, an arbitral award will come into effect upon its issuance.[13] If the debtor fails to perform according to the arbitral award during the performance period prescribed by the award and an enforcement application is made before a PRC court, the PRC enforcement court would likely impose the doubled interest on debt forward from the expiration date of the prescribed performance period up until to the date of actual payment.

If the seat of the arbitration is not in PRC but the enforcement application is made before a PRC court, doubled interest on debt might not be calculated until the date when the arbitral award is formally recognized by a PRC court, in accordance with the New York Convention or bilateral arrangements.

There is no statutory provision addressing whether the recognition must have a retrospective effect on doubled interest on debt in delayed execution. The law, therefore, does not specify whether, once arbitral awards are recognized by PRC courts, the doubled interest on debt should be calculated retrospectively from the date a debtor failed to timely perform its obligation as prescribed by the arbitral award.

It is the authors' view that, based on the wording of Article 253 of the Civil Procedure Law of the PRC, only a delay in performance of a PRC-recognized effective legal instrument can trigger the doubled interest on debt under Article 253. Therefore, the doubled interest on debt in delay execution cases should be calculated from the date the PRC courts formally recognize the arbitral awards.

VI EFFECT OF ENFORCEMENT ORDERS ON INTEREST ON THE AWARD ON BOTH THE SEAT AND ELSEWHERE

The enforcement orders will be the basis for enforcing the arbitral awards in PRC. However, there will be no impact on the award if enforcement is not sought in PRC.

VII POWERS OF THE COURT TO ORDER OR ADJUST POST-AWARD INTEREST

In general, interest is a matter of merits. Under PRC law, the grounds for refusal of enforcement of a foreign-related arbitral award are confined to procedural irregularities[14] and henceforth the enforcement courts do not have the power to adjust the interest awarded by an arbitral tribunal. Otherwise, it would go against the non-interference-of-merits policy in enforcement procedure. Accordingly, the enforcement courts may only recognize, deny or partially deny interest awarded that is beyond the arbitral tribunal's authority. The enforcement courts cannot adjust the rate or base for calculating such interest since it is considered an exclusive power of the arbitral tribunal.

13. Article 57 Arbitration Law, providing that "*The arbitral award takes legal effect upon its issuing.*"
14. Article 71 Arbitration Law and Article 274 of the Civil Procedure Law of the PRC.

Republic of India

Gopal Subramanium

INTRODUCTION

Arbitral tribunals in India are authorised to award (or refrain from awarding) post-award interest at a rate they deem appropriate. This authorisation flows from section 31(7)(b) of the Arbitration and Conciliation Act, 1996 (*the 1996 Act*). Section 31(7)(b) of the 1996 Act applies to domestic arbitrations and international commercial arbitrations seated in India.

Where awards are silent on matters concerning post-award interest, the 1996 Act mandates that such interest be imposed at a rate 2% higher than the prevailing '*current rate of interest*' as defined under the Interest Act, 1978. Tribunals can exercise their power to grant post-award interest irrespective of whether specific submissions have been made on the issue.

In India-seated arbitrations, where an award is under challenge, Indian courts may alter the rate at which post-award interest is awarded. Courts are authorised in such cases to reduce the rate awarded by a tribunal if, *inter alia*, it does not reflect prevailing economic conditions or is found unreasonable. The courts' determination will take notice of rates of interest prevalent internationally. Where an award emanates from an international commercial arbitration seated outside India, a party may object to its enforcement if post-award interest was awarded despite being barred under the arbitration agreement. Similarly, where the rate of post-award interest is unreasonably high, it is open to a party to contest enforcement on the ground that a usurious rate offends the public policy of India.

Section I of this chapter first begins by explaining the statutory authority behind the power of an arbitral tribunal in India to grant post-award interest. Next, section II explains the background behind the 1996 Act and how post-award interest in India is determined by the law of the seat. Section III discusses the practice of Indian courts using international standards when considering interest rates awarded by an arbitral tribunal.

Section IV of this chapter considers substantive law issues, including the mandate that arbitral tribunals take terms of the contract into account while provisioning for the late or non-payment of post-award interest. Next, section V discusses the main procedural law issues when considering post-award interest, including a detailed discussion of what the parties can expect when seeking corrections, pursuing a set aside of or accepting the arbitral award. Section VI explains the two stages of the effect of enforcement orders on interest, first in relation to the enforcement of foreign awards in India and next regarding execution proceedings originating from arbitrations in or outside of India.

Finally, section VII of this chapter discusses the power of enforcement courts in India to order or adjust post-award interest granted by an arbitral tribunal.

I POWER TO GRANT POST-AWARD INTEREST

1. Does an Arbitral Tribunal Have the Power to Grant Post-award Interest under National Law?

Yes, an arbitral tribunal in India has the power to grant post-award interest under the national law. The source of this power is in section 31(7)b of the 1996 Act, the Act which presently governs, *inter alia*, domestic arbitrations, international commercial arbitrations seated in India and the enforcement of foreign awards under the New York Convention.[1] The 1996 Act incorporated much of the United Nations Commission on International Trade (UNCITRAL) Model Law on International Commercial Arbitration while replacing the Arbitration Act of 1940.[2] Interestingly, the 1940 Act had no specific provision for granting either pre- or post-award interest, both of which were previously governed by section 34 of the Code of Civil Procedure, 1908.

Section 31(7) of the 1996 Act concerns the grant of both pre- and post-award interest. Under subsection (7)(a) of section 31, an arbitral tribunal can award pre-award interest from the date on which the cause of action arose to the date on which the award is made (or for any period in between). A tribunal's power to grant interest for the pre-award period is discretionary, leaving it to the arbitrators to decide whether interest should be granted at all and, in case it should, at what rate. However, this power is subservient to the principle of party autonomy. Subsection (7)(a) opens with the words '*Unless otherwise agreed by the parties*', indicating clearly that the discretion to grant pre-award interest is exercisable only if there is no agreement between the parties *quoad* pre-award interest. The Supreme Court of India held in *Sri Chittaranjan Maity v. Union of India*[3] that where the parties had agreed that interest shall not be payable, an arbitral tribunal had no power to grant pre-award interest. Expanding this ruling, the Supreme Court has also held that while it is permissible for parties to agree that no interest shall be payable, if the parties fail to raise a plea based on such a

1. Convention on the Recognition and Enforcement of Foreign Arbitral Awards (New York, 1958).
2. The 1996 Act also repealed and replaced the Arbitration (Protocol and Convention) Act, 1937 and the Foreign Awards (Recognition and Enforcement) Act, 1961.
3. [2017] 9 SCC 611, at [18]-[20].

contractual bar, they are deemed to have waived their right to object to the grant of interest.[4] Naturally, parties are also in a position to agree on the applicable rate of interest, and the language of subsection (7)(a) would bind the tribunal to such an agreement.

Section 31(7)(b) relates specifically to post-award interest. The power to grant interest from the date of the award to the date of payment is not (unlike subsection (7)(a)) subject to an agreement between the parties.[5] Subsection (7)(b) of section 31, as it presently stands, reads thus:

> A sum directed to be paid by an arbitral award shall, unless the award otherwise directs, carry interest at the rate of two percent higher than the current rate of interest prevalent on the date of the award, from the date of award to the date of payment.

Evidently, the 1996 Act gives an arbitral tribunal power to provide for post-award interest on money awards at such rate as it deems appropriate. An award may also refrain from granting any post-award interest, provided this decision is clearly expressed by the tribunal. Where the award is silent, the 1996 Act mandates that interest be payable from the date of the award to the date of payment at a rate 2% higher than the '*current rate of interest*'. It may be noted that the 1996 Act, as originally enacted, statutorily mandated the imposition of post-award interest at a rate of 18% per annum. Following an Amendment to the Act in 2015,[6] this rate has been altered to 2% higher than the '*current rate of interest*', an expression defined in the Interest Act 1978 as '*the highest of the maximum rates at which interest may be paid on different classes of deposits (other than those maintained by charitable or religious institutions) by different classes of scheduled banks in accordance with the directions given or issued to banking companies generally by the Reserve Bank of India under the Banking Regulation Act, 1949*'.

It is also relevant to note that following the decision of the Supreme Court of India in *Hyder Consulting (UK) Ltd. v. State of Orissa*,[7] post-award interest is not awarded on the principal money award rendered by a tribunal. Instead, it applies to the aggregate sum of the principal money award *and* pre-award interest. This has significant repercussions on the liability of an award-debtor who may now be liable to pay post-award interest on a sum much larger than the principal money award.

4. *Union of India v. Susaka Pvt. Ltd. & Ors.* [2018] 2 SCC 182, at [17], [27] and [31-35]. *See also Jaiprakash Associates v. Tehri Hydro Development* [2019] SCC OnLine SC 143.
5. *Vedanta Ltd. v. Shenzhen Shandong Nuclear Power Construction Co. Ltd.* [2018] SCC OnLine SC 1922.
6. The Arbitration and Conciliation (Amendment) Act, 2015 (No. 3 of 2016), with effect from 23 Oct. 2015. The 1996 Act, as amended, applies to arbitral proceedings and ancillary court proceedings that commenced on or after 23 Oct. 2015: *Board of Control for Cricket in India v. Kochi Cricket Pvt. Ltd.* [2018] 6 SCC 287.
7. [2015] 2 SCC 189. *See also UHL Power Company Ltd. v. State of Himachal Pradesh* [2022] 4 SCC 116.

2. Is the Power Exercisable Without a Request or Submission, or Is Such a Submission Required?

Yes, the power to award post-award interest can be exercised without a request or submission by the parties. This follows necessarily from the language of section 31(7)(b), which not only refrains from granting primacy to any agreement between the parties regarding post-award interest but also mandates the levy of interest until the date of payment in cases where the award is silent on the issue. Thus, for instance, where parties make no submissions regarding post-award interest, and where the award itself does not discuss the issue, interest at a rate 2% higher than the current rate of interest would automatically apply. Remarking on the mandatory character of post-award interest under the 1996 Act, the Supreme Court noted that '*post-award interest on the awarded sum is mandate of the statute ... if the Arbitral Tribunal has awarded post-award interest payable from the date of award to the date of payment at a particular rate in its discretion then it will prevail else the party will be entitled to claim post-award interest on the awarded sum at the statutory rate specified in clause (b) of Section 31(7) of the Act ...* '.[8]

Further, seen teleologically, the non-requirement for specific submission appears appropriate. While the purpose of pre-award interest is to compensate an award-holder for its '*foregone return on investment, or for the money withheld without justifiable cause*',[9] post-award interest seeks only to '*encourage early payment of the awarded sum and to discourage the usual delay, which accompanies the execution of the award*'.[10] Viewed thus, post-award interest serves an important public policy objective, i.e., to ensure a swift end to disputes, thus justifying the non-requirement for submissions.

It is important to note that while there is no requirement for submissions, the tribunal's discretion to award post-award interest is not unfettered. In *Vedanta Ltd. v. Shenzhen Shandong Nuclear Power Construction Co. Ltd*[11] (*Vedanta*), the Supreme Court laid down the factors that tribunals must consider in exercising their discretion to award interest:

> 12. The discretion of the arbitrator to award interest must be exercised reasonably. An arbitral tribunal while making an award for interest must take into consideration a host of factors, such as:
>
> (i) the 'loss of use' of the principal sum;
> (ii) the types of sums to which the interest must apply;
> (iii) the time period over which interest should be awarded;
> (iv) the internationally prevailing rates of interest;
> (v) whether simple or compound rate of interest is to be applied;
> (vi) whether the rate of interest awarded is commercially prudent from an economic stand-point;
> (vii) the rates of inflation;

8. [2015] 2 SCC 189. *See also UHL Power Company Ltd. v. State of Himachal Pradesh* [2022] 4 SCC 116.
9. *Vedanta*, at [4].
10. *Hyder*, at [9].
11. *Vedanta*.

(viii) proportionality of the amount awarded as interest to the principal sums awarded.

3. Is the Power Classified as One Under the Substantive Applicable Law or the Procedural Law of the Arbitration?

The power to grant post-award interest is classifiable as one under the procedural law or the *lex arbitri*, which in India's example would be the 1996 Act. However, as will be discussed in section II below, Indian law adopts the position taken under Article 1(2) of the Model Law,[12] namely, that for arbitrations seated in India, the procedural law will be the *lex loci arbitri* (the law of the seat).

II CHOICE OF LAW

4. What is the Law That Applies to Determine What the Post-award Interest Should Be? Would This Be the Governing Law of the Dispute or the Law of the Seat?

Post-award interest in India or, more particularly, the application of section 31(7)(b), is determined by the law of the seat. To fully understand this position, one must examine the structure of the 1996 Act. The 1996 Act is divided into four parts. Part I is titled '*Arbitration*' and covers areas including the powers of courts to grant interim relief, appoint arbitrators and set aside awards and the tribunal's power to award both pre- and post-award interest. Part II concerns the enforcement of awards under the New York and Geneva Conventions. Part III deals with conciliation, while Part IV prescribes certain supplementary provisions. For our present purposes, we are concerned only with Parts I and II.

In *Bhatia International v. Bulk Trading SA*,[13] the Supreme Court of India was called upon to determine whether Part I of the 1996 Act would apply to foreign-seated arbitrations. The court found that Parliament had not intended to exclude the applicability of Part I to arbitrations seated outside India, concluding that '*in cases of international commercial arbitrations held out of India, provisions of Part I would apply unless the parties by agreement, express or implied, exclude all or any of its provisions. In that case, the laws or rules chosen by the parties would prevail. Any provision, in Part I, which is contrary to or excluded by that law or rules will not apply*'.[14]

The decision in *Bhatia* continued to occupy the field until it came up for a detailed reconsideration in *Bharat Aluminium Co. Ltd. v. Kaiser Aluminium Technical Services* (*BALCO*).[15] Following the decision of the Supreme Court in *BALCO*, Part I of the 1996 Act applies only to domestic arbitrations and international commercial arbitrations

12. UNCITRAL Model Law on International Commercial Arbitration, 1985, as amended by the United Nations Commission on International Trade Law on 7 Jul. 2006, Article 1(2): '*The provisions of this Law, except Articles 8, 9, 17H, 17I, 17J, 35 and 36, apply only if the place of the arbitration is in the territory of this State*'.
13. [2002] 4 SCC 105.
14. [2002] 4 SCC 105.
15. [2012] 9 SCC 552.

seated in India.[16] The Supreme Court in *BALCO* concluded that the seat of arbitration was intended to be its '*centre of gravity*' and Parts I and II of the 1996 Act were mutually exclusive. For arbitrations seated outside India, the operation of Part I of the Act stood excluded.[17]

As already noted, section 31(7)(b) that empowers tribunals to grant post-award interest falls under Part I. It follows that the provision will apply in domestic arbitrations and international commercial arbitrations seated in India.

III DO THE COURTS TAKE INTO ACCOUNT INTERNATIONAL STANDARDS WHEN FACING CHALLENGES ON THE POST-AWARD INTEREST?

Yes, courts account for internationally prevalent standards in considering possible corrections to interest rates awarded by an arbitral tribunal. In her judgment in *Vedanta*,[18] Justice Malhotra lays down the principles which govern the award of interest in arbitrations. These principles expressly include a consideration of internationally prevalent rates of interest.

The arbitrators in *Vedanta* had granted a dual rate of interest for the post-award period (9% for 120 days post the award and 15% for any period thereafter, until the date of realisation). The arbitration in *Vedanta* was seated in India and the award was thus challenged by Vedanta, the award-debtor, before the Delhi High Court under section 34 of the 1996 Act. Vedanta's challenge was dismissed by the court, causing it to file an appeal before a Division Bench of the Delhi High Court. The Division Bench, too, dismissed Vedanta's appeal, finding no ground to disturb the award. Finally, Vedanta succeeded before the Supreme Court of India where it appealed the Division Bench's decision.

The Supreme Court held that the imposition of a dual rate of interest for the post-award period was unjustified, finding a higher rate of 15% to be arbitrary and excessive. Specifically, the court observed that the '*imposition of a high rate of interest @ 15 per cent post-120 days is exorbitant, from an economic standpoint, and has no co-relation with the prevailing contemporary international rates of Interest*'. Altering the

16. After the 2015 Amendment to the 1996 Act (*Supra* n. 6), unless the parties agree to the contrary, sections 9 (Interim measures, etc., by court), 27 (court assistance in taking evidence), 37(1)(a) and 37(1)(c) (Appealable orders) of Part I will also apply to international commercial arbitrations seated outside India.
17. *BALCO*, at [194]-[197]. Importantly, the law laid down in *BALCO* applies prospectively, i.e., to arbitration agreements executed after 6 Sep. 2012, the date on which the judgment was rendered. For agreements entered before this date, the law applicable would be that as laid down in *Bhatia.* However, even in such cases, were the court to arrive at the determination that the juridical seat of an arbitration was outside India or that a law other than Indian law governed the arbitration agreement, Part I of the 1996 Act would be excluded by necessary implication. *See Union of India v. Reliance Industries Ltd. & Ors.* [2015] 10 SCC 213, at [21].
18. *Vedanta.*

award, the court held, *inter alia*, that on the part of the award,[19] post-award interest would apply at a rate 3 percentage points higher than the prevailing London Interbank Offered Rate (LIBOR) rate of interest. (LIBOR indicates the borrowing cost between banks and offers an internationally accepted standard for determining rates of interest.)

IV SUBSTANTIVE LAW ISSUES

5. How Are Contractual Provisions on Late or Non-payment of Interest Relevant to Post-award Interest? Will These Be Considered By the Arbitral Tribunal?

Nothing in Indian law proscribes arbitral tribunals from relying on contractual provisions that concern the late or non-payment of post-award interest. On the contrary, section 28(3) of the 1996 Act places a general obligation on tribunals to take contractual terms *'into account'*:

> 28. Rules applicable to the substance of dispute –
>
> ...
>
> (3) While deciding and making an award, the arbitral tribunal shall, in all cases, take into account the terms of the contract and trade usages applicable to the transaction.

In light of the above, it is clear that contractual provisions concerning the late or non-payment of post-award interest must be considered by arbitrators. Further, in domestic arbitrations, it is of particular importance that contractual terms are followed by arbitrators. A failure to do so may cause the award to be set aside on the ground that it is patently illegal.[20]

6. How do the Procedural Rules of the Substantive Law Apply?

We have seen above that section 31(7)(b) would apply to domestic arbitrations and international commercial arbitrations seated in India. This statement would hold true to such arbitrations regardless of any requirement under substantive law, other than Indian law, to apply its procedural rules – a position that emerges from the absence of any condition giving primacy to an agreement between the parties on matters involving post-award interest. In other words, where Part I of the 1996 Act applies, section 31(7)(b) is mandatory and non-derogable.

Assuming the substantive law in a dispute is Indian law, it may be prudent to examine the procedural rules governing post-award or future interest, which are found in section 34 of the Code of Civil Procedure 1908 (*the Code*). Under this provision, where a decree is for the payment of money, a court may order future interest on the principal sum adjudged from the date of the decree to the date of payment or such earlier date as it considers appropriate. The rate of such future interest is capped by section 34 at 6%, a limit which is subject to the Proviso: *'that where the liability in*

19. The award in *Vedanta* contained amounts payable in both Indian Rupees and Euros. The LIBOR + 3% rate was applicable only to the Euro component of the award, while a uniform rate of 9% was made applicable to the Indian Rupee component for the post-award period.
20. *Indian Oil Corporation Ltd. v. Shree Ganesh Petroleum Rajgurunagar* [2022] 4 SCC 463, at [43].

relation to the sum adjudged had arisen out of a commercial transaction, the rate of such further interest may exceed six per cent per annum, but shall not exceed the contractual rate of interest or where there is no contractual rate, the rate at which moneys are lent or advanced by nationalised banks in relation to commercial transactions'. Section 34 also makes it clear that where a decree is silent with respect to future interest, the court is deemed to have refused to grant it.

Some relevant differences emerge between section 31(7)(b) of the 1996 Act and section 34 of the Code. The first of these involves the period for which future interest is granted. While the 1996 Act contemplates future interest from the date of the award to the date of payment, section 34 allows a court the discretion to order future interest up to a date earlier than the date of payment. A second notable distinction is the primacy section 34 accords to party autonomy insofar as the rate of future interest is concerned. We have seen above that the 1996 Act does not bind a tribunal to any agreement between the parties regarding the rate at which post-award interest is to be granted. The Code of Civil Procedure, however, expressly recognises that future interest may be granted at a rate in excess of 6% *provided* it does not exceed the contractual rate agreed by the parties. Lastly, an arbitral award carries post-award interest despite an award being silent about it. A court, however, is deemed under section 34, to have refused to order such interest where a decree is silent on the matter.[21]

In light of these differences, a question arises as to which of the two laws would apply where the substantive law governing a dispute is Indian law and the arbitration is seated in India. Section 34 of the Code has no application in arbitral proceedings, a position made clear by the Supreme Court of India in *Bhagawati Oxygen Ltd. v. Hindustan Copper Ltd.*[22] The procedural rules of the substantive law would thus have no bearing on post-award interest in India-seated arbitrations.

7. Whether the Award of Interest Can Be Subjected to Public Policy Objections, and if So, What Are They?

I will consider public policy objections in my response to Question 8 (below).

V PROCEDURAL LAW ISSUES

8. What Are the Main Procedural Law Issues When Considering Post-award Interest? How Are the Arbitration Laws and Other Laws or Regulations of the Seat Relevant?

As noted above, post-award interest is a means towards a vital public policy end – ensuring a speedy conclusion of disputes. In India's example, swift dispute resolution lessens a growing list of pending cases, while also increasing confidence among both foreign and domestic corporations with commercial ties to India.

21. *Kerala State Electricity Board & Anr. v. Kurien E. Kalathil & Anr.* [2018] 4 SCC 793, at [27] and [49.2].
22. [2005] 6 SCC 569, at [37]. *See also* The Arbitration and Conciliation Act, 1996, Section 19(1): '*The arbitral Tribunal shall not be bound by the Code of Civil Procedure, 1908 (5 of 1908) or the Indian Evidence Act, 1872 (1 of 1872).*'

In ensuring that this public policy objective is met, the procedural law of the arbitration and other laws of the seat become significant. The laws relevant here are the 1996 Act and the Code which deal, *inter alia*, with challenges to awards and the execution of decrees, respectively.

Once a final award is made in a proceeding to which Part I of the 1996 Act applies, the parties have three options before them. *First*, if the award contains errors or requires clarification, the parties may request the tribunal to make corrections or give an interpretation to certain parts of the award, as the case may be.[23] *Second*, a party may apply for the award to be set aside, challenging it on the limited grounds provided under section 34 of the 1996 Act, including the grounds of patent illegality and conflict with the public policy of India.[24] *Third*, the parties may accept the award as final and binding on them as well as on persons claiming under them.[25]

In exercising the *second* option, a party must make its application to set aside the award within three months from the date of the award.[26] The grounds on which such a party can challenge the award, listed in section 34 of the 1996 Act, correspond largely to those under Article 34 of the Model Law. In summary, courts may set aside awards under section 34 only if a party furnishes proof that (i) a party to the arbitration was under some incapacity, (ii) the arbitration agreement was invalid under the law to which the parties had subjected it, (iii) the party that challenges the award was not given proper notice of the appointment of an arbitrator, of the arbitral proceedings or was otherwise prevented from presenting its case, (iv) the award deals with a dispute that was outside the terms of the submission to arbitration or contained decisions on matters beyond the scope of the submission to arbitration, or (v) the composition of the arbitral tribunal or the arbitral procedure was not in accordance with the agreement of the parties.[27] In addition, courts may set aside awards on the grounds of (vi) conflict with the public policy of India or on the grounds of (vii) arbitrability (i.e., where they find that the subject matter of a dispute was incapable of settlement by arbitration).[28] For an award to be in conflict with the public policy of India, such an award must, *inter alia*, be induced by fraud or corruption, contravene the '*fundamental policy of Indian law*', or stand in conflict with '*the most basic notions of morality or justice*'.[29] In ascertaining whether any of these grounds are met, the court is prevented from conducting a review on the merits of the dispute.[30] Lastly, in the case of awards that

23. Arbitration and Conciliation Act, 1996. Section 33. Importantly, the '*errors*' that parties may seek a correction of do not include errors of law. Such errors are limited to '*computation errors, any clerical or typographical errors or any other errors of a similar nature*'.
24. Arbitration and Conciliation Act, 1996. Section 34.
25. Arbitration and Conciliation Act, 1996. Section 35.
26. Arbitration and Conciliation Act, 1996. Section 34(3). This period may be extended by a maximum of thirty days '*if the Court is satisfied that the applicant was prevented by sufficient cause from making the application*' within the prescribed three-month period.
27. Arbitration and Conciliation Act, 1996. Section 34(2)(a)(i)-(v).
28. Arbitration and Conciliation Act, 1996. Section 34(2)(b)(i)-(ii).
29. Arbitration and Conciliation Act, 1996. Section 34(2)(b), Explanation I.
30. Arbitration and Conciliation Act, 1996. Section 34(2)(a), Explanation II.

emanate from domestic arbitrations, courts may also set aside such awards on finding that (viii) they stand vitiated by patent illegality appearing on the face of the award.[31]

The grounds on which awards may be set aside are of particular importance to the issue of post-award interest. It is at this stage that courts of the seat are empowered to alter the rate at which such interest is awarded. Courts may reduce the interest rate awarded by an arbitral tribunal where such rate does not reflect prevailing economic conditions, where it is found unreasonable or where altering such rate would promote the interests of justice.[32]

If no application is made under section 34 before the three-month limitation period elapses, the parties are forced into the *third* option, and, resultantly, the award shall be enforced under the Code in the same manner as if it were a decree[33] of the court.[34] Where a party does file such an application within three months of the date of the award, the award may still be enforced under the Code if the court before which the application was filed has not ordered a stay on the operation of the award.[35] It appears, therefore, that while the 1996 Act describes which awards can be enforced and when they may be enforced, it does not prescribe a procedure for such enforcement. The 1996 Act overcomes this void by assigning to an award the character of a decree, thereby allowing for such an award to be enforced following the procedure for the execution of decrees contained in the Code. As the Preface to this book notes, '*an award is not worth the paper it is written on if an enforcement mechanism doesn't exist which encourages the award-debtor to pay up his debt promptly*' – this mechanism is discussed below.

For the purposes of execution proceedings under the Code, the award-holder is referred to as the '*decree-holder*',[36] while the award-debtor is characterised as the '*judgment-debtor*'.[37] Such proceedings are governed by Part II of the Code, which covers sections 36 to 74, and by Order XXI, which is contained in the First Schedule to the Code. To ensure that the award-debtor pays his debt, the '*executing court*' is empowered to order, *inter alia*, the delivery of property, the attachment or sale of property and the appointment of a receiver.[38] Where a decree is for the payment of money – as would invariably be the case in matters involving post-award interest – the court may also ensure execution by ordering the arrest and detention of the award-debtor in civil prisons.[39]

In conclusion, a number of issues pertaining to post-award interest may arise under the procedural law, which for India-seated arbitrations is the 1996 Act. Principal

31. Arbitration and Conciliation Act, 1996. Section 34(2A).
32. *Vedanta*, footnote 6 at [12].
33. Code of Civil Procedure, 1908. Section 2(2): '*"decree" means the formal expression of an adjudication which, so far as regards the Court expressing it, conclusively determines the rights of the parties with regard to all or any of the matters in controversy in the suit and may be either preliminary or final ...*' .
34. Arbitration and Conciliation Act, 1996. Section 36(1).
35. Arbitration and Conciliation Act, 1996. Section 36(2).
36. Code of Civil Procedure, 1908. Section 2(3).
37. Code of Civil Procedure, 1908. Section 2(10).
38. Code of Civil Procedure, 1908. Section 51.
39. Code of Civil Procedure, 1908. Section 51. *See also* sections 55-59 and Order XXI, Rules 30 and 37-40.

among these is the court's power to set aside the award, a power that includes the ability to alter the rate at which post-award interest is levied. Additionally, the relevance of other laws of the seat becomes clear through the Code, which provides the path an award-holder must follow to receive what he was awarded, i.e., the mechanism by which an arbitral award can be executed against the award-debtor.

VI EFFECT OF ENFORCEMENT ORDERS ON INTEREST ON THE AWARD ON BOTH THE SEAT AND ELSEWHERE

The effect of enforcement orders on interest may be understood at two stages: *first* in relation to the enforcement of foreign awards in India and *second* in relation to execution proceedings emanating from both arbitrations seated in or outside India. These aspects are discussed in turn.

Enforcing Foreign Awards

As supervisory jurisdiction over an award lies with the courts of the seat, courts in India have the power to set aside awards that arise from India-seated arbitrations, i.e., arbitrations governed by Part I of the 1996 Act. In the case of arbitrations seated outside India, Part II of the Act would apply. Lacking any supervisory authority over foreign awards, the power of Indian courts with respect to such awards is limited to their enforcement.

Under section 49 of the 1996 Act, '*where the court is satisfied that a foreign award is enforceable …, the award shall be deemed to be a decree of that court*'. The words '*where the court is satisfied*' are significant; foreign awards may only be enforced in India after a national court concludes that they are suitable for enforcement. Thus, at a stage anterior to enforcement, the court must be satisfied that certain conditions for the enforcement of foreign awards are met. These conditions, listed in section 48 of the 1996 Act, are not dissimilar to the grounds in section 34 under which awards may be challenged. An important difference between sections 34 and 48 is that under the former, domestic awards can be challenged on the grounds of '*patent illegality appearing on the face of the award*'; this ground is not available to contest the enforcement of foreign awards under section 48. Further, in dealing with foreign awards, Indian courts may refuse to enforce a foreign award where the courts of the seat have set it aside.

While the post-award interest component in a foreign award will not be governed by section 31(7)(b), such interest may nonetheless be a ground for objecting to its enforcement. For instance, a party may object to enforcement where post-award interest was awarded despite being barred under the arbitration agreement. Similarly, where the rate of post-award interest is unreasonably high, a party may contest enforcement on the ground that a usurious rate offends the public policy of India.[40] The

40. The expression '*public policy of India*' carries the same meaning under section 48 as it does under section 34: *Ssangyong Engineering & Construction Co. Ltd. v. National Highways Authority of India,* Civil Appeal No. 4779 of 2019. Judgment dated 08-05-2019.

enforcing court would, in such cases, have the power to alter the rate of post-award interest awarded by a tribunal.

Execution Proceedings

A foreign award that passes the scrutiny under section 48 is enforced as a decree under the Code. The procedure here is the same as that discussed in the section above. To ensure the enforcement of awards, the executing court has the power to pass a range of orders including, ordering the attachment of property and award-debtor's arrest in a civil prison.

Execution proceedings present the award-debtor with two modes of payment. Under Order XXI Rule 1 of the Code, the award-debtor may (i) deposit the award amount into the executing court by postal money order or through a bank or (ii) pay the award amount directly to the award-holder, either through a bank or through any other mode wherein payment is evidenced in writing.[41] Where the deposit is made into the court, the award-debtor is obligated to notify the award-holder of such deposit. In such cases, post-award interest shall cease to run from the date of service of such notice.[42] If the award-debtor chooses to pay the award-holder directly, post-award interest shall cease to run from the date of such payment.[43]

VII POWERS OF THE COURT TO ORDER OR ADJUST POST-AWARD INTEREST

9. Does the Indian Court Have the Power to Order or Adjust Post-award Interest, Assuming It Is Either the Seat Court or the Enforcing Court?

Yes, enforcing courts do enjoy the power to order post-award interest or adjust post-award interest awarded by a tribunal. The power to order such interest would naturally apply only where the arbitrators have passed no directions on the issue, in which case, and as seen above, the 1996 Act mandates the imposition of interest at a rate 2% higher than the '*current rate of interest*'. Following this statutory mandate, courts in such cases will order interest at the stage of enforcement. Further, as noted above, courts will exercise their power to adjust post-award interest in two cases: under Part I, where an award is under challenge, or under Part II, where the enforcement of a foreign award is contested.[44] Outside of these instances and appeals arising therefrom, no court has the power to order or adjust post-award interest. This bar continues to apply during execution proceedings. In *Rameshwar Dass Gupta v.*

---

41. Code of Civil Procedure, 1908. Order XXI, Rule 1(1) (a)-(b). However, the court may direct payment through additional means, *See* Order XXI Rule 1(1)(c).
42. Order XXI, Rule 1(4).
43. Order XXI, Rule 1(5).
44. It must be borne in mind, however, that in dealing with cases under both section 34 and 48, Indian courts are increasingly adopting the principle of minimal judicial intervention. Courts do not sit in appeal over arbitral awards and will not re-appreciate evidence or review the award on its merits. Moreover, even a contravention of the substantive of law of India would not, by itself, permit interference with an award: *Associate Builders v. Delhi Development Authority* [2015] 3 SCC 49. *See also Ssangyong Engineering.*

State of U.P. & Anr,[45] the executing court had granted a decree of interest – which was not part of the decree under execution – on the ground of undue delay in the execution proceedings. On appeal, the Supreme Court held that the executing court was barred from travelling beyond the decree (or award) under execution.

45. [1996] 5 SCC 728.

Republic of Indonesia

Andreas Hartono

INTRODUCTION

The Indonesian legal system is a confluence of three distinct systems. First, prior to the advent of Dutch traders and colonialists in the late sixteenth century and early seventeenth century, indigenous kingdoms ruled and applied a system of customary or *adat* law. Second, the colonization of Indonesia by the Dutch and their subsequent rule for the next 350 years until the end of World War II left a legacy of Dutch colonial law. Some of the legislations enacted by the Dutch colonialists are in operation even today. Third, after Indonesian independence on August 17, 1945, Indonesia began creating a national legal system based on Indonesian precepts of law and justice. Lastly, considering that the majority religion in Indonesia is Islam, Indonesia also adopted the Islamic law system only for the Muslim people.

Modern Indonesian law is a combination of the *adat* law, the Dutch colonial law and the national law, with Islamic law also influencing the legal system. For example, Indonesian commercial law is based on the Commercial Code of 1847, *Kitab Undang-Undang Hukum Dagang* or *Wetboek van Koophandel*, a relic of the colonial period. However, it is also supplemented by many new laws enacted since independence, including the Banking Law of 1992 (amended in 2020), Company Law of 2007, Capital Market Law of 1995, Antimonopoly Law of 1999 and the Oil & Natural Gas Law of 2001 (amended in 2020). The *adat* law, however, is less conspicuous. However, some *adat* principles such as "*consensus through decision making*" ("*musyawarah untuk mufakat*") still appear in modern Indonesian legislation.

The unique historical development of Indonesian law and the various sources of legislation act as a big hurdle for foreigners seeking to understand Indonesian law. To clarify the status of various types of legislation, through Law No. 12 of 2011 ("*Law No. 12*"), the Government of Indonesia stipulates the hierarchy of legislation as follows:

(i) 1945 Constitution or *Undang-Undang Dasar 1945.*
(ii) *Majelis Permusyawaratan Rakyat* (MPR) Resolution or *Ketetapan MPR.*

(iii) Law or *Undang-undang*/Government Regulation Substituting a Law or *Peraturan Pemerintah Pengganti Undang-undang.*
(iv) Government Regulation or *Peraturan Pemerintah.*
(v) Presidential Regulation or *Peraturan Presiden.*
(vi) Province Regulation or *Peraturan Daerah Provinsi.* and
(vii) Regency/Municipality Regulation or *Peraturan Daerah Kabupaten/Kota.*

In addition to these sources of law, Law No. 12 also regulates other sources of law issued by certain authorities that have regulatory and binding forces as long as their authorities are stipulated by higher rules of laws or established based on authority given by prevailing laws.

Once promulgated, legislation is published in the State Gazette of the Republic of Indonesia or *Lembaran Negara Republik Indonesia.* Certain types of legislation such as laws and government regulations are accompanied by an official explanatory memorandum called the Elucidation or *Penjelasan.* The Elucidation is published in Supplement to the State Gazette or *Tambahan Lembaran Negara* and is generally considered authoritative for interpretation purposes. In addition to the State Gazette, there is a sister publication called the State Report or *Berita Negara* which publishes government and public notices, ministerial regulations and supreme court regulations.

Post-award Interest in Indonesia

From the Indonesian law perspective, the post-award interest concept is known as forced money award or *dwangsom,* which under Article 606 section (a) of *Reglement op de Burgerlijke Rechtsverordering* (*the RV*) is stipulated as follows:

> As long as a judge's decision contains a sentence for something other than the payer of an amount of money, it can be determined, that as long as or whenever a person found guilty does not comply with the sentence/award, he must pay an amount of money as determined in the judge's decision/award, and the money is called forced money.

This Article can be applied in a condemnation decision containing a punishment against the parties, forcing them to undertake a certain action. For this reason, the plaintiff needs protection to ensure the implementation of the decision by imposing forced money. In other words, forced money will serve as a penalty to the defendant in case the defendant does not voluntarily enforce the court's decision. Another important point will be that the judges cannot apply for the force money within the decision without any claim statement from the plaintiff.

In the Indonesian arbitration regime, the arbitrator is positioned similarly to a judge in a court proceeding. This means that a panel of arbitrators in international arbitration with Indonesian law as the law of the seat must obey and comply with the provisions of Indonesian law if it is chosen to be the legal basis for the arbitration proceedings. If the decision is made not based on legal provisions or is not requested by the plaintiff in his statement claim, the decision can be annulled.

I POWER TO GRANT POST-AWARD INTEREST

1. Does an Arbitral Tribunal Have the Power to Grant Post-award Interest under Indonesian Law?

Article 56 of section (1) of Law Number 30 of 1999 requires a tribunal to make a decision based on the relevant provisions of law or based on justice and fairness or *ex aequo et bono*. Thus, this Article requires a tribunal to comply with the law agreed upon by the parties.

Indonesian law does not recognize the term post-award interest; however, it recognizes a concept similar to it known as forced money or *dwangsom*. According to Article 606 section (a) of the RV:

> As long as a judge's decision contains a sentence for something other than the payer of an amount of money, it can be determined, that as long as or whenever the find guilty person does not fulfil the sentence, he must submit an amount of money as resolute in the judge's decision, and the money is called forced money.

This article can be applied just in a condemnation decision (containing a point that punishes one of the parties). The decision requires the defendant to do something in the form of fulfilling achievement and recognizing the rights of the plaintiff. For this reason, the plaintiff needs protection from the implementation of the decision through forced money. Forced money forces the defendant to enforce the court decision by force (execution force). However, judges cannot grant forced money unless the plaintiff makes a claim to that end.

In Indonesia, the arbitrator is positioned similarly to a judge in a court proceeding. This means that a tribunal in arbitration with Indonesia as the seat must obey and comply with the provisions of Indonesian arbitration law. If the decision fails to consider Indonesian law or decides on a matter not claimed by the claimant, the decision can be annulled.

2. Is the Power Exercisable Without a Request or Submission, or Is Such a Submission Required?

As mentioned earlier, an arbitrator must render an award based on the relevant provisions of law. Post-award interest must be claimed by the claimant in its statement of claim for the tribunal to grant it.

3. Is the Power Classified As One under the Substantive Applicable Law or the Procedural Law of the Arbitration?

The power of the arbitration tribunal is stipulated under Law Number 30 of 1999. However, for granting post-award interest, the tribunal can only refer to Article 606 section (a) of the Rv, a source of civil procedure law in Indonesia.

II CHOICE OF LAW

4. What is the Law That Applies to Determine What the Post-award Interest Should Be? Would This Be the Governing Law of the Dispute or the Law of the Seat?

As this relates more to the authority of the arbitral tribunal than that of the subject matter of the dispute, the law of the seat shall be applied in determining the post-award interest.

III DO THE COURTS TAKE INTO ACCOUNT INTERNATIONAL STANDARDS WHEN FACING CHALLENGES ON THE POST-AWARD INTEREST?

Under Law No. 30 and Article V of the New York Convention, in facing any challenges against the enforcement of international arbitration awards, the Indonesian court only takes into account the law and public policy of Indonesia. The Indonesian court may only take any international standards into account if such standards have been adopted and subsequently ratified by the Government of Indonesia.

IV SUBSTANTIVE LAW ISSUES

5. How Are Contractual Provisions on Late or Non-payment of Interest Relevant to Post-award Interest? Will These Be Considered By the Arbitral Tribunal?

Contractual provisions on late or non-payment of interest shall only be applicable from the date when the default occurs or the notice of default is issued by the counterparty until the counterparty files its notice of arbitration to the relevant arbitration tribunal.[1] The contractual provisions regarding late or non-payment of interest shall cease to operate after the commencement of the arbitration. If its awarded by the arbitration tribunal based on the plaintiff's request, it will be continued by the post-award interest awarded by the arbitration tribunal.

The calculation of interest in Indonesian legal proceedings is based on the principle of propriety that applies in society. However, if there is a contractual provision on late or non-payment of interest that can be relied on by the plaintiff in calculating its request for post-award interest in its claim otherwise, the arbitration tribunal may determine the quantum of the post-award interest based on what they deem right or just.

6. How Do the Procedural Rules of the Substantive Law Apply?

Procedural Rules of the Indonesian substantive law are only applicable when the law of the seat is Indonesia.

1. Riau High Court Appeal Verdict No. 16/Pdt/2012/PTR, May 7, 2012.

7. Whether the Award of Interest Can Be Subjected to Public Policy Objections, and if So, What Are They?

In Indonesia, post-award interest is considered more of a procedural matter rather than a substantive one. Where Indonesian law applies, there are no public policy issues in granting post-award interest even if there is any contractual provision agreed upon by the parties in their underlying agreement.

If foreign law applies, there are also no public policy issues in recognition and enforcement of the awarded interest so long as the main decision supported by such post-award interest is not a decision instructing the defendant to pay its monetary obligation to the plaintiff.

V PROCEDURAL LAW ISSUES

8. What Are the Main Procedural Law Issues When Considering Post-award Interest? How Are the Arbitration Laws and Other Laws or Regulations of the Seat Relevant?

The main procedural law issue when considering post-award interest is that the post-award interest must be claimed in the statement of claim. Otherwise, the arbitration tribunal will not have the power to grant it.

Moreover, the main decision supported by such post-award interest is a decision other than a decision instructing the defendant to pay its monetary obligation to the plaintiff.

While Law Number 30 of 1999 is silent on post-award interest, Article 606 section (a) of the RV, which is a source of Indonesian civil procedural laws, regulates post-award interest.

VI EFFECT OF ENFORCEMENT ORDERS ON INTEREST ON THE AWARD ON BOTH THE SEAT AND ELSEWHERE

Indonesian courts shall enforce post-award interest so long as the order of post-award interest is based on the statement of claim of the claimant. If the tribunal grants post-award interest even when the claimant did not seek it, an Indonesian court may refuse to enforce the award because it is prohibited for a judge or arbitrator to decide beyond what is demanded *ultra petita* in Indonesia.

The prohibition on *ultra petita* decisions in Indonesia is within the scope of civil proceedings law Article 178 paragraphs (2) and (3) of the *Het Herziene Indonesisch Reglement* as well as Article 189 paragraphs (2) and (3) of the Ruth Bader Ginsburg (RBg). With respect to decisions that are deemed to have exceeded the limits of authority, the Supreme Court of Indonesia has the right to call off the decisions or the determination of the courts in all judicial environments.

VII POWERS OF THE COURT TO ORDER OR ADJUST POST-AWARD INTEREST

9. Does the Indonesian Court Have the Power to Order or Adjust the Post-award Interest, Assuming It Is the Seat Court of the Enforcing Court?

No, it does not. The enforcing court in Indonesia only has the power to verify whether the award containing an order for the payment of post-award interest has complied with all the requirements (including but not limited to not being in contradiction with the public policy) to be enforced in Indonesia. It does not have the authority to grant post-award interest for any international arbitration award that did not originally grant post-award interest.

Republic of Korea

Mino Han & Sameer Thakur

INTRODUCTION

Korea is a civil law jurisdiction and as such the legal system gives primacy to statutory law. The Korean legislative system consists of the Constitution as the paramount law, Acts particularizing the constitutional notions and administrative legislation (executive orders, decrees, ordinances, etc.) further implementing the Acts.

In terms of procedural rules, Korean court litigation is primarily governed by the Civil Procedures Act. Arbitrations seated in Korea are governed by the Arbitration Act (effective as of February 4, 2020),[1] which allows the parties to agree upon procedural rules, including institutional rules (e.g., KCAB Rules), to govern the arbitration procedure.[2] Even when procedural rules are agreed upon by the parties, the Arbitration Act could still apply to Korea-seated arbitrations as a supplement. There are also some mandatory rules in the Act which the parties cannot derogate from by agreement.[3]

It is important to note that the Arbitration Act prior to 2016 was previously silent on the matter of interest, but the 2016 amendment of the Arbitration Act introduced an express provision giving arbitral tribunals the power to grant interest. The intended purpose of the 2016 amendment was to grant tribunals with more power and allow for greater predictability in terms of execution.

1. Most of the provisions in the 2006 United Nations Commission on International Trade (UNCITRAL) Model law have been incorporated in the Arbitration Act.
2. Article. 20(2) Arbitration Act
3. *See* Kim, Kevin (Kap-You) et al., *Arbitration Law in Korea* (Pakyoungsa 2016) at p. [134].

I POWER TO GRANT POST-AWARD INTEREST

1. Does an Arbitral Tribunal Have the Power to Grant Post-award Interest Under Korea's Law?

Yes. It is largely accepted that arbitral tribunals in Korea-seated arbitrations have the power to grant interest including post-award interest.[4] Both pre- and post-award interest awards are frequently granted by tribunals, usually accruing until the date of complete performance of the payment of the principal obligation.[5]

The previous version of the Korean Arbitration Act (prior to the amendment of the Act as of November 30, 2016) was silent on the matter of interest. However, since the amendment of the Korean Arbitration Act as of November 30, 2016,[6] the Act addressed this gap by introducing an express provision (Article 34-3) stating that arbitral tribunals seated in Korea have discretionary power to grant interest.[7] An English translation of this provision is reproduced as follows:

> Article 34-3 (Delay Interest)
>
> Unless otherwise agreed by the parties, the arbitral tribunal, when rendering an arbitral award, may order payment of delay interest it deems appropriate considering all circumstances concerning the arbitration.

This provision is generally understood to empower an arbitral tribunal to award both pre- and post-award interest.[8] Since the Arbitration Act applies to all arbitration proceedings seated in Korea regardless of the governing law on the merits, Article 34-3 of the Arbitration Act applies even in cases where the applicable law of the subject matter is foreign law.

As expressly stated in Article 34-3, arbitral tribunals can only exercise discretion on interest if there is no separate agreement between the parties. Where there is an agreement between the parties regarding interest (for example, whether post-award interest may accrue upon delayed payment and if so the applicable interest rate), the tribunal is bound by that agreement.

4. *See* Kim, Kevin (Kap-You) et al., *Arbitration Law in Korea* (Pakyoungsa 2016) at p. [238]; Lim, Sungwoo (Sean), *International Arbitration* (Pakyoungsa 2016) at p. [310].
5. *See* Bae, Kim & Lee LLC, *Arbitration Law of Korea: Practice and Procedure* (Juris 2012) at pp. [211]-[212].
6. One recent amendment to Article 40 of the Arbitration Act became effective as of February 4, 2020, but any other provisions as amended in 2016 remain the same.
7. *See* Kim, Kevin (Kap-You) et al., *Arbitration Law in Korea* (Pakyoungsa 2016) at p. [238]; Lim, Sungwoo (Sean), *Proposed Amendments to the Korean Arbitration Act* (5th Issue, Korean Arbitration Review December 2015) at pp. [9]-[10].
8. *See* Suk, Kwang Hyun, *Major Contents of Amendment of the Arbitration Act of 2016 and Several Comments thereon* (Vol. 53, Chonbuk Law Review August 2017) at p. [246].

The International Arbitration Rules of the Korean Commercial Arbitration Board (*the KCAB*)[9] do not specifically address the matter of interest, similar to many other institutional rules.[10] In contrast, the KCAB Domestic Arbitration Rules[11] expressly provide that a tribunal may, to the extent reasonable, order payment of delay interest (Article 41(6) of the KCAB Domestic Arbitration Rules).

2. Is the Power Exercisable Without a Request or Submission, or Is Such a Submission Required?

It is not entirely clear whether a request or submission by a party on interest is required for the arbitral tribunal to exercise its power to award interest under Article 34-3. The language of this provision does not expressly require such party request or submission.

However, a Korean court may not rule on matters not pleaded and requested for (Article 203 of the Korean Civil Procedure Act) and under Korean law, an interest claim is considered a claim separate from the principal claim.[12] This principle of disposition is considered one of the fundamental principles of civil procedural law in Korea. Whether this principle would equally apply to an interest award in a Korea-seated arbitration (to which Article 34-3 applies) is yet to be seen.

Keeping the practice in Korean court litigation in mind, it is recommended that a party seeking interest should make sure to include an express seek of relief for interest in its submissions so that the award of interest is not later challenged as unenforceable because of it being outside of the scope of the parties' submissions.

3. Is the Power Classified as One under the Substantive Applicable Law or the Procedural Law of the Arbitration?

The Supreme Court of Korea has held that the issue of interest, including post-award interest, is a matter of substantive law applicable to the dispute (as further explained below in section II Question 4). Following this view, the arbitral tribunal's power to award post-award interest was also traditionally considered a matter of substantive law rather than one under the procedural laws of the arbitration.

However, since the introduction of the lately enacted Article 34-3 of the Arbitration Act, the arbitral tribunal's power to award interest may well be viewed as a matter to be determined under the procedural laws of the arbitration.

9. The KCAB International Arbitration Rules apply in circumstances where "*(i) the parties have agreed in writing to refer their disputes to arbitration under those Rules; or (ii) the parties have agreed in writing to refer their disputes to arbitration before the KCAB, and the arbitration is an International Arbitration*" (Article 3 of the KCAB International Arbitration Rules).
10. *See* Born, Gary B., *International Commercial Arbitration* (2nd edn, Volume III, Kluwer Law International 2014) at p. [3103]: "*Institutional Rules do not ordinarily address the subject of interest [...].*"
11. The KCAB Domestic Arbitration Rules apply in circumstances where "*(i) the parties have agreed in writing to refer their disputes to arbitration under those Rules; or (ii) the parties have agreed in writing to refer their disputes to arbitration before the KCAB, and the arbitration is a Domestic Arbitration*" (Article 3 KCAB Domestic Arbitration Rules).
12. Si Yoon Lee, *New Civil Procedure Act* (9th edn, Pakyoungsa 2015) at p. [315].

II CHOICE OF LAW

4. What Is the Law That Applies to Determine What the Post-award Interest Should Be? Would This Be the Governing Law of the Dispute or the Law of the Seat?

As explained above, the Supreme Court of Korea ruled in several cases that interest for delay in performing monetary obligations (including both pre- and post-award interest) should be determined in accordance with the governing law of the dispute.[13]

For instance, the Supreme Court ruled in its judgment dated January 27, 2011, Case No. 2009*Da*10249 as follows:

> Delay damages [i.e., delay interest] constitute compensation for delay in performance of an obligation, and payment thereof is incidental to the principal obligation; accordingly, delay damages should be determined in accordance with the *applicable law governing the principal claim and obligation.* (Emphasis added)

That said, to the extent that the arbitral tribunal's power to award interest is deemed a procedural law issue (due to the enactment of Article 34-3 of the Arbitration Act), the law applicable to determine what the post-award interest would be that of the seat. Notably, an authoritative scholar in Korea commented that Article 34-3 was enacted for the specific purpose of vesting arbitral tribunals with the power to award interest (especially post-award interest) at a rate it considers appropriate, taking into account all relevant circumstances.[14] This commentary appears to suggest that the issue of interest in arbitration should be considered a procedural matter subject to the procedural law of the arbitration; and as such, pursuant to Article 34-3, the arbitral tribunal should have full power to award interest at its discretion without being strictly bound to the standards under the substantive applicable law.

Given that the Korean courts' position of determining interest according to the substantive applicable law has been well established for a considerable period of time, it appears unlikely that they will now generally alter their position. Yet, it remains to be seen whether the newly enacted Article 34-3 will bring about future changes in the practice and perception of Korean courts and arbitral tribunals seated in Korea regarding the award of interest in an arbitration.

III DO THE COURTS TAKE INTO ACCOUNT INTERNATIONAL STANDARDS WHEN FACING CHALLENGES ON POST-AWARD INTEREST?

Yes. Article 7 of the Act of Private International Law provides that mandatory rules of Korea must be applied regardless of the applicable laws to the matter. Here, the

13. Supreme Court Judgment 95*Da*34385, May 9, 1997; Supreme Court Judgment 2009*Da*10249, January 27, 2011; Supreme Court Judgment 2009*Da*77754, October 25, 2012, etc.; *See* Kim, Kevin (Kap-You) et al., *Arbitration Law in Korea* (Pakyoungsa 2016) at p. [238]; Lim, Sungwoo (Sean), *International Arbitration* (Pakyoungsa 2016) at p. [310].
14. *See* Kwang Hyun Suk, *Major Contents of Amendment of the Arbitration Act of 2016 and Several Comments thereon* (Volume 53, Chonbuk Law Review August. 2017) at pp. [246]-[247].

mandatory rules of Korea are generally interpreted to include international standards. The Act of Private International Law, however, does not provide further guidance on what constitutes part of the *mandatory rules of Korea.*[15]

In addition, in a case regarding recognition of a foreign arbitration award, the Supreme Court has ruled that *Recognition or enforcement of arbitration awards can be denied if the enforcement of such award is in conflict with the state's public order pursuant to [the New York Convention]. The intent of such provision is to prevent enforcement of awards that will damage ethical beliefs and social order, so it must be interpreted restrictively considering both domestic circumstances and international transactional order.*[16] (Emphasis added)

In another case,[17] the Supreme Court acknowledged that *it is common practice to order payment of interest based on the appropriate international interest rate in international transactions* as it granted the enforcement of an international arbitration award which applied the international interest rate significantly higher than the statutory interest rates in Korea. It should be noted that the Supreme Court acknowledged the above under the pretense that *...since the generally recognized international interest rate is lower than the maximum legal interest rate in the Interest Limitation Act,*[18] *it is not against the public order of Korea.*

In short, it can be said that the Korean courts acknowledge international standards separate from domestic standards and also take them into consideration.

IV SUBSTANTIVE LAW ISSUES

5. How Are Contractual Provisions on Late or Non-payment of Interest Relevant to Post-award Interest? Will These Be Considered By the Arbitral Tribunal?

As stated above, pursuant to Article 34-3 of the Arbitration Act, the parties' agreement prevails over the tribunal's discretion in awarding interest. In other words, the tribunal is bound by the parties' agreement. Therefore, if contractual provisions dealing with late or non-payment interest exist, they will apply in deciding whether and how much interest is payable. If the contract is silent on the issue of interest, the tribunal may exercise discretion (*interest it deems appropriate*) which may include consideration of statutory rates of the Civil Act (5% per annum) or the Commercial Act (6% per annum).

6. How Do the Procedural Rules of the Substantive Law Apply?

Pursuant to Article 2 of the Arbitration Act, the Act applies to arbitration proceedings seated in Korea. Thus, the *procedural rules* of the substantive law, i.e., the Civil Procedures Act, are not directly applicable to an arbitration. It is also worth noting that the Civil Procedures Act of Korea does not contain an express provision on interest.

15. Hun-Mook Lee, *Arbitrability in Terms of International Mandatory Provisions* (Korea International Trade Law Association, December 30, 2013) at p. [23].
16. Supreme Court Judgment 2006*Da*20290, May 28, 2009.
17. Supreme Court Judgment 89*DaKa*20252, April 10, 1990.
18. Supreme Court Judgment 89*DaKa*20252, April 10, 1990.

7. Whether the Award of Interest Can Be Subjected to Public Policy Objections, and if So, What Are They?

As interest is regarded as a matter of substantive law, it is subject to public policy restrictions under the applicable law to the merits of the case. An award of interest can be subjected to public policy objections pursuant to Article 38 (domestic arbitral awards) or Article 39 (foreign awards) of the Arbitration Act. Both Articles 38 and 39 of the Arbitration Act state that an arbitral award may be denied of recognition or enforcement should such decision be in conflict with *the good morals and other forms of social order of Republic of Korea.* The violation of public policy can also be relied on as a ground for setting aside an award (Article 36).

In cases where Korean law is the governing substantive law, the following provisions are worthy of note:

Article 103 of the Korean Civil Act provides that juristic acts contrary to social order should be rendered null and void. Article 103 of the Korean Civil Act is a mandatory provision.

Further, Article 398 of the Korean Civil Act sets out that (i) the parties may determine in advance the amount of damages payable in the event of non-performance of an obligation (Article 398(1)), but (ii) if the amount of damages determined in advance is unduly excessive, the court may reduce the amount to a reasonable and appropriate sum (Article 398(2)). Pursuant to these provisions, if an agreement between parties for delay interest (including post-award interest) is found to be so unreasonable and excessive that it amounts to an act contrary to social order, the agreed interest may be reduced to a reasonable and appropriate sum by the arbitral tribunal.

In addition, Korea has in place a special law called the Interest Limitation Act. The provisions in the Interest Limitation Act are mandatory in nature. Article 6 of this Act sets out that, if the parties agree on an amount in advance as damages payable in the event of non-performance of a monetary obligation but that amount is found to be unreasonable in the court's view, the court may reduce that amount to a reasonable sum. The Act further provides, specifically in respect of interest rates under loan agreements, that the maximum interest rate agreeable by the parties shall not exceed the rate prescribed in the relevant Presidential Decree (Article 2 of the Interest Limitation Act). Currently, the relevant Presidential Decree (entered into force on February 8, 2018) identifies the maximum allowable interest rate as 24% per annum.[19] Therefore, in arbitral proceedings where the substantive law is Korean law and the dispute concerns a loan agreement, the arbitral tribunal is advised to consider the restriction imposed by the Interest Limitation Act on the maximum interest rate, and reduce any interest rates (including those on post-award interest) exceeding that threshold down to 24% per annum.

Public policy considerations may also come into play at the enforcement stage. Irrespective of whether Korean law is the governing law of the contract, the Korean

19. This is currently going through a revision process and is subject to change.

courts may refuse to enforce an award of interest or decide to set aside the award if such award is found to be contrary to the public policy of Korea.

However, the Supreme Court has ruled that *...even if the extinctive prescription (or limitation) period in the governing law (law of the Netherlands) is 30 years, such breach of mandatory provision of the Korean law*[20] *does not suffice to construe the foreign arbitration award to be in conflict with good morals,*[21] effectively ruling that a breach of a mandatory provision does not always result in a refusal of enforcement of an award or an award being set aside due to public policy.

There is also a case where a Korean court partially denied the enforcement of a foreign judgment concerning punitive damages pursuant to the Korean Civil Procedures Act's provision on the recognition of foreign judgments.[22]

Therefore, it is recommended that parties who pursue an arbitration or enforcement of an award in Korea be aware of the above mandatory provisions and principles to avoid and mitigate potential risks.

V PROCEDURAL LAW ISSUES

8. What Are the Main Procedural Law Issues When Considering Post-award Interest? How Are the Arbitration Laws and Other Laws or Regulations of the Seat Relevant?

As the Civil Procedures Act does not have a provision on interest, there are no particular procedural law issues when considering post-award interest. It may be worth reiterating that pursuant to Act 34-3 of the Arbitration Act, the tribunal has wide discretion in awarding post-award interest.[23]

Notably, Korea has a special law called the Special Act on Expedition of Legal Proceedings (*the Special Act*), which provides that a substantially higher interest rate (currently set at 12% per annum) shall be applied by a Korean court when awarding pre- and post-judgment interest from the date of the service of the complaint, provided that the claim amounts by the Plaintiff are upheld by the court in full.

A topic which has been the subject of considerable debate in Korea is whether such higher interest rate under the Special Act would be applicable only to interest ordered in domestic litigation proceedings, or whether it would also apply to interest awarded by arbitral tribunals (particularly those sitting in Korea and/or applying Korean law as the substantive law).[24] The debate has particularly been amplified by the fact that the practice of the KCAB has been inconsistent on this issue; some KCAB

20. Article 162 Civil Act, (Extinctive Prescription of Claims or Property Right), "*(1) The extinctive prescription of a claim shall become complete if not exercised for a period of ten years.*"
21. Supreme Court Judgment 93Da53054, February 14, 1995.
22. Article 217 Korean Civil Procedure Act, para. [1] sub-para. [3]: "*That the approval of such final judgment, etc. does not undermine sound morals or other social order of the Republic of Korea in light of the contents of such final judgment, etc. and judicial procedures;*" Seoul Eastern District Court Judgment 93Gahab19069, February 10, 1995.
23. Article 203, section 1 Civil Procedures Act.
24. *See* Kwang Hyun Suk, *Major Contents of Amendment of the Arbitration Act of 2016 and Several Comments thereon* (Volume 53, Chonbuk Law Review August. 2017) at p. [246].

tribunals have applied the Special Act interest rate when awarding interest while some have not.[25]

The starting point of this issue is to examine the language of Articles 1 and 3 of the Special Act, which state as follows:

> Article 1 (Purpose)
>
> The purpose of this Act is to prevent delay of litigation, to promote speedy implementation of claims and obligations, and to assist dispute resolution.
>
> Article 3 (Statutory Interest Rates)
>
> (1) In the event a judgment (which shall hereafter include adjudication) is pronounced ordering performance of all or a part of any monetary obligation, the statutory rate of interest applicable to the calculation of damages resulting from non-performance of the monetary obligation shall be, from the date following the date on which a complaint or an equivalent document is served to the obligor, in accordance with the interest rate which shall not exceed 40% per annum and shall be stipulated by the Presidential Decree in consideration of the delay interest rate applied by banks under the Banking Act and other circumstances of the economy. [...]
>
> (2) Where it is found that the obligor had adequate reasons to dispute the existence or the extent of its obligation until a judgment affirming the obligor's obligation to perform is pronounced by a body which has fact-finding jurisdiction, the above paragraph (1) shall not apply to such an extent.

The current version of the Presidential Decree (entered into force on May 21, 2019) referred to in Article 3(1) of the Special Act stipulates an interest rate of 12% per annum. The Special Act, therefore, empowers Korean courts to award interest accruing from the date of service of the complaint at a higher interest rate than the statutory rates provided under the Korean Civil Code and the Commercial Code. This is to encourage a speedy and effective resolution of court litigation. This interest rate of 12% per annum does not apply where it is found that Defendant had adequate reasons to dispute Plaintiff's claims (Article 3(2) of the Special Act).

As it currently stands, the prevailing view among Korean jurists appears to be that the Special Act should not be applied to arbitral awards absent mutual agreement by the parties.

First, the language of the Special Act itself indicates that the Special Act is intended to apply to *judgments* rendered by courts in *litigation* proceedings. There is no express basis upon which one can argue that the Special Act must be interpreted to cover *arbitral awards* issued for *arbitration* proceedings as well.[26]

Second, it could be said that there is a practical need to penalize a party who is unnecessarily delaying a court litigation proceeding. In contrast, in most international

25. *See* Young Seok Lee, *Interest in Korean Arbitration: Inconsistencies in Applying the Special Act on Expedition of Litigation* (Volume 3, Seoul National University (SNU) Law Review Dec. 2012) at p. [157]; Kevin Kim (Kap-You) et al., *Arbitration Law in Korea* (Pakyoungsa 2016) at p. [239].
26. *See* Bae, Kim & Lee LLC, *Arbitration Law of Korea: Practice and Procedure* (Juris 2012) at p. [212]; Kevin Kim (Kap-You) et al., *Arbitration Law in Korea* (Pakyoungsa 2016) at p. [239]; Young Seok Lee, *Interest in Korean Arbitration: Inconsistencies in Applying the Special Act on Expedition of Litigation* (Volume 3, SNU Law Review December 2012) at p. [166].

arbitration cases, the procedural timetable is often mutually agreed by the parties at an early stage of the proceedings, and even if it is later on amended, it is often done so upon the parties' agreement or by order of the tribunal. In such a case, the need to penalize a party for the unnecessary procedural delay is less justified.

For reference, Korean courts have consistently viewed that issues relating to interest should be determined pursuant to the governing law of the dispute, not the law of the seat. Accordingly, even if Korea is the seat of the arbitration, it does not logically follow that the Special Act should be applied.[27]

It is worth noting that prior to the enactment of Article 34-3 of the Arbitration Act, the Korean Supreme Court granted the enforcement of an arbitral award in which the interest rate under the Special Act was applied.[28] Since there has been no Supreme Court case on this issue after Article 34-3 of the Arbitration Act has become effective, it remains to be seen how the Korean courts will resolve the potential tension between the above decision and the approach to interpret Article 34-3 in a narrow fashion.

In theory, on the one hand, the enactment of Article 34-3 of the Arbitration Act allows the arbitral tribunal the freedom not to apply an interest rate of 12% per annum as prescribed in the Special Act. Article 34-3 was introduced directly in light of such discussions.[29] On the other hand, it may also give the tribunal the power to apply 12% per annum as the interest rate if deemed appropriate. As such, this issue remains unresolved and requires further guidance from the Korean courts.

VI EFFECT OF ENFORCEMENT ORDERS ON INTEREST ON THE AWARD ON BOTH THE SEAT AND ELSEWHERE

9. Legal Effect of Enforcement Orders By Korean Courts

A Korean court has ruled that *enforcement judgments empower arbitral awards with executive force so that one may pursue compulsory execution proceedings.*[30] Note that *enforcement judgments* in the Arbitration Act 1999 have been revised to *enforcement decisions* in the Arbitration Act 2016,[31] to accelerate the enforcement proceedings.[32]

27. *See* Kwang Hyun Suk, *Proposals for the Revision of the Korean Arbitration Act* (Volume 53 No. 3, Seoul Law Journal September 2012) at pp. [580]-[581]; Suk, Kwang Hyun, *Major Contents of Amendment of the Arbitration Act of 2016 and Several Comments thereon* (Volume 53, Chonbuk Law Review August 2017) at p. [246].
28. Supreme Court Judgment, 99*Da*13577, 13584, April 10, 2001; *see also* Supreme Court Judgment, 2004*Da*67264, 67271, May 13, 2005.
29. *See* Kwang Hyun Suk, *Proposals for the Revision of the Korean Arbitration Act* (Volume 53 No. 3, Seoul Law Journal September 2012) at pp. [580]-[581]; Suk, Kwang Hyun, *Major Contents of Amendment of the Arbitration Act of 2016 and Several Comments thereon* (Volume 53, Chonbuk Law Review August 2017) at p. [246].
30. Seoul High Court Judgment dated January 17, 2014, 2013*Na*13506.
31. Article 37(2), "*An arbitral award may be enforced only by a court's decision to enforce it upon the request of the parties.*"
32. Kwang Hyun Suk, *Changes of Legal Doctrines on Effect, Setting Aside, Recognition and Enforcement of Arbitral Awards under the Arbitration Act of 2016 of Korea* (Volume 34 Issue 1, Hanyang Law Review March 2017) at pp. [478]-[479].

Regarding the enforcement of arbitral awards, Korean courts tended to limit their role to merely confirming the award (in particular, the dispositive section which defines the contents and scope of civil execution in Korea) and turning it into an enforceable document. In that context, Korean courts have been reluctant to make any correction, revision or addition to the award.

An arbitration award carries the same effect on the parties as a final and conclusive judgment of the court,[33] and the Korean courts have repeatedly recognized the *res judicata* effect of arbitration awards.[34] Contrary to the United Kingdom (UK), France or International Centre for Settlement of Investment Disputes (ICSID) awards, in Korea, an arbitral award, whether domestic or international, is considered final and cannot be amended in court or elsewhere.[35] Therefore, Korean courts will not amend or complement an interest order at the enforcement stage or thereafter.

A relevant example would be a case before the Seoul Central District Court, where a party applied that a KCAB award ordering payment of interest at a rate of 6% per annum be enforced. While doing so, the applicant party argued that it was entitled to post-award interest at the rate stipulated under the Special Act and added a claim seeking payment of the difference between the amount of interest under the Special Act and that awarded by the arbitral tribunal. The Seoul Central District Court rejected the additional claim, pointing out that (i) the parties had entered into an arbitration agreement under which the parties agreed to finally resolve their dispute by arbitration, (ii) the claiming party had already received an award granting compensation for damages and delay interest thereon and (iii) as such, the additional claim for post-award interest pursuant to the Special Act was outside the scope of the arbitration agreement between the parties.[36]

10. What if Post-award Interest Is not Explicitly Stated in the Award?

It is debated whether a Korean court may independently order payment of post-award interest at the enforcement stage in circumstances where the arbitral tribunal has not expressly awarded any post-award interest. There are a few district court cases where the court additionally ordered payment of post-award interest despite there being no mention in the arbitral award.[37] However, there is no Supreme Court decision on this issue as of now, and there is a diversity of opinions among academia.

For instance: Some commentators have expressed the opinion that the Korean court should be permitted to reasonably supplement the award with an additional order for payment of post-award interest, so long as there is a clear legal basis (under the relevant applicable laws, for instance, the law of the arbitral seat) upon which

33. Article 35, Korean Arbitration Act.
34. *See*, e.g., Supreme Court Judgment 2006*Da*20290, May 28, 2009; Supreme Court Judgment 2004*Da*8814, December 23, 2005.
35. Young-jun Mok, Seung-jae Choi, *Commercial Arbitration Law* (ParkYoungSa 2018) at p. [246].
36. Seoul Central District Court Judgment 2012*Gahap*70260, 2013*Gahap*24257, May 31, 2013.
37. Seoul District Court Judgment 96*Gahap*64616, April 10, 1997; Seoul Western District Court Judgment 2008*Gahap*16806, July 15, 2010.

post-award interest may be granted.[38] They point out that, since an obligation to pay delay interest is *incidental* to the principal obligation,[39] it would be inappropriate and inconvenient if a separate award had to be obtained for delay interest simply because the previous award did not specifically mention it. They explain that the enforcing court's power to add post-award interest should be regarded as an exception to the general principle that the enforcing court should not correct, revise or supplement the contents of the award.

In contrast, others have opined that where post-award interest is not explicitly stated in the arbitral award, the Korean court should not itself order post-award interest at the enforcement stage.[40] The suggested reasons are that (i) the role of the Korean court when issuing an enforcement order is limited merely to converting the award into an enforceable document without making any amendments to the award (and disapproving enforcement if there are public policy concerns), and (ii) the issue of interest, including post-award interest, should be strictly considered an issue of substantive law and therefore a matter to be decided by the arbitral tribunal rather than the enforcing court.

A slightly different scenario is where the arbitral award includes an award of post-award interest, but the awarded interest rate is not stated in specific and concrete terms. For example, there may be cases where the arbitral award states that post-award interest shall be awarded *in accordance with the interest rates set by the Bank of England from time to time*, without specifying the exact interest rates to be applied. The problem with those awards is that they may not be regarded as enforceable under Korean law because the Korean execution court requires the dispositive section of judgments and awards to be sufficiently clear and specific.[41] That is to enable the execution authorities to proceed with compulsory execution based on the wording of the dispositive section alone.[42] While Korean courts have not yet expressly ruled on this matter, in practice, some enforcing courts have dealt with the problem by amending the wording of the dispositive section of the award when referring to it in its enforcement orders, so that it identifies the exact rates that are applicable.[43]

In sum, the power of the enforcing court to order post-award interest, where such an order is not clearly identified in the arbitral award, is subject to many uncertainties. It is thus advisable that any party seeking interest (including post-award interest)

38. *See* Moonchul Chang, *Commentary concerning Enforcement Proceedings for Foreign Arbitral Awards and Foreign Judgments* (Volume. 2, Korea Private International Law Journal December. 1997) at p. [674]; Kim, Kevin (Kap-You) et al., *Arbitration Law in Korea* (Pakyoungsa 2016) at pp. [312]-[313]; Kim, Soohyung, *Enforcement of Foreign Judgments* (Vol. 4, Korea Private International Law Journal December 1999) at pp. [506]-[507]; Suk, Kwang Hyun, *Essays in International Commercial Arbitration Law* (Vol. 1, 2007) at p. [334], etc.
39. *See,* e.g., Supreme Court Judgment 2009*Da*10249, January 27, 2011.
40. *See* Sungwoo Lim (Sean), *International Arbitration* (Pakyoungsa 2016) at pp. [337]-[339]; Yong Keun Sohn, *Articles: A Study on the Effect of Arbitral Awards* (Vol. 53, Lawyers Association Journal October. 2004) at p. [205], etc.
41. Seoul High Court Judgment 2013*Na*13506, January 17, 2014.
42. Seoul Southern District Court Judgment 2012*Gahap*15979, January 31, 2013, etc.
43. *See* Kevin Kim (Kap-You) et al., *Arbitration Law in Korea* (Pakyoungsa, 2016) at pp. [239], [316]; Seoul High Court Judgment 88*Na*8410, June 26, 1989, etc. Note that this was a case where the tribunal awarded interest but not the interest rate.

should explicitly seek interest in its submissions to the arbitral tribunal in clear and specific terms.[44]

VII POWERS OF THE COURT TO ORDER OR ADJUST POST-AWARD INTEREST

11. Does a Korean Court Have the Power to Order or Adjust the Post-award Interest Awarded By the Tribunal, Assuming It Is the Seat Court or the Enforcing Court?

Korean courts (whether in the capacity of the seat court or the enforcing court) have no power to adjust a post-award interest order awarded by the arbitral tribunal. As explained above, the power of a Korean court issuing an enforcement order is limited to converting the arbitral award into an enforceable document, and therefore the court has no power to correct, revise or supplement the contents of the award.[45]

A related question is whether the Korean court may adjust the post-award interest rate awarded by the tribunal (usually upwards) by applying the Special Act. For reference, in a case where a party was awarded delay interest of 6% per annum and filed for additional interest of 14% per annum to match the post-judgment award stipulated in the then effective Special Act (20% per annum), the court denied the claim on the ground that *seeking additional interest in an enforcement request is against the finality of the arbitration agreement.*[46]

44. *See* Kevin Kim (Kap-You) et al., *Arbitration Law in Korea* (Pakyoungsa, 2016) at p. [316].
45. *See* Sungwoo Lim (Sean), *International Arbitration* (Pakyoungsa, 2016) at pp. [339]-[340].
46. Seoul Central District Court judgment 2012*GaHab*70260, 2013*Gahab*24257, May 31, 2013. *See also* Kap-You Kim et al., *Arbitration Law in Korea* (Pakyoungsa 2016) at p. [314].

Republic of the Philippines

Jorge Alfonso C. Melo

INTRODUCTION

Arbitration in the Philippines is governed by the following laws: Title XIV of Republic Act (*R.A.*) No. 386, also known as the Civil Code of the Philippines("*the Civil Code*"),[1] R.A. No. 876, also known as The Arbitration Law,[2] R.A. No. 9285, also known as The Alternative Dispute Resolution Act of 2004,[3] DOJ Department Circular No. 098-09, also known as the Implementing Rules and Regulations of the Alternative Dispute Resolution Act of 2004,[4] A.M. No. 07-11-08-SC, also known as the Special Rules of Court on Alternative Dispute Resolution,[5] United Nations Commission on International Trade Law (*UNCITRAL*) Model Law ("*Model Law*"),[6] UNCITRAL Arbitration Rules[7] and 1958 Convention on the Recognition and Enforcement of Foreign Arbitral Awards ("*New York Convention*").[8]

The Philippines is among the first signatories of the New York Convention and acceded to the same as early as 1967. In addition, as a member of the UNCITRAL, the Philippines also adopted the UNCITRAL Model Law as the governing law on international commercial arbitrations. Hence, when the Philippine Congress enacted R.A. No. 9285, it incorporated the Model Law in its entirety.

1. Civil Code of the Philippines.
2. The Arbitration Law, Republic Act No. 876, June 19, 1953.
3. The Alternative Dispute Resolution Act of 2004, Republic Act No. 9285, April 2, 2004.
4. Implementing Rules and Regulations of the Alternative Dispute Resolution Act of 2004, DOJ Department Circular No. 098-09, December 4, 2009.
5. Special Rules of Court on Alternative Dispute Resolution, A.M. No. 07-11-08-SC, September 1, 2009.
6. United Nations Commission on International Trade Law (UNCITRAL) Model Law on International Commercial Arbitration 1985, with amendments as adopted in 2006.
7. United Nations Commission on International Trade Law (UNCITRAL) Arbitration Rules as amended in 2006.
8. New York Convention on the Recognition and Enforcement of Arbitral Awards, 1958.

Section I of this chapter examines the power of an arbitral tribunal to grant post-award interest based on the texts in the two paragraphs above. Next, Section II explains how a post-award interest rate is determined under the substantive law of the Philippines, both with and in the absence of an agreement. Section III of this chapter then briefly discusses the sources of international law recognized by the Philippines and their use in Supreme Court decisions related to international commercial arbitration.

Sections IV and V of this chapter examine issues regarding the award of post-award interest under substantive and procedural law. Section IV, for instance, discusses the controlling nature of contractual provisions concerning post-award interest and the limited circumstances when such interest may be adjusted. Section V then discusses the general procedural issues faced in ordinary court proceedings and their potential (and likely) application towards the award of post-award interest.

Section VI of this chapter provides a general overview of the legal effect of enforcement orders by Philippine courts and possible instances where post-award interest may still be granted when not explicitly awarded in the award itself. Finally, Section VII ends this chapter with a brief explanation of an enforcement court's authority to modify foreign arbitral awards and the extent to which this might be applied to awards of post-award interest.

I POWER TO GRANT POST-AWARD INTEREST

1. Does an Arbitral Tribunal Have the Power to Grant Post-award Interest under National Law?

None of the laws expressly give an arbitral tribunal the power to grant post-award interest. However, neither do these laws prohibit a tribunal from awarding such interest.

In the Philippines, post-award interest is generally classified as a form of compensatory damages (as opposed to punitive or exemplary damages) under the Civil Code.[9] It is not uncommon for courts to grant a post-award interest in court proceedings. In arbitration, however, the matter was only recently touched upon in *Mabuhay Holdings Corp. v. Sembcorp Logistics Limited*,[10] where the Philippine Supreme Court recognized and enforced an arbitral award imposing a 12% post-award interest rate, counted from the date of the final award until satisfaction. The contentious issue was whether the 12% rate of interest was against the public policy of the Republic of the Philippines and thus should not be enforced by the Philippine court. The Philippine

9. Article 2209 Civil Code of the Philippines; "*If the obligation consists in the payment of a sum of money, and the debtor incurs in delay, the indemnity for damages, there being no stipulation to the contrary, shall be the payment of the interest agreed upon, and in the absence of stipulation, the legal interest, which is six per cent per annum.*" *See also* *ECE Realty and Development, Inc. v. Hernandez* [August 6, 2014] G.R. No. 212689 (Resolution); *Sun Life of Canada (Phils.), Inc. v. Tan Kit* [October 15, 2014] G.R. No. 183272; *Spouses Abella v. Spouses Abella* [July 8, 2015] G.R. No. 195166.
10. *Mabuhay Holdings Corp. v. Sembcorp Logistics Limited* [December 5, 2018] G.R. No. 212734.

Supreme Court, implicitly recognizing that an arbitral tribunal has the power to grant post-award interest, upheld the grant of interest.

It is also worth noting that the Philippines adopted the UNCITRAL Model Law,[11] which espouses in Article 19 the principle that the arbitral tribunal may be afforded any powers as agreed by the parties, including the power to award post-award interest.

2. Is the Power Exercisable Without a Request or Submission, or Are Such Submissions Required?

Generally, under Philippine law, the ruling court can only grant reliefs which are prayed for and sufficiently established.[12] A court cannot grant a relief which a party has not prayed for, especially if it is a claim for a monetary award.[13]

The same rule is perhaps even stronger in an arbitration proceeding, where it is generally accepted that a tribunal can only rule on matters submitted to it by the parties. Thus, if a party fails to raise or claim post-award interest, the tribunal cannot grant it.[14] An arbitral award, which deals with an issue that is not contemplated by the parties or not falling within the terms of the submission to arbitration, may be set aside or refused recognition by the enforcing court.[15]

In Philippine court litigations, however, the prevailing rule is that post-judgment interest at the legal rate (at present) of 6% per annum from finality until its satisfaction may be imposed by the court with respect to a judgment for the payment of a sum of money, where there is no stipulation on the rate of interest.[16] This is imposed

11. United Nations Commission on International Trade Law (UNCITRAL) Arbitration Rules, as amended in 2006.
12. *Bucal v. Bucal* [June 17, 2015] G.R. No. 206957, where the Supreme Court nullified the order of a lower court granting "*visitation rights*" in a custody action and where the party concerned did not pray for such relief in the pleadings. The Supreme Court cited due process and fairness as reasons for the rule, to wit: "*It is improper to enter an order which exceeds the scope of relief sought by the pleadings, absent notice which affords the opposing party an opportunity to be heard with respect to the proposed relief.*"
13. *Diona v. Balangue* [January 7, 2013] G.R. No. 173559, where the Supreme Court nullified a ruling granting interest at a rate above what plaintiff sought.
14. Section. 20, The Arbitration Law states: "*the arbitrators shall have the power to decide only those matters which have been submitted to them. The terms of the award shall be confined to such disputes....*"
15. Sections. 12.4(a)(iii) and 13.4 (a)(iii), Special Rules of Court on Alternative Dispute Resolution, A.M. No. 07-11-08-SC, September 1, 2009, which mirror the relevant provisions in the UNCITRAL Model Law.
16. In *Nacar v. Gallery Frames* [August 13, 2013] G.R. No. 189871, the Supreme Court clarified the rule as follows: To recapitulate and for future guidance, the guidelines laid down in the case of *Eastern Shipping Lines* are accordingly modified to embody BSP-MB Circular No. 799, as follows: I. When an obligation, regardless of its source, i.e., law, contracts, quasi-contracts, delicts or quasi-delicts is breached, the contravenor can be held liable for damages. The provisions under Title XVIII on "*Damages*" of the Civil Code govern in determining the measure of recoverable damages. II. With regard particularly to an award of interest in the concept of actual and compensatory damages, the rate of interest, as well as the accrual thereof, is imposed, as follows: When the obligation is breached, and it consists in the payment of a sum of money, i.e., a loan or forbearance of money, the interest due should be that which may have been stipulated in writing. Furthermore, the interest due shall itself earn legal interest from the time it is judicially demanded. In the absence of stipulation, the rate of interest shall be 6% per annum to be computed from default, i.e., from judicial or extrajudicial demand under and subject to the provisions of Article 1169 of the Civil Code. When an obligation, not constituting a loan or

regardless of the presence of any prayer or submission by the claimant for post-judgment interest.

3. Is the Power Classified As One under the Substantive Applicable Law or the Procedural Law of the Arbitration?

There has been no specific or definitive pronouncement on this issue by the Philippine Courts. However, since post-award interest is viewed in the Philippines as a form of damages,[17] it can be surmised that the power to grant it springs from substantive law rather than procedural law.

Compensatory interest, as distinguished from monetary interest for the forbearance of money, refers to the damages imposed by the law and the courts under Articles 2209- 2212 of the Civil Code.[18] In *ECE Realty and Development Inc. v. Hernandez,*[19] the court recognized that the grant of interest is in the concept of compensatory damages under Article 2209 of the Civil Code. Here, the court granted the award of 6% interest per annum as a form of actual and compensatory damages from demand until the finality of the judgment; and from the finality of such judgment until its full payment, such total amount due would be compounded and earn interest of 6% interest per annum.[20]

II CHOICE OF LAW

4. What Is the Law That Applies to Determining What the Post-award Interest Should Be? Would This Be the Governing Law of the Dispute or the Law of the Seat?

In the Philippines, the determination of interest from the final judgment until full payment (or post-award interest as denominated in an arbitration proceeding) and the

forbearance of money, is breached, an interest on the amount of damages awarded may be imposed at the discretion of the court at the rate of 6 per cent per annum. No interest, however, shall be adjudged on unliquidated claims or damages, except when or until the demand can be established with reasonable certainty. Accordingly, where the demand is established with reasonable certainty, the interest shall begin to run from the time the claim is made judicially or extrajudicially (Article 1169, Civil Code), but when such certainty cannot be so reasonably established at the time the demand is made, the interest shall begin to run only from the date the judgment of the court is made (at which time the quantification of damages may be deemed to have been reasonably ascertained). The actual base for the computation of legal interest shall, in any case, be on the amount finally adjudged. When the judgment of the court awarding a sum of money becomes final and executory, the rate of legal interest, whether the case falls under para. 1 or para. 2, above, shall be 6% per annum from such finality until its satisfaction, this interim period being deemed to be by then an equivalent to a forbearance of credit.

17. Article 2209 Civil Code of the Philippines, states: "*If the obligation consists in the payment of a sum of money, and the debtor incurs in delay, the indemnity for damages, there being no stipulation to the contrary, shall be the payment of the interest agreed upon, and in the absence of stipulation, the legal interest, which is six per cent per annum.*"
18. *Sun Life of Canada (Phils.), Inc. v. Tan Kit* [October 15, 2014] G.R. No. 183272 states: There are two kinds of interest—monetary and compensatory. "*Monetary interest refers to the compensation set by the parties for the use or forbearance of money.*" No such interest shall be due unless it has been expressly stipulated in writing. "*On the other hand, compensatory interest refers to the penalty or indemnity for damages imposed by law or by the courts.*" The interest mentioned in Articles 2209 and 2212 of the Civil Code applies to compensatory interest.
19. G.R. No. 212689 [August 6, 2014] (Resolution).
20. G.R. No. 212689 [August 6, 2014] (Resolution).

rate of interest to be applied would be characterized as a governing substantive law issue, as discussed above.

The Philippines views the rate of interest as generally a matter of agreement or contractual stipulation between the parties and a matter governed by law in the absence of stipulation.

As a general rule, no interest on a loan can be charged or claimed unless there is a stipulation in the agreement.[21] However, in obligations consisting of payment of money, the creditor may claim damages in the form of interest under the Civil Code.[22] The application of this rule was explained in *Eastern Shipping Lines, Inc. v. Court of Appeals*.[23] While applying the Philippine Civil Code, the court ruled that the period from final judgment to the full satisfaction of the award is deemed to be an interim period equivalent to a forbearance of credit or payment of money.[24] Thus, the judgment obligee is entitled to interest at the stipulated rate, or in the absence of stipulation, at the legal rate of interest of 6% per annum from the finality of judgment until its satisfaction.[25]

III DO THE COURTS TAKE INTO ACCOUNT INTERNATIONAL STANDARDS WHEN FACING CHALLENGES ON THE POST-AWARD INTEREST?

The courts, where necessary, will generally apply foreign law in determining questions concerning interest. This may include resorting to the five general sources of international law recognized in the Philippines. These are customs, treaties and other international agreements, generally recognized principles of law, judicial decisions and teachings of highly qualified and recognized publicists.[26] In a number of cases dealing with international commercial arbitration, the Supreme Court has relied on and cited various sources from these five general sources.

In arbitration-related jurisprudence, the Philippine Supreme Court relied mostly on the 2016 UNCITRAL Secretariat Guide on the Convention on the Recognition and Enforcement of Foreign Arbitral Awards, judicial decisions from the United States, Hong Kong, England and Wales, Germany, Canada, etc. and commentaries of various highly qualified and recognized publicists, such as Gary Born, P. Capper, etc.

There has been no significant jurisprudence, however, dealing specifically with post-award interest where the Supreme Court relied on such international standards.

21. Article 1956 of Civil Code states: "*No interest shall be due unless it has been expressly stipulated in writing.*"
22. Article 2209 Civil Code.
23. *Eastern Shipping Lines, Inc. v. Court of Appeals* [12 July 1994] G.R. No. 97412. *See also Nacar v. Gallery Frames* [August 13, 2013] G.R. No. 189871.
24. *Eastern Shipping Lines, Inc. v. Court of Appeals* [12 July 1994] G.R. No. 97412. *See also Nacar v. Gallery Frames* [August 13, 2013] G.R. No. 189871.
25. *Eastern Shipping Lines, Inc. v. Court of Appeals* [12 July 1994] G.R. No. 97412. *See also Nacar v. Gallery Frames* [August 13, 2013] G.R. No. 189871. *See also Vitug v. Abuda* [11 January 2016] G.R. No. 201264; *see also* BSP Circular No. 799 [June 21, 2013] Series of 2013.
26. Bernas, Joaquin S.J., *Introduction to Public International Law* (September 2012).

IV SUBSTANTIVE LAW ISSUES

5. How Are Contractual Provisions on Late or Non-payment Interest Relevant to Post-award Interest? Will These Be Considered By the Arbitral Tribunal?

Generally, contractual provisions on late or non-payment of interest are considered, if not controlling, in determining the appropriate rate of post-award interest. Post-award interest would principally mirror or follow contractual provisions on late or non-payment interest. This is subject only to adjustment by the courts where such rate is considered unconscionable, exorbitant or contrary to public policy.[27]

To illustrate, the Supreme Court sustained the validity of an agreed late or non-payment interest rate of 21% in *Bautista*[28] and 24% in *Garcia.*[29] The Philippine Court invalidated the following interest rates due to unconscionability: an interest rate of 36% per annum in *Ruiz,*[30] 66% per annum in *Medel*[31] and 72% per annum in *Solangon.*[32]

6. How Do the Procedural Rules of the Substantive Law Apply?

The Philippines recognizes that the procedural rules of the substantive law in an arbitration should generally not apply.

The 2016 UNCITRAL Secretariat Guide on the New York Convention on the Recognition and Enforcement of Arbitral Awards states that, in accordance with the wording of Article III thereof, courts of the Contracting States have applied the procedural rules of their national laws only with regard to the recognition and enforcement of arbitral awards. Note that for recognition and enforcement of arbitral awards, the laws of the country where the arbitration took place are not applied. For example, a United States court rejected the application of English procedural rules to the recognition and enforcement of an arbitral award in the United States on the ground that enforcement was sought in the United States.[33]

In recognizing or enforcing a foreign arbitral award, the courts shall take into consideration the laws applied by the arbitral tribunal which is comprised of the substantive law of the contract and the procedural rules governing the conduct of arbitration proceedings.[34] In addition to the above, the procedural rules of the enforcement state shall also be applicable in so far as the enforcement of the award in that state is concerned.

---

27. *Bognot v. RRI Lending Corp.* [September 24, 2014] G.R. No. 180144, where the court nullified the interest rate of 5% per month (60% per annum) as unconscionable and excessive, and reduced it to 1% per month.
28. *Spouses Bautista v. Pilar Development Corp.* [August 17, 1999] G.R. No. 135046.
29. *Garcia v. Court of Appeals* [November 24, 1988] G.R. Nos. 82282-83.
30. *Ruiz v. Court of Appeals* [April 22, 2003] G.R. No. 146942.
31. *Medel v. Court of Appeals* [November 27, 1998] G.R. No. 131622.
32. *Spouses Solangon v. Salazar* [June 29, 2001] G.R. No. 125944.
33. 2016 UNCITRAL Secretariat Guide on the New York Convention on the Recognition and Enforcement of Arbitral Awards at p.. [83], para. [21].
34. *See Mabuhay Holdings Corp. v. Sembcorp Logistics Limited.*

7. Whether the Award of Interest Can Be Subjected to Public Policy Objections, and if So, What Are They?

Section. 45 of the Alternative Dispute Resolution Act of 2004[35] provides that the opposing party in an application for recognition and enforcement of the arbitral award in the Philippines may raise only those grounds that are enumerated under Article V of the New York Convention. One of those grounds to refuse recognition and enforcement is when doing so would be contrary to the public policy of the Philippines.[36]

Mabuhay Holdings Corp. v. Sembcorp Logistics Limited[37] clearly illustrates the Philippines' position in the application of public policy as a ground for refusing enforcement, especially that relating to the issuance of post-award interest. The Supreme Court stated that:

> *Under Article V (2) (b) of the New York Convention, a court may refuse to enforce an award if doing so would be contrary to the public policy of the State in which enforcement is sought. Neither the New York Convention nor the mirroring provisions on public policy in the Model Law and Philippine arbitration laws provide a definition of 'public policy' or a standard for determining what is contrary to public policy. Due to divergent approaches in defining public policy in the realm of international arbitration, public policy has become one of the most controversial bases for refusing enforcement of foreign arbitral awards.*
>
> Most arbitral jurisdictions adopt a narrow and restrictive approach in defining public policy pursuant to the pro-enforcement policy of the New York Convention. The public policy exception, thus, is 'a safety valve to be used in those exceptional circumstances when it would be impossible for a legal system to recognize an award and enforce it without abandoning the very fundaments on which it is based'. An example of a narrow approach adopted by several jurisdictions is that the public policy defense may only be invoked 'where enforcement [of the award] would violate the forum state's most basic notions of morality and justice'. Thus, in Hong Kong, an award obtained by fraud was denied enforcement by the court on the ground that fraud is contrary to Hong Kong's 'fundamental notions of morality and justice'. In Singapore, also a Model Law country, the public policy ground is entertained by courts only in instances where upholding the award is 'clearly injurious to the public good or ... wholly offensive to the ordinary reasonable and fully informed member of the public'.
>
> *'In Our jurisdiction, the Court has yet to define public policy and what is deemed contrary to public policy in an arbitration case. However, in an old case, the Court, through Justice Laurel, elucidated on the term 'public policy' for purposes of declaring a contract void:*
>
> > *At any rate, courts should not rashly extend the rule which holds that a contract is void as against public policy. The term 'public policy' is vague and uncertain in meaning, floating and changeable in connotation. It may be said, however, that, in general, a contract which is neither prohibited by law nor condemned by judicial decision, nor contrary to public morals, contravenes no public policy. In*

35. Section. 45 The Alternative Dispute Resolution Act of 2004: "*Section 45. Rejection of a Foreign Arbitral Award.— A party to a foreign arbitration proceeding may oppose an application for recognition and enforcement of the arbitral award in accordance with the procedural rules to be promulgated by the Supreme Court only on those grounds enumerated under Article V of the New York Convention. Any other ground raised shall be disregarded by the Regional Trial Court.*"
36. Rule 13.4, Special Rules of Court on Alternative Dispute Resolution.
37. *See Mabuhay Holdings Corp. v. Sembcorp Logistics Limited* [December 5, 2018] G.R. No. 212734.

the absence of express legislation or constitutional prohibition, a court, in order to declare a contract void as against public policy, must find that the contract as to the consideration or thing to be done, has a tendency to injure the public, is against the public good, or contravenes some established interests of society, or is inconsistent with sound policy and good morals, or tends clearly to undermine the security of individual rights, whether of personal liability or of private property'. (Emphasis ours)

An older case, Ferrazzini v. Gsell, defined public policy for purposes of determining whether that part of the contract under consideration is against public policy:

By 'public policy,' as defined by the courts in the United States and England, is intended that principle of the law which holds that no subject or citizen can lawfully do that which has a tendency to be injurious to the public or against the public good, which may be termed the 'policy of the law,' or 'public policy in relation to the administration of the law'. Public policy is the principle under which freedom of contract or private dealing is restricted by law for the good of the public. In determining whether a contract is contrary to public policy the nature of the subject matter determines the source from which such question is to be solved. (Emphasis ours and citation omitted)

In light of the foregoing and pursuant to the State's policy in favor of arbitration and enforcement of arbitral awards, the Court adopts the majority and narrow approach in determining whether enforcement of an award is contrary to our public policy. Mere errors in the interpretation of the law or factual findings would not suffice to warrant refusal of enforcement under the public policy ground. The illegality or immorality of the award must reach a certain threshold such that, enforcement of the same would be against Our State's fundamental tenets of justice and morality, or would blatantly be injurious to the public, or the interests of the society. (Citation omitted)

In the said case, *Mabuhay* opposed the enforcement of the arbitral award, arguing that the 12% post-award interest imposed by the arbitral tribunal is contrary to Philippine law (which specifies a default rate of 6%) and jurisprudence, thus making it contrary to public policy. It prayed that the enforcement of the award be negated. The Supreme Court ruled that the mere incompatibility of a foreign arbitral award with domestic mandatory rules on interest rates does not amount to a breach of public policy.

The Supreme Court continued to state that, "*some jurisdictions refused to recognize and enforce awards, or the part of the award which was considered to be contrary to public policy, where they considered that the awarded interest was unreasonably high.*" Nevertheless, the Supreme Court stated that the 12% interest rate imposed under the Final Award is not unreasonably high or unconscionable such that it violates the Philippines' "*fundamental notions of justice.*"

As previously discussed, the Supreme Court sustained the validity of agreed interest rates of 21% in *Bautista*[38] and 24% in *Garcia.*[39] However, the Philippine Court invalidated the following interest rates due to unconscionability: an interest rate of

38. *See Spouses Bautista v. Pilar Development Corp.* [August 17, 1999] G.R. No. 135046.
39. *Garcia v. Court of Appeals* [November 24, 1988] G.R. Nos. 82282-83.

36% per annum in *Ruiz*,[40] 66% per annum in *Medel*[41] and 72% per annum in *Solangon*.[42]

In line with this, the 2016 UNCITRAL Secretariat Guide on the New York Convention on the Recognition and Enforcement of Arbitral Awards has also cited cases where the enforcing court either "*severed the part of the award on interest as a whole or the part of the interest sum exceeding what would be considered appropriate in the enforcement State.*"[43] As noted previously, the Philippines is a member of the UNCITRAL and has also adopted the UNCITRAL Model Law as the governing law on international commercial arbitrations. The Philippine Supreme Court has also relied previously on the UNCITRAL Secretariat Guide as a persuasive legal basis.

V PROCEDURAL LAW ISSUES

8. What Are the Main Procedural Law Issues When Considering Post-award Interest? How Are the Arbitration Laws and Other Laws or Regulations of the Seat Relevant?

Where the Philippines is the seat of the arbitration, parties should be aware that the arbitration laws in the country do not explicitly lay down the rules relating to post-award interest. While guidance may be provided by recent jurisprudence, such as the case of *Mabuhay*, there is no certainty that future jurisprudence will follow the trend set by *Mabuhay*. Moreover, there is no ruling regarding the imposition of post-award interest absent a submission or request by a party.

However, it stands to reason that the same standards applied in ordinary court proceedings for the award of post-judgment interest can also be applied to arbitration awards. Thus, where Philippine law is the substantive governing law of the arbitration proceeding, the determination of the amount of post-award interest will be governed primarily by the agreement of the parties (subject to adjustment) or the current default rate of 6% in the absence of stipulation.

Where the Philippines is the enforcing court (not the seat), the following rules shall apply:

> Generally, where the arbitral tribunal grants interest where it was not submitted or claimed by the parties, the imposition of such interest may be questioned as one that goes beyond the authority of the tribunal.[44] Thus, Philippine procedural rules

40. *Ruiz v. Court of Appeals* [April 22, 2003] G.R. No. 146942.
41. *Medel v. Court of Appeals* [November 27, 1998] G.R. No. 131622.
42. *Spouses Solangon v. Salazar* [June 29, 2001] G.R. No. 125944.
43. 2016 UNCITRAL Secretariat Guide on the New York Convention on the Recognition and Enforcement of Arbitral Awards at p. [261].
44. Rule 12.4 (iii), Special Rules of Court on Alternative Dispute Resolution, A.M. No. 07-11-08-SC, September 1, 2009, which states: "*Rule 12.4. Grounds to set aside or resist enforcement.—The court may set aside or refuse the enforcement of the arbitral award only if: The party making the application furnishes proof that: (i) A party to the arbitration agreement was under some incapacity, or the said agreement is not valid under the law to which the parties have subjected it or, failing any indication thereof, under Philippine law; or (ii) The party making the application to set aside or resist enforcement was not given proper notice of the appointment of an arbitrator or of the arbitral proceedings or was otherwise unable to present his case; or (iii) The award deals*

allow a party to either set aside such part of the award or refuse its recognition and enforcement, as the case may be.

Specifically, for domestic arbitrations, if the grant of post-award interest is beyond the issues or matters submitted to the tribunal, a party may within 30 days of receipt of the award request that the arbitral tribunal correct or modify errors under section 25 of The Arbitration Law.[45]

In any case, mere incompatibility of a foreign arbitral award with Philippine laws or rules on interest rates does not necessarily amount to a breach of public policy, unless the post-award interest issued is unreasonably high or unconscionable.[46]

In international arbitrations, if the arbitral tribunal fails to deal with the issue of interest in its award despite it having been claimed, a party may request the arbitral tribunal to make an additional award under Article 33 of the UNCITRAL Model Law.

VI EFFECT OF ENFORCEMENT ORDERS ON INTEREST ON THE AWARD ON BOTH THE SEAT AND ELSEWHERE

Legal Effect of "Enforcement" Orders By Philippine Courts

In a petition for recognition and enforcement, the court only has two options. The court may either: (a) recognize and/or enforce or (b) refuse to recognize and enforce the arbitral award. A foreign arbitral award, when confirmed by a court of a foreign

---

with a dispute not contemplated by or not falling within the terms of the submission to arbitration, or contains decisions on matters beyond the scope of the submission to arbitration; provided that, if the decisions on matters submitted to arbitration can be separated from those not so submitted, only that part of the award which contains decisions on matters not submitted to arbitration may be set aside or only that part of the award which contains decisions on matters submitted to arbitration may be enforced; or (iv) The composition of the arbitral tribunal or the arbitral procedure was not in accordance with the agreement of the parties, unless such agreement was in conflict with a provision of Philippine law from which the parties cannot derogate, or, failing such agreement, was not in accordance with Philippine law; The court finds that: (i) The subject-matter of the dispute is not capable of settlement by arbitration under the law of the Philippines; or (ii) The recognition or enforcement of the award would be contrary to public policy. In deciding the petition, the Court shall disregard any other ground to set aside or enforce the arbitral award other than those enumerated above. The petition to set-aside or a pleading resisting the enforcement of an arbitral award on the ground that a party was a minor or an incompetent shall be filed only on behalf of the minor or incompetent and shall allege that (a) the other party to arbitration had knowingly entered into a submission or agreement with such minor or incompetent, or (b) the submission to arbitration was made by a guardian or guardian ad litem who was not authorized to do so by a competent court."

45. Section 25 of The Arbitration Law, states: "*Grounds for modifying or correcting award.—In any one of the following cases, the court must make an order modifying or correcting the award, upon the application of any party to the controversy which was arbitrated: (a) Where there was an evident miscalculation of figures, or an evident mistake in the description of any person, thing or property referred to in the award; or (b) Where the arbitrators have awarded upon a matter not submitted to them, not affecting the merits of the decision upon the matter submitted; or (c) Where the award is imperfect in a matter of form not affecting the merits of the controversy, and if it had been a commissioner's report, the defect could have been amended or disregarded by the court. The order may modify and correct the award so as to effect the intent thereof and promote justice between the parties.*"
46. *See Mabuhay Holdings Corp. v. Sembcorp Logistics Limited* [December 5, 2018] G.R. No. 212734.

country, shall be recognized and enforced as a foreign arbitral award and not as a judgment of a foreign court.[47] However, when it is confirmed by the Philippine court, it shall be enforced in the same manner as final and executory decisions of Philippine courts.[48]

Note that for foreign arbitral awards, an enforcement order may not substitute the judgment rendered by the arbitral tribunal with its own judgment.[49] The Special Rules of Court on Alternative Dispute Resolution provides that the courts shall not disturb the arbitral tribunal's determination of facts and/or interpretation of law.[50]

What if Post-award Interest Is Not Explicitly Stated in the Award?

It is generally viewed that if interest is not granted in the final award, the court may not subsequently grant post-award interest. The court, in a petition to recognize and enforce an award, cannot alter the merits of the award in any manner. This could be considered similar to the rule of immutability of judgments and *res judicata* in court judgments.[51] Nonetheless, there is no pronouncement under Philippine jurisprudence on the specific application of this rule to arbitration proceedings.

There are, however, some instances which may allow the grant of post-award interest where the award itself does not explicitly grant it.

---

47. Sections 40 and 44, Alternative Dispute Resolution Act of 200; *Korea Technologies Co., Ltd. v. Lerma* [January 7, 2008] G.R. No. 143581.
48. Sections 40 and 44, Alternative Dispute Resolution Act of 200; *Korea Technologies Co., Ltd. v. Lerma* [January 7, 2008] G.R. No. 143581.
49. *Fruehauf Electronics Philippines Corp. v. Technology Electronics Assembly and Management Pacific Corp.* [November 23, 2016] G.R. No. 204197. The Supreme Court in this case stated: "*We have deliberately refrained from passing upon the merits of the arbitral award—not because the award was erroneous—but because it would be improper. None of the grounds to vacate an arbitral award are present in this case and as already established, the merits of the award cannot be reviewed by the courts. Our refusal to review the award is not a simple matter of putting procedural technicalities over the substantive merits of a case; it goes into the very legal substance of the issues. There is no law granting the judiciary authority to review the merits of an arbitral award. If we were to insist on reviewing the correctness of the award: (or consent to the CA's doing so), it would be tantamount to expanding our jurisdiction without the benefit of legislation. This translates to judicial legislation—a breach of the fundamental principle of separation of powers. The CA reversed the arbitral award—an action that it has no power to do – because it disagreed with the tribunal's factual findings and application of the law. However, the alleged incorrectness of the award is insufficient cause to vacate the award, given the State's policy of upholding the autonomy of arbitral awards.*"
50. Rule 11.9, Special Rules of Court on Alternative Dispute Resolution, states in part: "*In a petition to vacate an award or in petition to vacate an award in opposition to a petition to confirm the award, the petitioner may simultaneously apply with the Court to refer the case back to the same arbitral tribunal for the purpose of making a new or revised award or to direct a new hearing, or in the appropriate case, order the new hearing before a new arbitral tribunal, the members of which shall be chosen in the manner provided in the arbitration agreement or submission, or the law. In the latter case, any provision limiting the time in which the arbitral tribunal may make a decision shall be deemed applicable to the new arbitral tribunal. In referring the case back to the arbitral tribunal or to a new arbitral tribunal pursuant to Rule 24 of Republic Act No. 876, the court may not direct it to revise its award in a particular way, or to revise its findings of fact or conclusions of law or otherwise encroach upon the independence of an arbitral tribunal in the making of a final award.*"
51. *See Republic v. Heirs of Gotengco* [January 24, 2018] G.R. No. 226355, where the Supreme Court ruled, in part, that the decision had become final and that the petitioners slept on their rights and failed (after several years) to correct the omission of the interest from the decision.

For domestic arbitration, Rule 11.4 (B) of the Special Rules on Alternative Dispute Resolution states that the court may correct or modify a domestic arbitral award not later than 30 days from receipt of the arbitral award in case the arbitrators have omitted to resolve an issue submitted to them for resolution.[52] Thus, if post-award interest was one of the issues submitted to the tribunal, the failure of the tribunal to rule on that matter may be reviewed by the court, which may then modify the award to include such interest.

In international commercial arbitration, Article 33 of the UNCITRAL Model Law will apply. Thus, if the arbitral tribunal fails to deal with the issue of interest in its award despite it having been claimed, a party may request the arbitral tribunal to make an additional award. If, however, the tribunal fails or refuses to make an additional award, there is no provision of law or procedural rule authorizing the court to correct or modify the foreign arbitral award. As previously mentioned, for international commercial arbitral awards being enforced in the Philippines, the court cannot substitute or alter the judgment rendered by the arbitral tribunal. The Special Rules of Court on Alternative Dispute Resolution provides that the courts shall not disturb the arbitral tribunal's determination of facts and/or interpretation of law.[53] This is viewed to extend the presence or absence of an award of post-award interest.

However, in a decision of the United States Court of Appeals, Second Circuit, entitled *Waterside Ocean Navigation Inc. v. International Navigation Ltd.*[54] ("the *Laurentian Forest*"), it was found that district courts had the power to grant post-award and pre-judgment interest for cases brought under the New York Convention when the arbitral tribunal failed to do so. It remains to be seen whether the Philippine courts will adopt the same perspective, although jurisprudence from the United States is generally accorded persuasive status in the Philippines in the absence of relevant rulings in local jurisprudence.[55]

52. Section. 11.4(B) of the Special Rules on ADR states: "*(B) To correct/modify an arbitral award.—The Court may correct/modify or order the arbitral tribunal to correct/modify the arbitral award in the following cases: a. Where there was an evident miscalculation of figures or an evident mistake in the description of any person, thing or property referred to in the award; b. Where the arbitrators have awarded upon a matter not submitted to them, not affecting the merits of the decision upon the matter submitted; c. Where the arbitrators have omitted to resolve an issue submitted to them for resolution; or d. Where the award is imperfect in a matter of form not affecting the merits of the controversy, and if it had been a commissioner's report, the defect could have been amended or disregarded by the Court.*"
53. Rule 12.13 of the Special Rules of Court on Alternative Dispute Resolution provides: "*Rule 12.13. Judgment of the court.—Unless a ground to set aside an arbitral award under Rule 12.4 above is fully established, the court shall dismiss the petition. If, in the same proceedings, there is a petition to recognize and enforce the arbitral award filed in opposition to the petition to set aside, the court shall recognize and enforce the award. In resolving the petition or petition in opposition thereto in accordance with the Special ADR Rules, the court shall either set aside or enforce the arbitral award. The court shall not disturb the arbitral tribunal's determination of facts and/or interpretation of law.*"
54. 737 F.2d 150 (2d Cir. 1984).
55. *Philippine Health Care Providers, Inc. v. Commissioner of Internal Revenue* [September 18, 2009] G.R. No. 167330 (Resolution); *Rodriguez v. Commission on Elections* [July 24, 1996] G.R. No. 120099; Repide *v. Afzelius* [November 20, 1918] G.R. No. 13438.

VII POWERS OF THE COURT TO ORDER OR ADJUST POST-AWARD INTEREST

9. Does the Philippine Court Have the Power to Order or Adjust the Post-award Interest, Assuming It Is Either the Seat Court or the Enforcing Court?

Generally, a party may challenge a domestic award by applying to vacate it under section 41 of the Alternative Dispute Resolution Act,[56] or it may reject enforcement of a foreign arbitral award under section 45 of the same Act.

The enforcing court in a domestic arbitration can also modify or correct the award where the tribunal failed or omitted to rule on a matter submitted to it.[57]

In addition, an enforcing court in a domestic or foreign arbitration can vacate, set aside or refuse recognition to (as the case may be) an arbitral award for post-award interest where it can be considered contrary to public policy.[58]

Save for these exceptional cases (and possibly a case that will call for the application of the *Laurentian Forest* case), it is questionable and highly doubtful whether the court has the authority to order or adjust post-award interest where the issue has been determined by the arbitral tribunal.

56. Alternative Dispute Resolution Act of 2004.
57. Article 33 Alternative Dispute Resolution Act.
58. Articles 34 and 36 Alternative Dispute Resolution Act.

Singapore

Michael Hwang S.C. & Yin Wai Chan

INTRODUCTION

Under the Singapore International Arbitration Act 1994 (2020 Revised Edition) (*the IAA*), arbitral tribunals in Singapore-seated arbitrations are afforded broad discretion on matters concerning post-award interest. Subject to the parties' agreement, arbitral tribunals have the power to award post-award interest on a simple or compound basis, from such date at such rate and with such rest as they consider appropriate.

While the public policy of Singapore does not prohibit the award of interest, any award of interest should be compensatory or restitutionary in nature and cannot be penal in character. It is arguable that, in certain circumstances, an award of interest based on a penalty clause may be viewed as being contrary to the public policy of Singapore and may be liable to be set aside or refused enforcement. An award of interest, like any other award of an arbitral tribunal, is final and binding as to the matters determined. It may be challenged or enforced in the same manner as any other award issued by an arbitral tribunal.

The first part of this chapter discusses an arbitral tribunal's power and discretion when awarding post-award interest. Part two considers the choice of law issues concerning the award of post-award interest.

The third part of this chapter briefly discusses the applicability of international standards in challenges on post-award interest before the Singapore courts. Part four then examines substantive law issues associated with the award of post-award interest in Singapore.

The fifth part of this chapter explores procedural law issues related to post-award interest, including those errors in computation and omission of interest claims, the limitations period for enforcing an award of interest and the enforceability of such an award.

Finally, the sixth and seventh parts of this chapter focus on the overall enforceability of and powers of the Singapore courts to order or adjust post-award interest.

I POWER TO GRANT POST-AWARD INTEREST

1. Does an Arbitral Tribunal Have the Power to Grant Post-award Interest under the Singapore Law?

Yes, under sections 12(5)(b) and 20 of the IAA, arbitral tribunals are provided with the statutory power to award post-award interest.

Section 12(5)(b) of the IAA provides that:

> (5) Without prejudice to the application of Article 28 of the [1985 UNCITRAL Model Law on International Commercial Arbitration ("*Model Law*")], an arbitral tribunal, in deciding the dispute that is the subject of the arbitral proceedings –
>
> *[...]*
>
> (b) may award simple or compound interest on the whole or any part of any sum in accordance with section 20(1).

Section 20 of the IAA provides that:

> 20—(1) Subject to subsection (3), unless otherwise agreed by the parties, an arbitral tribunal may, in the arbitral proceedings before it, award simple or compound interest from such date, at such rate and with such rest as the arbitral tribunal considers appropriate, for any period ending not later than the date of payment on the whole or any part of —
>
> (a) any sum which is awarded by the arbitral tribunal in the arbitral proceedings;
>
> (b) any sum which is in issue in the arbitral proceedings but is paid before the date of the award; or
>
> (c) costs awarded or ordered by the arbitral tribunal in the arbitral proceedings.
>
> (2) Nothing in subsection (1) affects any other power of an arbitral tribunal to award interest.
>
> (3) Where an award directs a sum to be paid, that sum, unless the award otherwise directs, carries interest as from the date of the award and at the same rate as a judgment debt.

The phrase '*unless otherwise agreed by the parties*' in section 20(1) of the IAA indicates that parties are free to determine the arbitral tribunal's power to award interest and may choose to limit or exclude the arbitral tribunal's power to award such interest.[1]

Pursuant to section 20(1) of the IAA, arbitral tribunals have the power to award simple or compound interest. If the successful claimant can show that it was living with the burden of having to pay its financiers compound interest, it would obviously have a strong case for seeking compound interest from the respondent which had wrongly

1. It has been suggested that '*clear words of exclusion are necessary (such as an express reference to exclusion of the statutory power; a clause in a contract simply providing that a party is not entitled to interest would be treated as precluding contractual rights to interest but not otherwise):*' see commentary on a similar provision under the 'Hong Kong Arbitration Ordinance' in John Choong and Romesh Weeramantry (eds.), The Hong Kong Arbitration Ordinance: Commentary and Annotations (2nd edn, Sweet & Maxwell 2015), at para. [79.11].

denied the claimant's claim and therefore causing the claimant's extra loss of compound interest. Reimbursement of a claimant's actual losses by way of compound interest is, therefore, easier to justify than a simple claim for compound interest without showing actual suffering of compound losses.

Arbitral tribunals also have broad discretion to determine the date of commencement of accrual, interest rate, period of interest and such rest as they consider appropriate. If an award does not provide for post-award interest, the default position is that a sum awarded by the arbitral tribunal will automatically carry simple interest from the date of the award at the rate of 5.33 % per annum.[2] It is important to note that arbitral tribunals are not prohibited from awarding interest higher than the statutory rate of 5.33 per annum.

Section 20(2) of the IAA clarifies that an arbitral tribunal's statutory power to award post-award interest under section 20(1) of the IAA does not affect any other power that it may have to award interest. Such other power may, for example, be provided by contract.[3]

There are no legislative provisions which prescribe the factors that arbitral tribunals must take into account when exercising their discretion under sections 12(5)(b) and 20(1) of the IAA. In practice, arbitral tribunals will consider the contractual provisions (if any) that impose interest rates in respect of late or non-payment, the currency of the award and the place of payment.

2. Is the Power Exercisable Without a Request or Submission, or Is Such a Submission Required?

Sections 12(5)(b) and 20 of the IAA do not expressly provide that interest must be specifically pleaded before the tribunal in order for it to exercise its power to grant post-award interest.

In the context of litigation before a Singapore court, it has been held that '*it was not necessary to specifically plead interest for the court to exercise its discretion to award it*'.[4] Similarly, in the context of arbitration, it has been held that '*it was in the court's view implicit in a reference or submission to arbitration that parties have conferred power on the arbitrator to award interest as if the matter in difference were litigated in a court of law*'.[5] It would therefore appear that the arbitral tribunal's power to award interest is exercisable even without a request or submission from a party.

However, in light of the modern arbitration practice, the better view may be that an arbitral tribunal should not normally exercise its power to award interest in the absence of a request for the same and without first giving each party a reasonable

2. Section 20(3) IAA read with O 17 r 5 Rules of Court 2021.
3. This provision is particularly relevant in cases (such as those involving banking loan contracts) where the contract provides for a particular rate of interest (which may be different from the statutory default rate) on an 'as well after as before judgment' basis. In such cases, the arbitral tribunal can then rely on the parties' agreed contractual rate to award interest for both before and after the award.
4. *Ng Swee Kin v. Ng Tian Hock and other appeals* [1992] 1 SLRI 266, at para. [8].
5. *Ahong Construction (S) Pte Ltd v. United Boulevard Pte Ltd* [1994] 3 I(R) 669, at para. [19].

opportunity to present its case. This is to ensure due process and the equal treatment of the parties, the failure of which may expose the eventual award to a challenge.

3. Is the Power Classified as One Under the Substantive Applicable Law or the Procedural Law of the Arbitration?

When interest is claimed under the IAA, the arbitral tribunal's power to award post-award interest under the IAA is generally considered to be a procedural matter governed by *lex arbitri*.

However, when a claim for interest is based on a contractual provision, the power should be properly classified as one under the substantive applicable law (i.e., the governing law of the contract). Accordingly, where the substantive applicable law operates to render a contractual provision for interest unenforceable, the arbitral tribunal will have no power under the contractual provision to award interest and doing so will amount to an excess of jurisdiction.[6]

II CHOICE OF LAW

4. What Is the Law That Applies to Determine What the Post-award Interest Should Be? Would This Be the Governing Law of the Dispute or the Law of the Seat?

When a claim for interest is based on a contractual provision (e.g., when a contract provides for the payment of interest for late or non-payment of sums due), the award of such interest will be determined by the substantive law applicable to the contract. This is consistent with section 20(2) of the IAA which provides that the statutory power to award interest under section 20(1) of the IAA does not affect any other power that the arbitral tribunal may have to award interest.

Arbitral tribunals also have the statutory power to award post-award interest under section 20(1) of the IAA. Under the common law in Singapore, a distinction is drawn between (i) the entitlement to interest and (ii) the rate at which interest so payable is to be paid.[7] There is the view that the former is governed by the substantive applicable law while the latter is governed by the procedural law. However, it would appear that, under section 20(1) of the IAA, an arbitral tribunal is not bound to apply this choice of law analysis given that it has broad discretion to award interest based on what it considers appropriate. This is analogous to the *voie directe* approach that is used in the context of determining the applicable law governing the substance of the dispute.[8] Thus, in the absence of contrary agreement between the parties, the arbitral tribunal is vested with the power to select the appropriate law or rules of law to directly

6. *CBX and anor v. CBZ and ors* [2021] SGCA(I) 3, paras [86]-[100].
7. Lord Collins of Mapesbury (ed.), *Dicey, Morris & Collins on the Conflict of Laws* (15th edn, Sweet & Maxwell 2012), at para. [7-098]: '*the existence of a right to claim interest is properly classified as a substantive matter and thus should be referred to the lex causae of the relevant claim.*' Paul Carruthers (ed.), *Cheshire, North & Fawcett: Private International Law* (15th edn, OUP 2017), at p. [96]: '*Where damages for breach of contract are being claimed, rather than a debt, then the right to interest on the damages is governed by the law applicable to the contract*'.
8. For a general discussion of the difference between *voie directe* and *voie indirecte* approach, *see*: Doug Jones, 'Choosing the Law or Rules of Law to Govern the Substantive Rights of the Parties:

determine the applicable interest to be awarded, taking into account elements such as the substantive contract, the commercial circumstances of the case and the submissions of the parties.

Although arbitral tribunals are afforded broad discretion to award interest, this discretion must be exercised judicially and fairly. Further, the tribunal must particularly keep in mind any express duty it has to render a valid and enforceable award. For example, under Rule 41.2 of the Singapore International Arbitration Centre SIAC Rules 2016, '*the Tribunal shall act in the spirit of these Rules and shall make every reasonable effort to ensure [...] the enforceability of any Award*'. In this regard, it has been commented that '*the tribunal should be cognisant of any potential issues arising out of the mandatory substantive laws which may be determined to be applicable and should consider any public policy implications which may affect the enforceability of the award when determining the applicable substantive law*'.[9]

III DO THE COURTS TAKE INTO ACCOUNT INTERNATIONAL STANDARDS WHEN FACING CHALLENGES ON THE POST-AWARD INTEREST?

There are no reported cases where the Singapore courts have considered international standards when faced with a challenge on an award for post-award interest.

However, the Singapore courts have recognised that the provisions of the IAA must be applied in consonant with the underlying philosophy of the Model Law, which is to de-emphasise the importance of the seat of arbitration and facilitate the uniform treatment of international arbitration awards.[10] It can therefore be expected that the Singapore courts will not adopt a parochial approach in considering matters relating to the IAA, and will take into account international standards and practices when such considerations are relevant.

IV SUBSTANTIVE LAW ISSUES

5. How Are Contractual Provisions on Late or Non-payment of Interest Relevant to Post-award Interest? Will These Be Considered By the Arbitral Tribunal?

Yes, contractual provisions on late or non-payment of interest will generally be considered to give effect to the parties' contractual agreement.

6. How Do the Procedural Rules of the Substantive Law Apply?

A Discussion of *voie directe* and *voie indirecte*' in Chan Leng Sun SC & Michael Hwang SC (eds), Conflict of Laws in Arbitration (Singapore Academy of Law Journal, 2014), at pp. [911]-[941].

9. Doug Jones, 'Choosing the Law or Rules of Law to Govern the Substantive Rights of the Parties: A Discussion of *voie directe* and *voie indirecte*' in Chan Leng Sun SC & Michael Hwang SC (eds), Conflict of Laws in Arbitration (Singapore Academy of Law Journal, 2014), at para. [13].
10. *PT First Media TBK (formerly known as PT Broadband Multimedia TBK) v. Astro Nusantara International BV and others and another appeal* [2014] 1 SLR 372, at paras [53]-[55], [57]-[62] and [64].

If the parties choose Singapore to be the seat, the procedural rules of the substantive law (if other than Singapore law) would not normally be applicable.

So, for example, the choice of law rules (being procedural rules) of the substantive applicable law would not normally be applicable, consistent with Article 28(1) of the Model Law which provides that '*any designation of the law or legal system of a given State shall be construed, unless otherwise expressed, as directly referring to the substantive law of that State and not to its conflict of laws rules*'.

7. Whether the Award of Interest Can Be Subjected to Public Policy Objections and if So, What Are They?

It is not against Singapore's public policy to award interest. However, an award of interest under Singapore substantive law should be compensatory or restitutionary in nature, not penal. It is arguable that an award enforcing a penalty clause or providing for interest that is penal in nature may be viewed as being contrary to the public policy of Singapore. Such awards may risk being set aside (pursuant to Article 34(2)(b) of the Model Law) or refused enforcement (pursuant to section 31(4)(b) of the IAA and Article 36(1)(b)(ii) of the Model Law) for being contrary to Singapore's public policy.[11]

Under Singapore substantive law, a penalty clause is defined as a deterrent clause which is not a genuine pre-estimate of loss. To determine if a clause constitutes a genuine pre-estimate of loss, the Singapore courts have applied the following test as formulated in the English case of *Dunlop Pneumatic Tyre Company Limited v. New Garage and Motor Company Limited.*[12]

(a) A clause will be held as a penalty if the stipulated sum is extravagant and unconscionable in comparison with the greatest loss that could conceivably be proved to have followed from the breach.
(b) A clause will be held as a penalty if the breach consists only in not paying a sum of money, and the sum stipulated is a sum greater than the sum which ought to have been paid.
(c) The presumption is that a clause is a penalty if it is payable in a number of events of varying gravity.
(d) A clause would not be treated as penal by reason only of the impossibility of precisely pre-estimating the true loss.

11. *See* further discussion at Section VII below.
12. *Dunlop Pneumatic Tyre Company Limited v. New Garage and Motor Company Limited* [1915] 1 AC 79; followed in *Denka Advantech Private Limited & another v. Seraya Energy Pte Ltd & another* [2020] SGCA 119, and where the Court of Appeal declined to adopt the wider approach developed by the United Kingdom (UK) Supreme Court in *Cavendish Square Holding BV v. Makdessi* [2016] AC 1172.

V PROCEDURAL LAW ISSUES

8. What Are the Main Procedural Law Issues When Considering Post-award Interest? How Are the Arbitration Laws and Other Laws or Regulations of the Seat Relevant?

Errors in Computation of Interest and Omissions of Interest Claims

If an arbitral tribunal makes an error in computation of the interest, or any clerical or typographical error or any error of similar nature in the award, the aggrieved party may, with notice to the other party, request the arbitral tribunal within 30 days of receipt of the award to correct the error (unless another period of time has been agreed upon by the parties).[13] If the arbitral tribunal considers the request to be justified, it shall make the correction within 30 days of receipt of the request.[14] Even if no such request is made, the arbitral tribunal may correct the error on its own initiative within 30 days of the date of the award.[15]

If the arbitral tribunal omits to address a claim of interest made in the proceedings in its award, a party may, with notice to the other party, request the arbitral tribunal to make an additional award within 30 days of the date of the award (unless another period of time has been agreed upon by the parties).[16] If the arbitral tribunal considers the request to be justified, it shall make the additional award within 60 days.[17]

Limitation Periods for Enforcing an Award Including Interest

The limitation period for an action to enforce an award is six years from the date on which the award was rendered.[18]

Irreversibility of Awards on Interest/Enforceability of Contractual Clause on Interest

Once the arbitral tribunal has delivered its decision on interest and/or the enforceability of a contractual clause on interest, the award on those issues is final and binding and cannot be reopened.[19] This is unless a party is seeking a variation, amendment, correction, review, addition or revocation of the award pursuant to Articles 33 and 34(4) of the Model Law.[20]

---

13. Article 33(1)(a) Model Law.
14. Article 33(1) Model Law.
15. Article 33(2) Model Law.
16. Article 33(3) Model Law.
17. Article 33(3) Model Law.
18. Section 6(c) Limitation Act 1959 (2020 Revised Edition).
19. Section 19B IAA. In *PT Perusahaan Gas Negara (Persero) TBK v. CRW Joint Operation* [2015] SGCA 30, the Singapore Court of Appeal stated that section 19B IAA was '*intended to restore or restate the established law that once a tribunal has issued an award (be it an interim, interlocutory, partial or final award), the tribunal is functus officio in relation to the specific issue(s) dealt with by the award* – i.e., *the tribunal cannot revisit its decision and change it even if it turns out to be wrong*'.
20. Section 19B(2) IAA.

VI EFFECT OF ENFORCEMENT ORDERS ON INTEREST ON THE AWARD ON BOTH THE SEAT AND ELSEWHERE

This question appears to be in reference to the effect of enforcement of an award (domestic and foreign) for interest by the Singapore courts.

In relation to a domestic arbitral award for interest, section 19 of the IAA provides that such awards may, '*by leave of the General Division of the High Court, be enforced in the same manner as a judgment or an order to the same effect and, where leave is so given, judgment may be entered in terms of the award*'. O 48 r 6 of the Rules of Court 2021 sets out the procedure for making an application to enforce an award. Once judgment is entered in terms of the award, the judgment can then be enforced like any other judgment of court.

In relation to a foreign arbitral award for interest, section 29(1) of the IAA provides that such awards may be enforced in the same way as a domestic arbitral award (as set out in the preceding paragraph).

Once leave is granted for the enforcement of an award (whether domestic or foreign), the award creditor can then take steps to enforce the award in Singapore by (for example) commencing garnishee proceedings or obtaining a writ of seizure and sale in respect of the award debtor's assets in Singapore.

VII POWERS OF THE COURT TO ORDER OR ADJUST POST-AWARD INTEREST

9. Do the Singapore Courts Have the Power to Order or Adjust Post-award Interest, Assuming It Is Either the Seat Court or the Enforcing Court?

Treatment of Post-award Interest Granted By the Tribunal

An award for post-award interest may be enforced like any other arbitral award.[21] And like any arbitral award that is sought to be enforced, a party may resist its enforcement based on one of the recognised grounds.[22] An award for post-award interest may also be challenged under one of the prescribed grounds for setting aside an award pursuant to section 24 of the IAA and Article 34(2) of the Model Law.

If a party makes an application to the Singapore courts to enforce an award (whether domestic or foreign), the Singapore courts will ordinarily enforce the award, together with any post-award interest that may have been awarded. As the Law Reform Committee of the Singapore Academy of Law observed in its 2005 Report on Pre- and Post-Judgment Interest:

21. *See* discussion on enforcement at Section VI above.
22. Grounds for resisting the enforcement of a foreign arbitral award are set out in section 31 of the IAA. For a domestic arbitral award, reference should be made to the grounds set out in Article 36 of the Model Law, which although not expressly incorporated into Singapore law (*see* section 3(1) of the IAA), are nevertheless available to a party resisting enforcement under section 19 of the IAA: *see PT First Media TBK (formerly known as PT Broadband Multimedia TBK) v. Astro Nusantara International BV and others and another appeal* [2014] 1 SLR 372, at para. [84].

> [...] there is a stronger case to give effect to the arbitrator's decision on the post-award interest, because the award is the result of the agreement of the parties, and because the judicial system plays only a supervisory role in arbitration and a supportive role in lending its enforcement machinery to arbitration awards. Thus, the interest rate awarded by the arbitral tribunal should be followed at the enforcement stage, unless the award itself is challenged. Unlike the case of judgments, it does not make sense to distinguish between local and foreign arbitral awards where post-award interest is concerned.[23]

There is no provision under Singapore law that allows the Singapore courts to vary the rate of interest imposed by the arbitral tribunal. An aggrieved party will therefore have to apply for setting aside of the award of interest or resist enforcement of the award of interest under one of the prescribed grounds as provided under the IAA and the Model Law.

In *BRQ v. BRS*,[24] the respondent sought to set aside an award for pre-award interest on the basis that the tribunal had acted in breach of natural justice by ordering the interest to run from an earlier date though neither of the parties had pleaded it. The Singapore High Court dismissed the application and held that '*[under Section 20(1) of the IAA] the award of interest is a matter entirely at the tribunal's discretion. [...] The tribunal was entitled to grant pre-award interest in its discretion commencing from a date that it considered appropriate. Its omission to give reasons for choosing the date does not render this part of its award vulnerable to being set aside*'.[25] This case demonstrates that the Singapore courts will generally be slow to intervene in the decision of an arbitral tribunal, consistent with the policy of minimal curial intervention and the need to promote the finality of the arbitral process.

Post-award Interest Granted By the Singapore Courts

Post-award interest may be ordered by the Singapore courts when an award is enforced by entering judgment in terms of the award. In such circumstances, the award creditor may seek from the court an order for interest from the date of the judgment.[26] The judgment debt will carry simple interest at the statutory rate of 5.33% per annum.[27]

Treatment of an Arbitral Tribunal's Decision to Uphold a Contractual Provision on Interest

Like any arbitral award, an arbitral tribunal's decision to uphold a contractual provision on interest may be challenged under one of the prescribed grounds for setting aside an award pursuant to section 24 of the IAA and Article 34(2) of the Model Law.

---

23. Law Reform Committee, Singapore Academy of Law, *Report of the Law Reform Committee on Pre- and Post- Judgment Interest* (August 2005), at para. [200].
24. *BRQ and another v. BRS and another and another matter* [2019] SGHC 260. For other examples, *see also*: *Ahong Construction (S) Pte Ltd v. United Boulevard Pte Ltd* [1994] 3 SLR(R) 669; *AUF v. AUG and other matters* [2016] 1 SLR 859.
25. *BRQ and another v. BRS and another and another matter* [2019] SGHC 260, at para. [163]. Although this case concerns the award of pre-award interest, the principles are equally applicable to situations concerning the award of post-award interest.
26. Timothy Cooke, *International Arbitration in Singapore: Legislation and Materials* (Sweet & Maxwell 2018), at para. [1.158].
27. O 17 r 5 of the Rules of Court 2021.

A party may also choose to resist the enforcement of an arbitral tribunal's decision pursuant to section 31 of the IAA and Article 36 of the Model Law.

As indicated above,[28] it is arguable that an award upholding a penalty clause (or an award of interest that is penal in nature) may be viewed as being contrary to Singapore's public policy and may be liable to be set aside (pursuant to Article 34(2)(b) of the Model Law) or refused enforcement (pursuant to section 31(4)(b) of the IAA and Article 36(1)(b)(ii) of the Model Law).

However, it should be noted that the standard required to succeed on the ground of public policy is extremely high. In *PT Asuransi Jasa Indonesia (Persero) v. Dexia Bank SA*,[29] the Singapore Court of Appeal held that an award only conflicts with Singapore's public policy if upholding the award would '*shock the conscience,*' is '*clearly injurious to the public good or wholly offensive to the ordinary reasonable and fully informed member of the public*' or where it '*violates the forum's most basic notion of morality and justice*'. Instances of corruption, bribery or fraud and similar serious cases would suffice.[30] Errors of law or fact do not.[31]

While there is yet no Singapore case law that addresses this question, the position under English law (which has a similar rule against penalties) may provide some indication as to how the Singapore courts might address this question when so confronted.

In *Pencil Hill Limited v. US Citta Di Palermo S.p.A.*,[32] the English High Court has held that an award of interest may be enforced notwithstanding that the interest was awarded pursuant to a penalty clause. In that case, the respondent sought to resist enforcement of a Swiss-seated arbitral award made by the Court of Arbitration for Sport (CAS) on the ground that the award included interest based on a penalty clause, contrary to English public policy prohibiting the enforcement of penalty clauses. While the court acknowledged that the rule against penalties was an '*important public policy,*' the court found that it was not a rule that protected a '*universal principle of morality*' and was not so clearly '*injurious to the public good*' that enforcement should, without more, be refused. The court ultimately held that '*the public policy of upholding international arbitral awards [...] outweighs the public policy of refusing to enforce penalty clauses*'. Significant weight was also placed on the fact that the governing law (i.e., Swiss law) chosen by the parties empowered the Swiss courts to interfere with a penalty by reducing it. This power to reduce the penalty was in fact exercised, and as a result, the interest awarded was no longer considered excessive or objectionable under the governing law. The court reasoned that, in the eyes of Swiss law, the variation of the payment obligation changed the nature of the obligation. What had been a penalty payment was changed into a non-penalty payment. The position was, therefore, not that Swiss law upheld a penalty, rather it was that Swiss law removed a penalty and replaced it with an obligation to pay a sum it regarded as neither exorbitant

28. *See* discussion at section IV above.
29. *PT Asuransi Jasa Indonesia (Persero) v. Dexia Bank SA* [2006] SGCA 41.
30. Howard Holtzmann and Joseph Neuhaus, *A Guide to the UNCITRAL Model Law on International Commercial Arbitration* (Kluwer Law 1989) at p. [913].
31. *PT Asuransi Jasa Indonesia (Persero) v. Dexia Bank SA* [2006] SGCA 41.
32. *Pencil Hill Limited v. US Citta Di Palermo S.p.A.* [2016] EWHC 71 QB.

nor unconscionable. Accordingly, the court allowed the award to be enforced in its entirety.

This decision suggests that a breach of the rule against penalties may not be sufficient, in and of itself, to refuse enforcement on public policy grounds. This is consistent with the high bar that has been set by the Singapore courts for setting aside or refusing enforcement of arbitral awards in general.

State of Qatar

Thomas Williams, Ahmed Durrani & Umang Singh[*]

INTRODUCTION

Qatar is a civil law jurisdiction. The primary legislation which deals with private civil law is Law No. 22 of 2004 (*the Qatar Civil Code*). In addition, Qatar hosts an offshore business and financial centre, with a separate regulatory, commercial and legal framework, called the Qatar Financial Centre (*the QFC*). In comparison to Qatar's civil law tradition, QFC's legal system is based on common law. The QFC was established by Law No. 7 of 2005 (*the QFC Law*).

The Mainland Arbitration Law is Law No. 2 of 2017 (*the Mainland Arbitration Law*) and the QFC's arbitration regime is set out in the QFC Arbitration Regulations 2005 (*the QFC Arbitration Law*). The Mainland Arbitration Law is the applicable curial law to Doha-seated arbitrations, and the QFC Arbitration Law applies to QFC-seated arbitrations.[1]

The position on post-award interest differs under each of these regimes.

Mainland Qatari law

Qatar is an Islamic country. It is an accepted principle that interest is prohibited under the Islamic Sharia law, which forms the basis of Qatari law, further to Article 1(2) of the Qatar Civil Code[2] and Article 1 of the Constitution of the State of Qatar.[3]

However, in recent years, Qatari Courts have upheld awards in Doha-seated arbitrations (governed by mainland Qatari law) in which post-award interest was awarded to the winning party. In other words, Qatari Courts found that post-award

* The authors are grateful to Shehzadul Haq and Shanu Jain for their research and valuable input.

1. *See* Article 2 of Arbitration Law and Article 6(1) of the Arbitration Regulations.
2. Article 1(2) of the Qatar Civil Code provides: '*Where there is no statutory provision, the Judge shall rule according to the relevant provision of the Islamic Sharia, if any, otherwise the Judge shall rule according to the customary practice or in accordance with the rules of justice*'.
3. Article 1 Constitution of Qatar: '*Qatar is an independent sovereign Arab State. Its religion is Islam and the Sharia Law shall be a principal source of its obligations …*'

interest in arbitral awards is not contrary to public policy. The basis of such findings has in large measure been similar: Qatari Courts have treated post-award interest as compensation for delayed payments.

By way of example, in Appeal No. 31/CCA/2019, the Qatari Court of Appeal (the Competent Court under the Mainland Arbitration Law) upheld an award in which the arbitral tribunal had granted post-award interest. That case concerned a dispute between a United Arab Emirates (UAE) construction company, in its capacity as the main contractor ('*the UAE Company*') on a tower project, and its Qatari subcontractor ('*the Qatari Company*'). The governing law of the underlying subcontract was Qatari law. The arbitral tribunal rendered the final award in favour of the Qatari Company and granted post-award interest at the rate of 5% if the awarded amount was not paid within 30 days by the UAE Company. The award was subsequently challenged by the UAE Company pursuant to Article 33 of the Mainland Arbitration Law. One of the grounds for the challenge was that the Tribunal's decision to grant 5% post-award interest was contrary to public policy. However, the Qatari Court of Appeal rejected that ground and ruled as follows:

> In the sixth ground, the Appellant alleges that the award violated the public order of the state of Qatar when it ruled the interest of 5% for the delay of paying the ruled amount. Compelling the Plaintiff to pay interests only serves as compensation for delaying the implementation of its obligations. The law of the Qatari Central Bank allowed banks to receive interests on the debts due from the debtor. This shows that the Qatari legislator did not consider receiving interests for the delay of paying payments as violation of the construction or Islamic Sharia. Therefore, the court is of the opinion that ruling the interests does not form a violation of the public order. Therefore, the denouncement is not grounded and the whole appeal is not factually or lawfully grounded because of absence of one of the cases stipulated in Article 33 of the Law No. 2 / 2017 concerning arbitration in civil and commercial matters related to annulment. Therefore, the court rules to dismiss the lawsuit as outlined in the wording.[4]

As part of its reasoning, the Qatari Court of Appeal drew an analogy with banking transactions, particularly the receipt of interest on delayed payments. Such banking transactions are permitted under Qatari law, including the payment of interest on credit facilities granted by licensed financial institutions in Qatar.[5] As indicated by the Qatari Court of Appeal, the legalisation of such banking transactions shows that, as a matter of principle, the Qatari legislature does not consider interest in delayed payments to be a violation of Islamic Sharia law. The same principle was then applied to the interest for delaying the payments which became due further to an arbitral award. The Qatari Court of Appeal's finding in Appeal No. 31/CCA/2019 is indeed consistent with its previous findings.[6]

4. Qatar Court of Appeal: Appeal No. 31/CCA/2019.
5. Article 70 of Qatar Law No. 13/2012 Promulgating the law of Qatar Central Bank and the Regulation of Financial Institutions; *see also* Part 2 of the Qatar Central Bank's '*Instruction to Banks – September 2013.*'
6. Noelle Tannous, *The Qatari Courts' Approach to Awarding Interest*, Al Tamimi & Co., https://www.tamimi.com/law-update-articles/the-qatari-courts-approach-to-awarding-interest/; *see also*

The analogy used by the Qatari Court of Appeal can be construed in two ways. First, it is arguable that interest can be granted either if it is expressly agreed in the underlying contract or by way of compensation pursuant to an arbitral tribunal's general discretion to grant compensation for delayed payments under Article 268 of the Qatar Civil Code. Alternatively, it could be argued that interest can only be granted as compensation for delayed payment if there is an underlying agreement to that effect. The second interpretation should be preferred: it is a more cautious approach which would not jeopardise the integrity of any award. Arbitral tribunals also tend to prefer a circumspect approach. For example, an International Chamber of Commerce (ICC) arbitral tribunal in a Doha-seated arbitration, governed by Qatari law, rejected interest claims due to the absence of any agreement between the parties. That tribunal did not explore whether or not it had a standalone power to grant interest by way of compensation under Article 268.

The QFC Law

Under the QFC Law, the award of interest is expressly permitted. Article 104 of the QFC Contract Regulations[7] provides that, '*if a party does not pay a sum of money, the aggrieved party is entitled to interest upon such sum from the time when payment is due to the time of payment*'. Although Article 104 does not expressly refer to post-award interest, it is broad enough to encompass the same.

Under the QFC Arbitration Law, an arbitral tribunal is expressly allowed to grant interest. Article 38 of the Arbitration Regulations provides that:

> Article 38 – Costs of Proceedings and Interest
>
> Unless the parties to an Arbitration Agreement have (whether in the agreement or in any other document in writing) otherwise agreed, an Arbitral Panel may in making an Award:
>
> (1) direct to whom, by whom, and in what manner, the whole or any part of the costs that it awards shall be paid;
> (2) fix the amount of costs to be paid or any part of those costs; and
> (3) award interest on any sums it directs to be paid. (Emphasis added)

Currently, there are no precedents on the application of Article 38(3) which could explain whether its scope encompasses post-award interest; however, on its proper construction, Article 38(3) indicates that an arbitral tribunal can grant post-award interest.

Notably, Article 38 permits parties to limit the arbitral tribunal's power to award interest. This can be done by way of the arbitration agreement or through any other binding instrument.

Sarah ElJaili, Awarding Interest in Arbitral Awards, Sultan Al-Abdulla & Partners (March 16, 2020), https://qatarlaw.com/awarding-interest-in-arbitral-awards.html.

7. Article 104, QFC Contract Regulations, September 2005.

I POWER TO GRANT POST-AWARD INTEREST

1. Does an Arbitral Tribunal Have the Power to Grant Post-award Interest under Qatari Law?

There is no specific provision under the Mainland Arbitration Law that empowers an arbitral tribunal to grant post-award interest. On the one hand, as discussed in the introductory part of this article, recent judgments of the Qatari Court of Appeal indicate that post-award interest may be granted by way of compensation for delayed payment of the awarded amount if there is an underlying agreement between the parties to that effect.

On the other hand, in the context of QFC-seated arbitrations, Article 38 of the QFC Arbitration Law expressly grants power to the arbitral tribunal to grant interest, which should include post-award interest.

2. Is the Power Exercisable Without a Request or Submission, or Is Such a Submission Required?

Under mainland Qatari law, a party cannot seek relief (such as interest) unless that party expressly requests for the same in the proceedings.[8] As such, where a party seeks to claim interest as compensation for delay in payments, it should make appropriate submissions to the arbitral tribunal. This is corroborated by Article 23(1) of the Mainland Arbitration Law, which requires statements of case to set out a party's '*requests*' for relief.

In the QFC, the answer is unclear. This is because Article 38 of the QFC Arbitration Law does not mandate any request or submission. However, Article 29(1) of the QFC Arbitration Law states that statements of case must set out the relief or remedy sought by a party, unless agreed otherwise. Therefore, if a party wishes to seek interest, it ought to ask for that relief in its statement of case, unless there is an agreement to the contrary.

However, it is open to an argument that no express request is required. Pursuant to the Practice Direction No. 3/2021 on post-judgment interest ('*the Practice Direction*'),[9] if the QFC court does not make an order for interest, a default compensatory rate of interest of 5% is applied to judgments. In other words, the Practice Direction does not foreshadow any requirement for a request or submission for post-judgment interest. Therefore, it is possible that, in a QFC-seated arbitration, even if a party has not expressly sought post-award interest, an arbitral tribunal could follow the practice of the QFC court, as per the Practice Direction, to grant post-award interest.

However, in the authors' view, such an approach would be incorrect. This is because the curial law of a QFC-seated arbitration is the QFC Arbitration Law, and the procedures of the QFC court should bear no relevance to how the arbitration is conducted. Overall, arbitral tribunals in QFC-seated arbitrations should exercise

8. Qatar Court of Cassation: Judgment no. 133/2015.
9. *Practice Direction No. 3/2021: Award of Post Judgment Interest by the Court*, Qatar International Court and Dispute Resolution Centre (August 16, 2021), https://www.qicdrc.gov.qa/courts/court/regulations-and-procedural-rules.

caution: arbitral tribunals are a creature of the parties' contract, and their purpose is to decide those matters or disputes which are expressly referred to them. Granting post-award interest in circumstances where no corresponding relief is sought might render any award susceptible to challenge.

3. Is the Power Classified As One under the Substantive Applicable Law or the Procedural Law of the Arbitration?

In mainland Qatari law, the power to grant interest is a substantive issue. This is because interest can only be granted if it is agreed in the underlying contract and as compensation for delayed payments of amounts awarded in the final award. The Mainland Arbitration Law or the Qatar Civil Code does not otherwise confer a standalone power to an arbitral tribunal to grant post-award interest.

Under the QFC Law, the position is unclear. First, under Article 104 of the QFC Contract Regulations, the right to claim interest is a substantive right. Therefore, the award of interest by an arbitral tribunal should be treated as a substantive issue.

However, the power to grant interest is derived from Article 38 of the QFC Arbitration Law. Additionally, because Article 38 deals with costs of arbitration and interest together, post-award interest is arguably treated as a procedural matter.

II CHOICE OF LAW

4. What is the Law That Applies to Determine What the Post-award Interest Should Be? Would This Be the Governing Law of the Dispute or the Law of the Seat?

From a Qatari perspective, the answer would depend on whether the arbitration is governed by mainland Qatari law or QFC Law.

In an arbitration governed by mainland Qatari law and seated in Doha, the substantive law would govern the issue of post-award interest. This is because interest is prohibited under Qatari law, unless expressly permitted under the contract and granted as compensation for delayed payments. Therefore, in a Qatari-law-governed contract, in the absence of the parties' agreement on right to claim interest, an arbitral tribunal cannot award interest, including post-award interest even if the law of the seat empowers the tribunal to grant interest. The upshot of the above is that, by way of example, in a QFC-seated arbitration where the governing law is mainland Qatari law, an arbitral tribunal should tread cautiously when considering the question of post-award interest.

In an arbitration governed by the QFC Law, the position would be different:[10] arbitral tribunals will have the authority to award interest, irrespective of the fact that the arbitration is seated in Doha or the QFC.

10. Article 104, QFC Contract Regulations, September 2005.

III DO THE COURTS TAKE INTO ACCOUNT INTERNATIONAL STANDARDS WHEN FACING CHALLENGES ON THE POST-AWARD INTEREST?

There is no provision under Qatari law which requires the Qatari courts to consider international standards in any legal disputes. Judgments of the Qatari courts and courts of other Middle Eastern jurisdictions, i.e., Egypt, can have persuasive value but are not binding.

Likewise, there are no QFC court precedents which show the QFC court's inclination (or aversion) to looking at international standards on post-award interest. However, as a matter of general principle, in *Chedid & Associates Qatar LLC v. Said Bou Ayash*,[11] the court held as follows:

> [O]n behalf of the Defendant it was submitted that in order to resolve the issue of… the Court should be guided by English case law. This is not the correct approach. QFC Regulations set out detailed codes of employment law and general law. Some of the provisions reflect principles of common law, but in many respects conditions in Qatar differ markedly from conditions in England and other common law countries. Where an issue is governed by a QFC Regulation, the correct approach is to apply that Regulation according to its natural meaning and having particular regard to conditions in Qatar. Foreign jurisprudence can sometimes be of assistance, but it should be used sparingly as a last and not as a first resort.

Therefore, it is likely that the QFC court might not consider international standards when looking at post-award interest, if it is of the view that the QFC Law adequately addresses the issue. This approach is corroborated by the court's reliance on the Practice Direction in respect of post-judgment interest findings,[12] wherein the court did not consult any international standards.

IV SUBSTANTIVE LAW ISSUES

5. How Are Contractual Provisions on Late or Non-payment of Interest Relevant to Post-award Interest? Will These Be Considered By the Arbitral Tribunal?

As discussed above, an arbitral tribunal can only grant post-award interest if the contract prescribes interest for delayed payments where agreements are governed by Qatari law.

In the QFC, contractual provisions are also relevant because they would determine the scope of the arbitral tribunal's powers under Article 38 of the QFC Arbitration Law. Article 38 sets out the default rule that arbitral tribunals can grant post-award interest, subject to the parties' agreement. Any prohibition on interest in the underlying contract would mean that the tribunal cannot grant any interest.

6. How Do the Procedural Rules of the Substantive Law Apply?

11. [2015] QIC (A) 2.
12. Appellate Division of the Qatar International Court: *Qatar Financial Centre Regulatory Authority v. Horizon Crescent Wealth LLC and the Practice Direction* [2021] QIC (A) 5.

Doha-seated arbitrations were governed by the provisions of the then Articles 190 to 210 of Qatar's Civil and Commercial Procedures Law (*'the Procedural Law'*) prior to the enactment of the Mainland Arbitration Law. However, Article 4 of the Arbitration Law has expressly repealed those provisions. Therefore, the procedural rules of the local courts would not apply in a Qatari-law-governed arbitration.

Similarly, the QFC Arbitration Law governs the arbitral process in the QFC. Therefore, any procedural rules applicable to the QFC court are not directly applicable. However, as discussed previously, some arbitral tribunals might be open to taking guidance from the Practice Direction on post-award interest.

7. Whether the Award of Interest Can Be Subjected to Public Policy Objections and if So, What Are They?

In mainland Qatar, as a matter of principle, an award of interest can be subjected to public policy objections, pursuant to Articles 33(3) and 35(2)(b) of the Mainland Arbitration Law. Article 33(3) concerns the annulment of an arbitral award for public policy reasons, whereas Article 35(2)(b) relates to the refusal to recognise or enforce an arbitral award on public policy grounds.

Interest is generally prohibited under Qatari law. Therefore, any arbitral award which grants interest, save for contracts which permit interest as compensation for delayed payments, is likely to be challenged on public policy grounds in accordance with Article 33(3) or 35(2)(b). On the one hand, there are no reported judgments which record a successful challenge of an arbitral award on these grounds.

On the other hand, any award which grants interest should not be subjected to a challenge on public policy grounds in the QFC. This is because the QFC Laws permit interest,[13] and the QFC court grants post-judgment interest itself.

V PROCEDURAL LAW ISSUES

8. What Are the Main Procedural Law Issues When Considering Post-award Interest? How Are the Arbitration Laws and Other Laws or Regulations of the Seat Relevant?

There is no guidance in the Mainland Arbitration Law regarding post-award interest because interest is generally prohibited. However, as discussed above, an arbitral tribunal should consider the following criteria when addressing post-award interest based on some judicial precedents: (i) is there agreement between the parties for post-award interest as a means for compensating delayed payments, and (ii) has the party seeking post-award interest made an appropriate request or submissions.

After the tribunal satisfies itself as to the above criteria and it is minded to give interest on awarded amounts, it should specify a time period for compliance with the award, failing which the award debtor would be liable to compensate the award creditor by way of post-award interest.

The QFC regime also does not prescribe any particular procedural rules for post-award interest. As discussed previously, Article 38 of the QFC Arbitration Law

13. Article 104, QFC Contract Regulations, September 2005.

grants the tribunal a broad power in awarding post-award interest. Although it is not binding, arbitral tribunals could take guidance from the Practice Direction as to the procedure to follow when considering post-award interest. Among others, the Practice Direction provides that the QFC court should specify the date from which in case party fails to comply with the judgment, an enhanced rate of interest should apply. It also sets out a non-exhaustive list of relevant considerations for the imposition of such an enhanced rate.

VI EFFECT OF ENFORCEMENT ORDERS ON INTEREST ON THE AWARD ON BOTH THE SEAT AND ELSEWHERE

Legal Effect of 'Enforcement' Orders By Qatari Courts

Under Article 34(1) of the Mainland Arbitration Law, arbitral awards have the status of res judicata, and are enforceable. For a Doha-seated award, after the time for filing an annulment application has lapsed or the annulment challenge has been unsuccessful, a party can file an application to a competent judge to enforce the award. This would include the interest component in the award.

For arbitrations seated elsewhere, recognition and enforcement proceedings are governed by Article 35 of the Mainland Arbitration Law. In particular, under Article 35(2), a competent judge may on their own volition refuse recognition or enforcement if they consider the arbitral award to be contrary to public policy. Therefore, if a foreign-seated award grants post-award interest without satisfying the criteria under Qatari law identified above, it is possible that its enforcement might be refused in Qatar.

The QFC Arbitration Law contains a similar enforcement regime under Articles 42 and 43. In other words, awards issued in QFC-seated arbitrations are binding and enforceable. As far as non-QFC awards are concerned, the QFC court has the power to refuse recognition or enforcement if it considers the award to be contrary to the QFC's public policy. Given that the QFC is a separate offshore jurisdiction, it is arguable that the public policy of the QFC, as a matter of principle, should be narrower than the public policy of Qatar. In the context of post-award interest, public policy considerations would not be relevant for enforcement because granting interest is expressly permitted in the QFC.

What if Post-award Interest Is Not Explicitly Stated in the Award?

Given the similarity in the regimes, it is very unlikely for an enforcement court to grant post-award interest when the same is not granted in the award. There is no precedent, particularly in the QFC court, which demonstrates otherwise.

VII POWERS OF THE COURT TO ORDER OR ADJUST POST-AWARD INTEREST

9. Does a Qatari Court Have the Power to Order or Adjust the Post-award Interest Awarded By the Tribunal, Assuming It Is the Seat Court or the Enforcing Court?

There is no power conferred under the Mainland Arbitration Law to an arbitral tribunal to adjust post-award interest. This is consistent with the res judicata status afforded to arbitral awards under the Mainland Arbitration Law. Similarly, such a power does not exist under the QFC regime.

As a matter of principle, the role of recognition and enforcement courts (whether in mainland Qatar or in the QFC) is limited to issues concerning challenges to awards or their enforcement and does not encapsulate any jurisdiction to make corrections or adjustments to awards.[14]

14. Articles 41, 42 and 43 Arbitration Regulations.

Taiwan

Nigel N.T. Li & Joyce N. Chang

INTRODUCTION

Taiwan is of a civil law jurisdiction, and the power to charge interest is vested by the legislators in the courts. In Taiwan, unlike some common law jurisdictions, the amount of interest is predetermined by the legislators, who have not delegated the discretion to courts to directly grant interest to creditors. Issues related to interest are regulated in the Civil Code, and therefore, the courts take the creditor's right to interest as a claim of the creditor, granted by the legislators, that is subordinate to the major claim for the principal.[1]

There are two primary sources for the applicable interest rate. First, when the interest rate has been agreed on by the parties, the courts will enforce the agreement of the parties to the extent permitted by law. Interest rates determined by the parties are recognized as a right of the creditor under the substantive law if they do not exceed the ceiling set forth in law. Profiteering is expressly prohibited for public-policy reasons. Article 205 of the Civil Code states: "*If the agreed rate of interest exceeds sixteen percent (16 per cent) per annum, the part of the agreement stipulating the excess is invalid.*"[2] To

1. Supreme Court Judgment 109-Tai-Shang-Zi No. 2810 [2020]; Supreme Court Judgment 106-Tai-Shang-Zi No. 171 [2017]; Supreme Court Judgment 104-Tai-Shang-Zi No. 1376 [2015]; Supreme Court Judgment 104-Tai-Shang-Zi No. 538 [2015]; Supreme Court Decree 99-Tai-Kang-Zi No. 561 [2010].
2. Before July 20, 2021, Article 205 of the Civil Code read: "*If the agreed rate of interest exceeds twenty per cent (20 per cent) per annum, the creditor shall not be entitled to claim any interest over twenty per cent (20 per cent).*" The legislative intent sets out two major reasons for the recent amendment. First, the interest rate for deposits has been significantly lowered compared to when the Civil Code was first enacted; therefore, the interest cap should be adjusted for alignment with the current economy. Second, the original Article deprived the creditor of the right to claim interest over 20% without invalidating the agreement on the interest rate between the parties. To strengthen the regulatory effect of the cap on interest and protect the underprivileged, the legislators nullified any interest rate agreement over 16% per annum. Parenthetically, by Article 10-1 of the Enforcement Act of the Part of Obligations of the Civil Code, this amendment also applies to agreements predating it under which interest continues to accrue after the amendment

safeguard the underprivileged in the context of contractual relations, this clause imposes a limit on the party that leverages economic dominance to reap unjust benefits. The concept is similar to "*undue influence*" in common law. Also, under Article 207 of the Civil Code, simple interest is the standard and compound interest is the exception.

The second source of the interest rate is the legal rate, when no interest rate has been fixed by the parties. Article 203 states: "*In the case of a debt bearing interest, if no rate has been fixed by the contract or by the act, the rate shall be five percent (5 per cent) per annum.*"

Without explicitly offending the stipulated public policy, the parties are given the freedom to decide the applicable interest rate under the substantive law, while the discretion of the courts is circumscribed.

Section I of this chapter begins by further discussing the extent of an arbitral tribunal's power when granting post-award interest. Section II then provides an in-depth analysis of choosing the applicable law for selecting a post-award interest rate. Section III explores the circumstances Taiwan courts are willing to accept international standards for setting interest rates.

Section IV of this chapter explains substantive law issues associated with the post-award interest, including not allowing creditors to exceed the 16% (previously 20%)cap of interest cited above. Section V then discusses the procedural law issues concerning post-award interest, primarily the consideration of Taiwan courts when dealing with interest rates under foreign laws and judgments.

Section VI discusses the effect of enforcement orders by Taiwan courts and most courts' reluctance to grant interest ex officio. Section VII concludes with a brief discussion concerning Taiwan courts and their absence of authority to adjust post-award interest by an arbitral tribunal.

I POWER TO GRANT POST-AWARD INTEREST

Unlike the laws in other jurisdictions, the Arbitration Act[3] in Taiwan does not specifically regulate the arbitral tribunal's power to impose interest, much less the power to grant post-award interest. This may be due to the general view of interest as a substantive law issue and as a right of the creditor. Only when a party raises a claim for interest should the court take the claim into consideration. This is a striking difference between the laws of Taiwan, which belongs to the family of civil law

comes into force. *Most of the judgments cited below were entered before July 20, 2021, so the twenty per cent cap on interest was applied.*

3. The R.O.C. Arbitration Act, effective as of November 24, 1998. Articles 7, 8, 47, 54 and 56 of the Arbitration Act were amended in 2002, 2009 and 2015. One of the most important amendments is the amendment to Article 47(2). It was amended to expressly provide that foreign arbitral awards recognized by Taiwanese courts have the same legal effect as that of a final judgment. Taiwan has not been able to accede to the New York Convention of 1958. The Arbitration Act contains a number of provisions to incorporate the New York Convention nearly verbatim to ensure foreign arbitral awards will be recognized and enforced by the courts in Taiwan as if Taiwan were a party State.

jurisdictions, and the common law system. In common law jurisdictions, interest is considered a procedural issue, and therefore the court may order interest when it thinks fit.[4]

This difference can also be further understood from the long-standing debate on the juridical nature of arbitration. In *Applicable Law in International Commercial Arbitration: A Study in Commercial Arbitration Awards*, Julian D. M. Lew introduced four theories concerning the nature of arbitration: the Jurisdictional Theory, the Contractual Theory, the Mixed or Hybrid Theory and the Autonomous Theory.[5]

The Jurisdictional Theory recognizes arbitration as a dispute settlement mechanism with authority from the State. Arbitrators are quasi-judges exercising judicial power under the control of the State. After an award is made, it can be appealed to the courts. (In English practice, the awards were subject to appeal until the late twentieth century.)[6] This doctrine remains a clear theoretical cornerstone in some laws in Taiwan. For instance, the Arbitration Act provides that schedules of arbitration fees are subject to regulations enacted and promulgated jointly by the Judicial Yuan and the Executive Yuan,[7] as arbitration is considered synonymous with the judicial power of the State, with the arbitration institution as a Non-Governmental Organization (NGO) subject to the oversight of the agency in charge under the Executive Yuan. Another good example is the Criminal Code which provides that an arbitrator is similar to a judge; if his judgment or award has violated the law deliberately, he is subject to criminal penalties. In short, arbitrators are under a legal duty to adjudicate according to law, like judges.[8]

Supporters of the Contractual Theory emphasize that the origin of arbitration is the agreement of the parties. Arbitrators are not state-appointed bureaucrats, and

4. Philip Yang (楊良宜), Shijie Mo (莫世杰) and Ernest Yang (楊大明), *Arbitration Law: From holding hearings to making and enforcing arbitral awards* (仲裁法：從開庭審理到裁決書的作出與執行) (2010), at pp. [209]-[221].
5. Julian D.M. Lew, *Applicable law in international commercial arbitration: A study in commercial arbitration awards* (1978), at pp. [51]-[66].
6. Para. 1, section 69 of the Arbitration Act 1996 states: "*Unless otherwise agreed by the parties, a party to arbitral proceedings may (upon notice to the other parties and to the tribunal) appeal to the court on a question of law arising out of an award made in the proceedings. An agreement to dispense with reasons for the tribunal's award shall be considered an agreement to exclude the court's jurisdiction under this Section.*" Article 29.2 of the London Court of International Arbitration (LCIA) Arbitration Rules 1998 states: "*To the extent permitted by the law of the seat of the arbitration, the parties shall be taken to have waived any right of appeal or review in respect of any such decisions of the LCIA Court to any state court or other judicial authority.*" As section 69 of the Arbitration Act 1996 is not a mandatory provision, the effect of Article 29.2 of the LCIA Arbitration Rules 1998 is to oust the right of appeal even on a point of law. The current applicable law is the LCIA Arbitration Rules 2020, and the content of Article 29.2 remains the same.
7. Article 54, para. 2 of the Arbitration Act: "*Regulation(s) or guideline(s) of organization, establishment approval, revocation or repeal of approval, arbitrators' registration, cancellation of arbitrators' registration, arbitration fees, mediation procedures and fees of an arbitration institution shall be jointly provided by the Executive Yuan and the Judicial Yuan.*" The Rules on Arbitration Institution, Mediation procedures and Fees were jointly promulgated by Executive Yuan and Judicial Yuan in 1999.
8. Article 124 of the Criminal Code: "*A public official vested with judicial functions or an arbitrator who renders an illegal decision or arbitral award shall be sentenced to imprisonment for not less than one year but not more than seven years.*"

therefore, should not be seen as judges or quasi-judges serving the State. Also, in the absence of the parties' agreement, no one shall be forced to enter an arbitration process. This theory is not the common view in practice in Taiwan, as the Securities and Exchange Act and the Act for Settlement of Labour-Management Disputes both stipulate compulsory arbitration,[9] under the sway of the Jurisdictional Theory.

Proponents of the Mixed or Hybrid Theory try to define the nature of arbitration based on the elements of the above two theories;[10] however, it is not the dominant view in Taiwan either.

The leading theory next to the Jurisdictional Theory, and the most recent, is the Autonomous Theory. The core concept of it is that the parties are the owners of the dispute; therefore, the owners have the right to decide how to dispose of such dispute. This concept is similar to "*the procedural autonomy right*" provided in civil procedures and embedded in the fundamental right to lodge legal actions, which the Constitution explicitly safeguards.[11] That said, the mission of the State is to make courts available to adjudicate, not to force people to file lawsuits. Unlike the Contractual Theory, which only recognizes the effect of arbitration coming from the consent of the parties, the Autonomous Theory goes further to acknowledge the parties' autonomy right to resolve disputes through means of Alternative Dispute Resolution (ADR). Under the Autonomous Theory, awards are enforceable not because of their contractual nature, but because the State must respect the way people choose to resolve their own

9. Article 166 of the Securities and Exchange Act: "*I. Parties to any dispute arising under securities transactions executed pursuant to this Act may, pursuant to their agreement, resolve their disputes by arbitration. Any disputes arising between the stock exchange and securities firms, or between securities firms shall be resolved by arbitration regardless whether there is an agreement to arbitration between the parties. II. Unless otherwise provided under this Act, the arbitration referred to in the proceeding, two paragraphs shall be governed by the Arbitration Act.*" Article 25, para. 4 of the Act for Settlement of Labor-Management Disputes: "*When an interest dispute is not successfully concluded, the municipal or county (city) competent authority regards that the dispute is of great impact on livelihood and interests of the public or receives the request of the competent authority of related business, and may ex officio hand over the dispute to arbitrate and notify both parties.*"
10. Julian DM Lew, *Applicable law in international commercial arbitration: A study in commercial arbitration awards*, at p. [57]: "*He [Professor Sauser-Hall] consequently defined arbitration as 'a mixed juridical institution, sui generis, which has its origin in the [parties'] agreement and draws its jurisdictional effects from the civil law.*"
11. Interpretation 591, Constitutional Court, Judicial Yuan: "*The types of civil disputes have tended to become more and more diverse as the social and economic circumstances have constantly changed. In order to determine the relative duties of disputing parties and thus to resolve disputes, the State has established such mechanisms as arbitration and other non-litigious means in addition to the litigation systems. Under the doctrine of national sovereignty and the constitutional guarantee of the people's fundamental rights, the people should assume principal roles in the procedure so as to enjoy the rights of procedural disposition and procedure option whereby they are enabled to choose through mutual agreement to resolve a dispute by means of litigation or any other statutorily prescribed non-litigious dispute resolution procedure to the extent that public interests are not contravened since they are the subjects of rights under private law. Arbitration is a system under which the parties, according to the law and based on the principle of freedom of contract, choose through mutual agreement to resolve a dispute via non-litigious means. The system has the dual effects of both procedural and substantive laws and possesses the quality of autonomous resolution of disputes arising from private causes, which is acknowledged by the Constitution.*"

disputes, and the State is bound to support arbitration by recognizing the validity of arbitral awards.[12]

As regards interest, from the perspective of the Jurisdictional Theory, arbitration is the exercise of the State's judicial power, and arbitrators exercise similar judicial powers as judges in courts. If judges do not have the power to grant interest without a request, nor do arbitrators. Under the sway of the Jurisdictional Theory embedded in Taiwan's current legal system, courts often see arbitration more as a dispute mechanism arising out of public policy consideration than a product of the "*procedural autonomy right*" of the parties.

1. Does an Arbitral Tribunal Have the Power to Grant Post-award Interest under Taiwanese Law?

Yes. As issues regarding interest are explicitly regulated in Taiwan's Civil Code,[13] an arbitral tribunal that applies the Civil Code as the applicable law over the dispute does have the power to grant post-award interest.

2. Is the Power Exercisable Without a Request or Submission, or Is a Submission Required?

No. If the parties have not agreed and the Arbitration Act is silent on certain procedural issues, the tribunal may choose to adopt the Code of Civil Procedure or any other procedural rules it deems proper.[14]

Article 388 of the Code of Civil Procedure states: "*Except as otherwise provided, the court may not enter any judgment on claims which are not raised by parties.*" In other words, the judges are not to make judgments beyond what has been requested or submitted by the parties. The Supreme Court has elaborated:

> The courts shall not grant interest to parties that have not asked for interest. Only when the creditor claims for interest lawfully shall the court calculate and grant interest to the creditor.[15]

To summarize, according to the Civil Code, the tribunal cannot grant a party post-award interest without a request or submission by the party. An arbitral tribunal granting post-award interest without a request or submission would be considered delivering an award on matters beyond the scope of the submission to arbitration. The award would be vulnerable to challenges to set aside actions.[16]

12. Interpretation 591, Constitutional Court, Judicial Yuan.
13. Articles 203–207 of the Civil Code.
14. Article 19 of the Arbitration Act: "*In the absence of an agreement on the procedural rules governing the arbitration, the arbitral tribunal shall apply this Law. Where this Law is silent, the arbitral tribunal may adopt the Code of Civil Procedure mutatis mutandis or other rules of procedure which it deems proper.*"
15. Supreme Court Jurisprudence 19-Shang-Zi No. 128 [1930], Supreme Court Judgment 109-Tai-Shang-Zi No. 2760 [2020] and Supreme Court Judgment 109-Tai-Shang-Zi No. 2545 [2020] also indicated the same view.
16. Article 40 of the Arbitration Act.

3. Is the Power Classified as One under the Substantive Applicable Law or the Procedural Law of the Arbitration?

Interest rates are a subject well covered in the Civil Code. As stated above, creditors are not entitled to claim interest over 16% per annum. If the parties have not agreed on a certain rate in the contract, the legal rate shall apply, i.e., 5% per annum. Therefore, the power to grant interest is clearly classified as a substantive right in the eyes of the legislators.

II CHOICE OF LAW

4. What Is the Law That Applies to Determining What the Post-award Interest Should Be? Would It Be the Governing Law of the Dispute or the Law of the Seat?

	The Governing Law: Taiwan Law (the Civil Code)	*The Governing Law: Foreign Substantive Law Without Interest Rate Regulations*
The Law of the Seat: *Taiwan Law (the Arbitration Act)*	When deciding the interest rate of a case, the arbitrators shall first look at the governing law of the case. As the Civil Code does stipulate regulations concerning interest rates, the Civil Code shall apply.	The governing law lacks regulations concerning interest rates and so does the law of the seat. There are two ways to solve this problem. First, the arbitrators may see foreign procedural law concerning interest rates as substantive rules in the procedural law and directly adopt them as the governing law of the case. Second, according to Article 19 of the Arbitration Act, the arbitral tribunal may adopt other rules of procedure which it deems proper. This way, they may still adopt the procedural law of the country of the governing law.
The Law of the Seat: *Foreign Procedural Law with Interest Rate Regulations*	The governing law and the law of the seat both contain regulations concerning interest rates. The arbitrators shall apply the governing law of the case, which is the Civil Code of Taiwan.	As the governing law and the law of the seat are from the same jurisdiction, the arbitrator shall apply any rules concerning interest rates; in this case, the law of the seat shall apply.

For an arbitrator seated in Taiwan with a foreign law as the governing law, the foreign substantive laws would determine what the post-award interest should be if such foreign laws also consider the issue a substantive law issue instead of a procedural law issue. It would be a different story if the foreign applicable law takes it as a procedural matter.

For example, if the governing law is Hong Kong law and the seat of arbitration is Taiwan, arbitrators will look into the substantive law of Hong Kong to find authority to grant post-award interest. However, in this case, the arbitrators may not be able to find any regulations in the substantive law because Hong Kong sees the granting of interest as a procedural issue and regulates it in the procedural law. The arbitrators may explore the possibility of taking these rules as substantive rules in the procedural law and directly adopt them as the governing law of the case. Taiwan's Arbitration Act may prove to be helpful here. Since it is the applicable procedural law at the seat of arbitration, the arbitrators may invoke a provision therein, giving the tribunal free rein to adopt related procedural laws of Hong Kong if they deem it proper.[17] Under the Hong Kong Arbitration Ordinance,[18] the arbitrators enjoy the power to determine the amount of interest.

If the governing law is Taiwan law and the seat of arbitration is a foreign jurisdiction, the arbitral tribunal may not decide the amount of interest ex officio and should follow the rules of interest set forth in the Taiwan Civil Code.

Regarding the recognition and enforcement of foreign arbitral awards, if a winning party petitions for post-award interest in the enforcement procedure, the Taiwan court will not entertain the claim because it would be considered a de novo claim to be heard by another arbitrator or a separate action in court.

III DO THE COURTS TAKE INTO ACCOUNT INTERNATIONAL STANDARDS WHEN FACING CHALLENGES ON THE POST-AWARD INTEREST?

Whether international standards are taken into account is an issue often seen in common law jurisdictions. The issue surfaces only when the courts have the power to decide the interest rate. For a civil law system such as the one existing in Taiwan, as the legislators have already set the legal rate at 5% per annum, the courts in Taiwan do not have discretion to set the interest rate.

Nevertheless, if the governing law is a foreign law and the courts in that jurisdiction do have discretion to set the interest rate and do take international standards into account, the courts in Taiwan are ready to accept international standards. There are already many court judgments recognizing and enforcing foreign

17. Article 19 of the Arbitration Act.
18. Section 79 of the Arbitration Ordinance: "*Arbitral tribunal may award interest (1) Unless otherwise agreed by the parties, an arbitral tribunal may, in the arbitral proceedings before it, award simple or compound interest from the dates, at the rates, and with the rests that the tribunal considers appropriate, subject to Section 80, for any period ending not later than the date of payment—(a)on money awarded by the tribunal in the arbitral proceedings; (b)on money claimed in, and outstanding at the commencement of, the arbitral proceedings but paid before the award is made or (c)on costs awarded or ordered by the tribunal in the arbitral proceedings. (2) Subsection (1) does not affect any other power of an arbitral tribunal to award interest. (3) A reference in subsection (1)(a) to money awarded by the tribunal includes an amount payable in consequence of a declaratory award by the tribunal.*"

judgments in Taiwan. If foreign judgments adopt an international standard rate, such as the Singapore Interbank Offered Rate (SIBOR) rate or the London Interbank Offered Rate (LIBOR) rate, the courts in Taiwan will recognize and enforce such judgments.[19] Hence, it is safe to say that when the governing law of an arbitration is a foreign law and the arbitrators adopt international standards to determine the amount of interest in the arbitral award, Taiwan courts would be willing to recognize and enforce such award.

Taiwan's legal rate of 5% per annum is definitely not a low figure compared with the floating SIBOR and LIBOR rate.[20] That said, if a foreign arbitral award adopts the SIBOR or LIBOR rate as the interest rate, the parties to the dispute cannot ask Taiwan courts not to recognize such award on the grounds that such interest rate defies the public policy of Taiwan.

IV SUBSTANTIVE LAW ISSUES

5. How Are Contractual Provisions on Late or Non-payment Interest Relevant to Post-award Interest? Will These Be Considered by the Arbitral Tribunal?

Under the Civil Code,[21] the interest rate agreed on by the parties trumps the fixed 5% per annum. Therefore, contractual provisions concerning late or non-payment interest apply in deciding whether and how interest should be calculated. For contracts sans such provision, where Taiwan law is the governing law, the tribunal is to grant the creditor 5% interest per annum without discretion.

6. How Do the Procedural Rules of the Substantive Law Apply?

Other than what the Civil Code provides regarding the interest rate, there are no other procedural rules designed for granting interest. Hence, there are no applicable procedural rules in the substantive law.

7. Can the Award of Interest Be Subjected to Public Policy Objections and If So, What Are They?

The Arbitration Act in Taiwan incorporates the 1958 New York Convention's provisions almost verbatim.[22] The courts will recognize and enforce a foreign arbitral award like any court in a New York Convention (NYC) Member State jurisdiction. The public-policy test is one of the listed grounds for the court to deny recognition. In

19. A judgment which recognized the SIBOR rate: Chiayi District Court Judgment 98-Zhong-Su-Zi No. 3 [2009].Judgments which recognized the LIBOR rate: Taiwan High Court Judgment 102-Shang-Yi-Zi No. 465 [2013]; Shilin District Court Judgment 100-Su-Zi No. 1327 [2011]; Taipei District Court Judgment 92-Kuo-Mao-Zi No. 3 [2003].
20. The 1-month SIBOR rate was 2.31125% per annum on August 3, 2022. The one-month LIBOR rate was 2.37629% per annum on August 3, 2022.
21. Article 203 of the Civil Code.
22. Article 49 of the Arbitration Act: "*The court shall issue a dismissal with respect to an application submitted by a party for recognition of a foreign arbitral award, if such award contains one of the following elements: 1. Where the recognition or enforcement of the arbitral award is contrary to the public order or good morals of the Republic of China.*"

practice, Taiwan courts seldom cite the test for refusing to recognize and enforce arbitral awards.[23]

Is an Award Granting Interest at More Than 16% (Previously 20%) Per Annum Contrary to the Public Policy of Taiwan?

While no court precedent has dealt with such awards before, the common view of the courts is that foreign laws and judgments which grant interest at more than 20% per annum are not considered *per se* contrary to the public policy of Taiwan.

The Supreme Court stated in two judgments:

> Article 25 of the Act Governing the Choice of Law in Civil Matters Involving Foreign Elements (before amendments) stipulates that if the result of the application of foreign law leads to a violation of the public order or boni mores of Taiwan, that law shall not apply. This is an exception clause, and therefore shall be strictly interpreted. To elaborate, according to Article 205 of the Civil Code, if the parties' agreed rate of interest exceeds 20 per cent per annum, the creditors cannot claim for more than 20 per cent, while the exceeding part is not invalid under the law. Thus, in cases in which the governing laws are foreign laws, if the courts correctly apply foreign laws and grant interest at more than 20 per cent per annum respecting the parties' agreement, such judgments are not contrary to the public policy of Taiwan.[24]

In at least two cases, the court recognized judgments of mainland China that granted interest at 24% per annum. The Taipei District Court explained: "*Different countries and regions have different social climates, cultural histories, and values, and the laws enacted based on their respective social environment are different. Therefore, the judgment of mainland China shall not be deemed contrary to the public policy of Taiwan simply because the laws of mainland China are different from ours. Instead, we shall consider whether the judgment is in line with our society's general interests and moral values.*"[25]

However, one cannot read these decisions and leap to the conclusion that parties agreeing on an interest rate in cross-border transactions need not heed public policy. There are cases where the agreed interest rate is entirely incompatible with the previous legal ceiling of 20% per annum. In these cases, even though the agreed rate was lawful under the governing law of the contract, the court still refused to grant the creditor the part of the interest rate exceeding 20% per annum. Specifically, in a case where the agreed late-payment interest was 70.56% per annum and 81.84% per annum, the High Court recognized that Israeli law, the governing law of the case, did

23. There are many similar judgments, some of which are as follows: Taiwan High Court Decree 109-Fei-Kang-Zi No. 82 [2020]; Taiwan High Court Decree 102-Fei-Kang-Zi No. 41[2013]; Taiwan High Court Taichung Branch Decree 92-Kang-Zi No. 559 [2003]; Taiwan High Court Taichung Branch Decree 92-Kang-Zi No. 260 [2003]; Taiwan High Court Taichung Brach Decree 89-Kang-Zi No. 81 [2000].
24. Supreme Court Judgment 103-Tai-Shang-Zi No. 1957 [2014]; Supreme Court Judgment 101-Tai-Shang-Zi No. 883 [2012].
25. The case numbers of the first case are Taiwan High Court Decree 108-Fei-Kang-Zi No. 76 [2019] and Taipei District Court Judgment 108-Kang-Zi No. 228 [2019]. The case number of the second case is Taipei District Court 108-Lu-Hsu-Zi No. 6 [2019].

not prescribe any cap on the interest rate. Notwithstanding the same, the High Court found that as the agreed interest rate is three or four times higher than the cap on the interest rate in the Civil Code (i.e., 20% per annum), the excess is violative of the public policy of Taiwan.[26]

The recent amendment to Article 205, which came into effect on July 20, 2021, lowered the rate ceiling to 16% per annum and invalidated any *agreement on the part of the interest rate over 16% per annum. The legislators strengthened the regulatory effect to curb financial exploitation and equalize the bargaining positions of the transaction parties. The parties cannot exclude such provisions, and whether the courts will refuse to recognize any award granting interest at more than 16% per annum owing to the amendment remains to be seen.*

In contrast, the default legal rate provision is not mandatory and can be superseded by the agreement of the parties. To elaborate, for an arbitral tribunal seated in Taiwan with the substantive governing law being Taiwanese Law, agreed interest rates grossly exceeding 20% per annum will be subject to scrutiny by courts in Taiwan under the Arbitration Act.[27] However, when the tribunal grants interest at less than 5% per annum on the basis of, say, the current Copenhagen Interbank Offered Rate (CIBOR) rate or LIBOR rate, the courts in Taiwan will recognize and enforce the award without concerns about the public-policy test.

To summarize, based on the previous practice of the court, in cases where the governing law is Taiwan law or the interest rate grossly exceeds 20% per annum, an arbitral award granting interest at over 20% per annum will be neither recognized nor enforced by the courts in Taiwan.

Another provision of the Civil Code forbids manipulation by creditors for interest above the legal ceiling through discounts or otherwise.[28] In two cases where the respective interest rates amounted to 54% per annum and 77.87% per annum under the loan agreements, the Taoyuan District Court declared that such provision was the legislative embodiment of Taiwan's public policy, on the basis of which the court refused to apply Philippine laws to grant the creditors interest in excess of 20% per annum.[29]

26. Taiwan High Court Judgment 98-Shang-Geng-Yi-Zi No. 39 [2009].
27. Article 40 of the Arbitration Act: "*A party may apply to a court to set aside the arbitral award in any of the following circumstances: 1. The existence of any circumstances stated in Article 38.*" Article 38 of the Arbitration Act: "*The court shall reject an application for enforcement in any of the following circumstances where: 1. The arbitral award concerns a dispute not contemplated by the terms of the arbitration agreement, or exceeds the scope of the arbitration agreement, unless the offending portion of the award may be severed and the severance will not affect the remainder of the award; 2. The reasons for the arbitral award were not stated, as required, unless the omission was corrected by the arbitral tribunal; 3. The arbitral award directs a party to act contrary to the law.*"
28. Article 206 of the Civil Code: "*The creditor shall not cunningly obtain interests by discounting or by any other way, except the interest specified in the preceding Article.*"
29. Taoyuan District Court Judgment 107-Tao-Jian-Zi No. 1209 [2018]; Taoyuan District Court Judgment 107-Tao-Jian-Zi No. 787 [2018].

V PROCEDURAL LAW ISSUES

8. What Are the Main Procedural Law Issues When Considering Post-award Interest? How Are the Arbitration Laws and Other Laws or Regulations of the Seat Relevant?

Interest is considered a substantive law issue rather than a procedural law issue under Taiwan law. However, in some jurisdictions interest is regulated in the procedural laws. In cases where parties seek to enforce a foreign arbitral award in Taiwan, the procedural law of the seat may be considered by the courts.

Foreign Judgments and Foreign Laws with Interest Rates Other Than 5% Per Annum

Several courts have made clear their positions on enforcing foreign judgments with an interest rate higher than Taiwan's fixed 5% per annum rate.[30] The Supreme Court takes the view that a judgment made in the United Kingdom is subject to section 17 of the Judgments Act 1838.[31] The Supreme Court held that the debtor shall pay interest at 8% per annum, and the courts in Taiwan have no reason not to enforce such judgment in Taiwan. The Taiwan High Court further elaborated that the fixed 5% interest rate is not an imperative rule. Taiwan's public policy does not prevent the court from applying a different interest rate pursuant to the governing law of a foreign jurisdiction. The Kaohsiung District Court had once made a judgment in accordance with the law of Singapore.[32] According to Singapore law, the judges have discretion as to the rate of interest as well as the period during which interest will accrue.[33] Since interest at 5% per annum far exceeds international practice, and the plaintiff did not have any urgent financial need, the judges decided to grant interest at 2% per annum.

Foreign Laws with Interest Rates Higher Than 20% Per Annum

In another case dealt by a Taiwan Court,[34] the applicable law was Singapore law.[35] Since the Singapore rule honors the parties' agreement on the interest rate, the Taiwan High Court decided to grant the creditor interest at 2% per month. The High Court

30. Supreme Court Judgment 104-Tai-Shang-Zi No. 1085 [2015]; Taiwan High Court Judgment 101-Zhong-Shang-Zi No. 92 [2012]; Taiwan High Court Judgment 92-Shang-Zi No. 802 [2003].
31. Section 17 of the Judgments Act 1838: "*Every judgment debt shall carry interest at the rate of 8 pounds per centum per annum from such time as shall be prescribed by rules of court until the same shall be satisfied, and such interest may be levied under a writ of execution on such judgment.*"
32. Kaohsiung District Court Judgment 99-Marinetime-Zi No. 11[2010]. Even though a part of the holding of the judgment was discarded by Taiwan High Court Judgment 103-Marinetime-Shang-Geng-Yi-Zi No. 1, the interest rate was maintained.
33. *Holdings Ltd. (formerly known as Export Credit Insurance Corp of Singapore Ltd.) v. TKM (Singapore) Pte. Ltd.* [1994] 2SLR137CA, para [9].
34. Taiwan High Court Judgment 95-Zhong-Shang-Zi No. 551 [2006].
35. Para. 12 of the Civil Law Act (Chapter 43) of Singapore states: "*In any proceedings tried in any court of record for the recovery of any debt or damages, the court may, if it thinks fit, order that there shall be included in the sum for which judgment is given interest at such rate as it thinks fit on the whole or any part of the debt or damages for the whole or any part of the period between the date when the cause of action arose and the date of the judgment.*" Order 42, Rule 12 of the Rules of Court of Singapore 2006 provides: "*Except when it has been otherwise agreed between the parties, every judgment debt shall carry interest at the rate of 6 per cent per annum.*"

further elaborated that such agreement made by the parties shall not be ignored on the grounds of inconsistency with Article 205 of the Taiwan Civil Code.

Foreign Judgments with Compound Interest Rates

In a case where a party sought to enforce a U.K. judgment in Taiwan, the opponent challenged the judgment for violating Article 207 and, thus, the public policy of Taiwan. The opponent's argument was based on the fact that the U.K. court granted a compound interest rate to the creditor.[36] Applying the applicable U.K. rules, the U.K. court divided interest on damages into interest accrued before the date of the judgment and interest accrued after the date of the judgment, which resulted in the compound interest rate. Invoking the Code of Civil Procedure,[37] the Taiwan High Court recognized the judgment and took the view that the U.K. judgment applied U.K. law correctly and the result of the application does not defy Taiwan's public policy or any fundamental values of Taiwan law.[38]

The Civil Code permits the creditor to ask for a compound interest rate if the trade custom allows it.[39] Taiwan courts have recognized that the banking industry has a custom of applying compound interest rates.[40] In cases where the parties to the dispute were not in the banking industry and the requesting party was not able to prove with evidence an existing trade custom, courts would not grant compound interest to the requesting party.[41] An arbitral tribunal certainly enjoys the power to decide whether a trade custom exists and justifies claims based on a compound rate.

---

36. Rule 40.8 of the Civil Procedure Rule of the United Kingdom (UK): "*(1) Where interest is payable on a judgment pursuant to Section 17 of the Judgments Act 1838 or Section 74 of the County Courts Act 1984, the interest shall begin to run from the date that judgment is given unless—(a) a rule in another Part or a practice direction makes different provision; or (b) the court orders otherwise. (2) The court may order that interest shall begin to run from a date before the date that judgment is given.*"
37. Article 402 of the Code of Civil Procedure: "*I. A final and binding judgment rendered by a foreign court shall be recognized, except in case of any of the following circumstances: 1. Where the foreign court lacks jurisdiction pursuant to the R.O.C. laws; 2. Where a default judgment is rendered against the losing defendant, except in the case where the notice or summons of the initiation of action had been legally served in a reasonable time in the foreign country or had been served through judicial assistance provided under the R.O.C. laws; 3. Where the performance ordered by such judgment or its litigation procedure is contrary to R.O.C. public policy or morals; 4. Where there exists no mutual recognition between the foreign country and the R.O.C. II. The provision of the preceding paragraph shall apply mutatis mutandis to a final and binding ruling rendered by a foreign court.*"
38. Taiwan High Court Judgment 99 Zhong-Shang-Geng-Yi-Zi No. 145 [2010]. A more recent judgment, Taiwan High Court Kaohsiung Branch Decree 109-Fei-Kang-Zi No. 6 [2020], also recognized a Singaporean award granting a compound interest rate, and indicated that recognizing the award did not defy Taiwan's public policy.
39. Article 207 of the Civil Code.
40. Supreme Court Jurisprudence 43-Tai-Shang-Zi No. 477 [1954]; Taiwan High Court Judgment 90-Zhong-Shang-Zi No. 140 [2001].
41. Supreme Court Judgment 106-Tai-Shang-Zi No. 409 [2017]; Supreme Court Judgment 93-Tai-Shang-Zi No. 1367 [2004].

VI EFFECT OF ENFORCEMENT ORDERS ON INTEREST ON THE AWARD ON BOTH THE SEAT AND ELSEWHERE

Legal Effect of "Enforcement" Orders by Taiwan Courts

The Arbitration Act specifically confers on arbitral awards seated in Taiwan the same binding force as a final, unappealable judgment of the court.[42] An arbitral award can be enforced by a court only after an enforcement order has been issued upon the application of the party. Following the principle of the 1958 New York Convention, courts in Taiwan do not review the merits of the award, and consciously limit their review to a formalistic review without ever making corrections, revisions or additions to an award.

The court will refuse to issue an enforcement order over an award to the extent that it is ultra vires or directs the party to act contrary to the law.[43] It means that the court may refuse to enforce interest on an award if the court finds the adopted interest rate runs afoul of public policy. If the tribunal fails to state in the award the reasoning for its decision to apply an interest rate different from that legally prescribed, the award would be enforced only after the omission is corrected by the tribunal.

As for a foreign award,[44] it will be enforceable after the court issues an order of recognition upon the party's application.[45] The applicable legal grounds for denying recognition of a foreign award in the Arbitration Act are identical to those in the New York Convention.[46] Awards with recognition orders are legally enforceable awards.

42. Article 37, para. 1 of the Arbitration Act: "*The award shall, insofar as relevant, be binding on the parties and have the same force as a final judgment of a court.*"
43. Article 38 of the Arbitration Act.
44. The Arbitration Act adopts the New York Convention definition of foreign award more broadly, and thus enlarges the scope of application of New York Convention principles over foreign awards. Para. 1 of Article 47 of the Arbitration Act: "*A foreign arbitral award is an arbitral award which is issued outside the territory of the Republic of China or issued pursuant to foreign laws within the territory of the Republic of China.*"
45. Article 48, para 1 of the Arbitration Act: "*To obtain recognition of a foreign arbitral award, an application shall be submitted to the court and accompanied by the following documents: 1. The original arbitral award or an authenticated copy thereof; 2. The original arbitration agreement or an authenticated copy thereof; 3. The full text of the foreign arbitration law and regulation, the rules of the foreign arbitration institution or the rules of the international arbitration institution which applied to the foreign arbitral award.*"
46. Article 49 of the Arbitration Act: "*I. The court shall issue a dismissal with respect to an application submitted by a party for recognition of a foreign arbitral award, if such award contains one of the following elements: 1. Where the recognition or enforcement of the arbitral award is contrary to the public order or good morals of the Republic of China. 2. Where the dispute is not arbitrable under the laws of the Republic of China. II. The court may issue a dismissal order with respect to an application for recognition of a foreign arbitral award if the country where the arbitral award is made or whose laws govern the arbitral award does not recognize arbitral awards of the Republic of China.*" Article 50 of the Arbitration Act: "*If a party applies to the court for recognition of a foreign arbitral award which concerns any of the following circumstances, the respondent may request the court to dismiss the application within twenty days from the date of receipt of the notice of the application: 1. The arbitration agreement is invalid as a result of the incapacity of a party according to the law chosen by the parties to govern the arbitration agreement. 2. The arbitration agreement is null and void according to the law chosen to govern said agreement or, in the absence of choice of law, the law of the country where the arbitral award*

What if Post-award Interest Is Not Explicitly Stated in the Award?

No court precedents explicitly state that the courts do not have the power to order post-award interest at the enforcement stage. However, in practice, most courts are willing to enforce only the holdings of foreign judgments. As a result, holdings in foreign judgments granting interest will lead to a court order of recognition/enforcement granting interest calculated on the basis of the principal. By the same token, if no interest is awarded, the court would not award interest ex officio. Again, interest rate is considered an issue under the substantive law, and enforcement of judgments/awards is considered non-contentious proceedings. Therefore, in spite of parties' expressly requesting for the same, most courts hold that they do not have the power to grant post-judgment interest short of trial if it is not explicitly stated in the foreign judgment.[47]

Nevertheless, the Taiwan High Court had once questioned the majority view of the courts in its Judgment 92-Shang-Zi No. 802(2003):

> Whether or not courts attach orders of interest rate to judgments varies around the world. If we only observe judgments in form and refuse to recognize and enforce interest rates that are not specified in the judgments, enforcement orders will vary from jurisdiction to jurisdiction. This is not appropriate. Furthermore, if the interest rate is stipulated in the governing law, interest shall accrue automatically with the principal, and the amount can be specified easily. If the party that wins in a foreign lawsuit has to file a lawsuit again in Taiwan to ask for the missing interest rate, the party's right will be prejudiced. ... Therefore, this Court hereby recognizes the ruling of the U.K. Supreme Court and grants the winning party 8 per cent interest rate per annum according to the Civil Procedure Rules of the U.K.[48]

As discussed above, most courts are willing to enforce only the holdings of foreign judgments. This may mean that the winning party who chooses to file a lawsuit in Taiwan seeking interest would incur substantial time and financial investments. However, there is a fix. In cases where the arbitral award does not include an order for interest, the winning party may apply for an enforcement order from the court that contains an order of interest in the seat of arbitration and then petition the Taiwan court to recognize and enforce such "*enforcement order.*" Needless to say, the winning

---

was made. 3. A party is not given proper notice whether of the appointment of an arbitrator or of any other matter required in the arbitral proceedings, or any other situations which give rise to lack of due process. 4. The arbitral award is not relevant to the subject matter of the dispute covered by the arbitral agreement or exceeds the scope of the arbitration agreement, unless the offending portion can be severed from and not affect the remainder of the arbitral award. 5. The composition of the arbitral tribunal or the arbitration procedure contravenes the arbitration agreement or, in the absence of an arbitration agreement, the law of the place of the arbitration. 6. The arbitral award is not yet binding upon the parties or has been suspended or revoked by a competent court."

47. Supreme Court Judgement 95-Tai-Shang-Zi No. 293 [2006]; Taiwan High Court Judgement 99-Zhong-Shang-Geng-Yi-Zi No. 145 [2010]; Taiwan High Court Judgement 95-Shang-Geng-Yi-Zi No. 36 [2006].
48. Rule 40.8.1 of the Civil Procedure Rule of the UK states: "*Where interest is payable on a judgment pursuant to Section 17 of the Judgments Act 1838 or Section 74 of the County Courts Act 1984, the interest shall begin to run from the date that judgment is given unless—(a) a rule in another Part or a practice direction makes different provision; or (b) the court orders otherwise.*"

party will need to convince the court that the enforcement order is a final and binding judgment pursuant to the Code of Civil Procedure of Taiwan.[49]

VII POWERS OF THE COURT TO ORDER OR ADJUST POST-AWARD INTEREST

9. Does the Taiwan Court Have the Power to Order or Adjust Post-award Interest, Assuming It Is Either the Seat Court or the Enforcing Court?

No. As stated above, Taiwan courts consciously stay away from reviewing the merits of the awards and make enforcement orders strictly based on the awards. We are not aware of any precedent in which the courts were willing to consider the request of a party and make corrections, revisions or additions to an award. However, if the enforcement order of an award was made in a foreign country, and the foreign court has granted the applying party post-award interest, the courts in Taiwan may enforce such enforcement order pursuant to the Code of Civil Procedure.

49. Article 402 of the Code of Civil Procedure.

Thailand

Pathorn Towongchuen, Jedsarit Sahussarungsi & Napassorn Panitchewakul

INTRODUCTION

In Thailand, interest is a matter of substantive law under the Thai Civil and Commercial Code (as amended) (*the CCC*) and is not a matter specifically covered under the Arbitration Act B.E. 2545 (2002) (as amended) (*the AA*). Like many other civil law jurisdictions, the authority to enforce arbitral awards on interest is vested in the competent Thai court.

Although the CCC separates interest into pre-default and post-default interest categories, most, if not all, cases of post-award interest are consequences of disputes between parties and/or parties failing to satisfy their agreed-upon obligations. The post-award interest discussed in this chapter shall refer to cases of post-default interest only.

Post-award interest awarded by an arbitral tribunal may be at the post-default rates agreed upon between the parties (on a contractual basis) and/or the rates stipulated by the applicable substantive law. Under the CCC, the statutory post-default interest rate is 5% per annum.[1] However, the parties are generally free to agree on a specific interest rate (i.e., higher or lower than the statutory interest rate). Arbitral awards granting compound interest may also be set aside or have their enforcement refused by the Thai courts due to lack of sufficient evidence or in the interests of public policy under the AA.

It is also important to note that the Thai courts (as the enforcing courts) will not grant post-award interest unless it is expressly provided by the arbitral award in question. Thus, it is recommended that the relevant parties in the arbitration proceedings include post-award interest in the relief sought, and ensure, to the extent possible, that the arbitral award includes sections on post-award interest.

1. The Royal Emergency Decree Amending the Civil and Commercial Code B.E. 2564 (2021), effective on April 11, 2021. Prior to this, the statutory post-default interest rate was 7.5% per annum.

Section I of this chapter initially explores an arbitral tribunal's power to grant post-award interest under Thai law and its inability to grant such interest without a request or submission therefor by any of the parties. It concludes with the authors' view that the arbitral tribunal's power to grant post-award interest may be classified under substantive law.

Section II of this chapter examines the applicable law when determining post-award interest. Depending on the circumstances, the applicable law may be the governing law of the dispute or of the seat of arbitration. Section III of this chapter then briefly discusses the adoption of international standards when enacting the AA.

Section IV of this chapter explores the substantive law issues associated with granting post-award interest, including the relevancy of late or non-payment interest, the AA's governance of procedural rules in the dispute and when the award of interest can be set aside based on public policy grounds. Awards considered as going against the public policy of Thailand include those which imposed compound interest or interest at a rate exceeding the statutory post-default interest rate without legitimate grounds.

Section V of this chapter discusses circumstances that can be classified as procedural law issues, in which the Supreme Court refused to enforce awards of interest beyond the scope of those awards. Section VI then provides an analysis of the legal effect of enforcement orders granting a post-award interest in and outside of Thailand. Section VI also explains the limitations of a Thai court's authority when granting post-award interest.

Finally, Section VII of this chapter examines the circumstances when a Thai court may utilize its discretion to partially set aside an award or refuse to enforce some parts of an award based on interest that is contrary to the public policy of Thailand.

I POWER TO GRANT POST-AWARD INTEREST

1. Does an Arbitral Tribunal Have the Power to Grant Post-award Interest under National Law?

Yes, although the AA does not contain a specific provision granting an arbitral tribunal seated in Thailand the power to grant post-award interest, an arbitral tribunal may grant post-award interest by referring to the provisions of the relevant agreements and/or the substantive applicable law of the relevant agreements (including the law chosen by the parties to the relevant agreements).[2]

2. Section 34 of the AA states that, "*The arbitral tribunal shall decide the dispute in accordance with the governing law chosen by the parties. Any designation of law or legal system of a country shall be construed, unless otherwise expressed, as directly referring to the substantive law of the country and not to its conflict of laws rules. Failing any designation by the parties, the arbitral tribunal shall decide the dispute in accordance with Thai laws, save where there is a conflict of laws, the arbitral tribunal shall apply the law determined by the principle of conflict of laws it considers appropriate. The parties may expressly stipulate that the arbitral tribunal shall determine the dispute ex aequo et bono. The arbitral tribunal shall decide in accordance with the terms of the contract and shall take into account the trade usage applicable to the transaction.*"

In the case where Thai substantive law applies (as the substantive law chosen by the parties or otherwise), it is worth noting that interest under the CCC can be broadly divided into two categories, i.e., ordinary (pre-default) interest and post-default interest. As post-award interest (i.e., interest granted by an arbitral tribunal and added to the amount specified in the award, until such amount is paid in full) is in most, if not all, cases post-default interest, this chapter will thus refer to and analyze post-award interest as post-default interest.

Under Thai law, post-award interest that is granted by an arbitral tribunal may be subject to either (i) the (post-default) interest rates as specified in the relevant agreements (i.e., contractual interest rates) or (ii) the (post-default) interest rates as stipulated in the relevant laws (i.e., statutory interest rates). As a general principle, post-award interest must be subject to the statutory interest rate of 5% per annum, unless the award creditor is able to legitimately demand a higher interest rate (e.g., by referring to contract-contractual rates).[3] On the one hand, if the parties did not specify any post-default interest rate in the relevant agreements, the post-award interest rate under Thai law (as the statutory interest rate) shall be 5% per annum. On the other hand, if the relevant agreements between the parties specify post-default interest rates, such post-default interest shall be considered as a penalty under section 379 of the CCC,[4] which may be reduced by the arbitral tribunal at its discretion.[5]

In the case where foreign substantive law applies, the interest rates shall be as determined under such foreign law. However, in practice, for an arbitral tribunal seated in Thailand, foreign substantive law is applicable to the extent to which the award rendered by such a tribunal is not set aside or does not have its enforcement refused by the Thai courts.[6] Pursuant to the AA, one of the grounds for setting aside or

3. Section 224 of the CCC states that, "*A monetary obligation shall produce interest during the default of an obligation at the rate stipulated in Section 7 plus the add-on rate at 2 percent per annum. If the creditor can demand higher rate of interest by referring to any other legitimate ground, such interest shall continue to be paid. The interest payable for default shall not apply to interest. Proof of further damage is permissible.*" Section 7 of the CCC states that, "*Whenever interest is to be paid, and the rate is not fixed by a juristic act or by an express provision of law, it shall be 3 percent per annum. The rate stipulated in the foregoing paragraph may be adjusted downwards or upwards in accordance with the economic situation of the country by a Royal Decree. Generally, the Ministry of Finance shall review the interest rate every 3 years, taking into account the interest rates of deposits and loans of commercial banks.*"
4. Section 379 of the CCC states that, "*If the debtor promises the creditor that he will pay a sum of money as a penalty in case that he does not perform his obligation or does not perform it in the proper manner, the penalty is forfeited if he is in default. If the performance shall be conducted by omitting any act, the penalty is forfeited as soon as any act in contravention of the obligation is committed.*"
5. Section 383 of the CCC states that, "*Where a penalty claimed is disproportionately high, the court may reduce it to a reasonable amount. In considering the reasonableness of the amount to be determined, the court shall take into account all the legitimate gains or losses, which shall not be limited only to property-related, of the creditor. Where the penalty is paid, the right to request the reduction shall become extinguished. Besides the cases mentioned in Sections 379 and 382, the same shall also apply to the case where a person promises a penalty for a commission or omission of an act.*"
6. Section 40 of the AA states that, "*Challenge of an arbitral award may be made by a motion for setting aside to the competent court in accordance with this Section. Within ninety days after receipt of a copy of the award or after the correction or interpretation or the making of an additional award, a party may file a motion for setting aside of the award with the competent court. The court*

refusing the enforcement of arbitral awards is the circumstances in which the recognition or enforcement of the arbitral awards would be contrary to public policy. The Thai Supreme Court has previously ruled that the post-default interest rate issue is not in itself an issue of public policy since section 224 of the CCC (which specifies the statutory post-default interest rate) does not prohibit an award creditor, in absolute terms, from applying post-default interest rates which are higher than 5% per annum.[7] Thus, as long as there are legitimate grounds on which an award creditor can rely for collecting post-award interest at a rate higher than 5% per annum (e.g., by referring to the provisions of the relevant agreements or the statutory interest rates stipulated in the applicable foreign substantive law), an arbitral award will be legally enforceable in Thai courts.

shall set aside the arbitral award in the following cases: The party filing the motion can furnish proof that: (a) A party to the arbitration agreement was under some incapacity under the law applicable to that party; (b) The arbitration agreement is not binding under the law of the country agreed to by the parties. Or failing any indication thereon, under the law of Thailand; (c) The party making the application was not given proper advance notice of the appointment of the arbitral tribunal or of the arbitral proceedings or was otherwise unable to defend the case in the arbitral proceedings; (d) The award deals with a dispute not within the scope of the arbitration agreement or contains a decision on matter beyond the scope of the arbitration agreement. However, if the award on the matter which is beyond the scope thereof can be separated from the part that is within the scope of arbitration agreement, the court may set aside only the part that is beyond the scope of arbitration agreement or clause; or (e) The composition of the arbitral tribunal or the arbitral proceedings was not in accordance with the agreement of the parties or, unless otherwise agreed by the parties, in accordance with this Act. (2) Where the court finds that: (a) The award deals with a dispute not capable of settlement by arbitration under the law; or (b) The recognition or enforcement of the award would be contrary to public policy. In considering application for setting aside an award, if a party so requests and the court considers it reasonably justified, the court may adjourn the hearing of the case as it deems fit so that the arbitral tribunal can resume the case or carry out any act as it deems fit to eliminate the grounds for setting aside." Section 43 of the AA states that: "*The court may refuse enforcement of the arbitral award, irrespective of the country in which it was made, if the person against whom the award will be enforced furnishes proof that: (1) A party to the arbitration agreement was under some incapacity under the law applicable to that party; (2) The arbitration agreement is not binding under the law of the country agreed to by the parties, or failing any indication thereon, under Thai law; (3) The party making the application was not given proper advance notice of the appointment of the arbitral tribunal or of the arbitral proceedings or was otherwise unable to defend the case in the arbitral proceedings; (4) The award deals with a disputed not falling within the scope of the arbitration agreement or contains a decision on matter beyond the scope of the arbitration agreement. However, if the award on the matter which is beyond the scope thereof can be separated from the part that is within the scope of arbitration agreement, the court may set aside only the part that is beyond the scope of arbitration agreement or clause; (5) The composition of the arbitral tribunal or the arbitral proceedings was not in accordance with the agreement of the parties or, if not otherwise agreed by the parties, in accordance with this Act; or (6) The arbitral award has not yet become binding, or has been set aside or suspended by a competent court or under the law of the country where it was made. Save where the setting aside or suspension of the award is being sought from the competent court, the court may adjourn the hearing of this case as it thinks fit; and if requested by the party making the application, the court may order the party against whom enforcement is sought to provide appropriate security.*" Section 44 of the AA states that: "*The court may dismiss the application for enforcement under Section 43 if it finds that the award involves a dispute not capable of settlement by arbitration under the law or if the enforcement would be contrary to public policy.*"

7. Supreme Court Decision No. 1916/2544, in which the Supreme Court decided that the arbitral tribunal could render an award granting post-default interest at the rate of 1.5% per month (i.e., 18% per annum).

2. Is the Power Exercisable Without a Request or Submission, or Are Such Submissions Required?

No, the power to grant post-award interest is not exercisable without a request or submission. The second paragraph of section 37 of the AA stipulates that "*[u]nless otherwise agreed by the parties, the award shall clearly state the reasons for making such decisions. However, it shall not prescribe or decide on any matters falling beyond the scope of the arbitration agreement or the relief sought by the parties, except awards rendered in accordance with the settlement agreements under Section 36, or the fixing of arbitration fees, expenses or remunerations of the arbitrator under Section 46.*" In the same vein, the Thai Supreme Court has, on at least one occasion, decided that an award rendered by an arbitral tribunal must be in accordance with the claims or requests submitted by the parties to the arbitration proceedings.[8]

A similar concept to this is also reflected in section 142 of the Thai Civil Procedure Code, which applies to litigation in Thai courts and provides that, unless an exception applies, "*[j]udgment or order of the Court shall be adjudicated on every claim in the plaint, but no judgment or order shall be rendered exceeding or beyond the claims contained in such plaint ...*"[9] Thus, according to the second paragraph of section 37 of the AA, an arbitral tribunal must exercise its power, including the power to grant

8. Supreme Court Decision No. 9477/2558, in which the Supreme Court decided that "*[E]ven though the debt under the sale agreement on which the award is based on is a monetary debt, whereby the law permits calculation of interest to be made from the default date onwards, the arbitral award however must be in accordance with the claims and the request for arbitration. As the request for arbitration of the petitioner does not include a claim for post award interest, and the arbitral tribunal adjudicated on the interest only as requested. When the petitioner requested for enforcement of the award, the petitioner thus shall not request for enforcement beyond the scope of the arbitral award....*"
9. Section 142 of the Civil Procedure Code states that: "*Judgment or order of the Court shall be adjudicated on every claim in the plaint, but no judgment or order shall be rendered exceeding or beyond the claims contained in such plaint, except that: (1) in the case claiming for immovable property which is deemed to be of the same kind as a plaint claiming for eviction of the defendant, the Court, if rendering judgment in favor of the plaintiff, may, when he deems appropriate, order the eviction of the defendant; such order shall apply to all relatives and dependents of the defendant, who dwell on immovable property and are not able to show the Court any distinctive entitlement; (2) in the case where the plaintiff claims for any property, but during the trial it is found that he or she is only entitled to a portion thereof, the Court may, when he deems appropriate, render a judgment in favor of the plaintiff for merely such portion; (3) in the case where the plaintiff claims for any payment together with accrued interest up to the date of the entry of the plaint, the Court may, when he deems appropriate, render a judgment ordering a payment of the interest up to the date when full payment was settled according to the judgment; (4) in the case where the plaintiff claims for any rent or compensation calculated up to the date of the entry of the plaint, the Court may, when he deems appropriate, render a judgment ordering payment of rent and compensation up to the date when full payment was settled according to the judgment; (5) in the case where the issue of law concerning public order could have been raised, the Court may, when he deems appropriate, raise that issue for the purpose of making a decision and render a judgment; (6) in the case where the plaintiff claims for any payment together with accrued interest, which the interest rate is not specified by any agreement, the Court may, when he deems appropriate, by taking in to account the reasonable grounds and good faith of the defense, render the judgment to cover the interest exceeding the interest rate which the plaintiff is entitled thereof according to the law, but not exceeding fifteen percent per year as from the date of entry of the plaint, or any other later date.*"

post-award interest (if applicable), in accordance with the relevant agreements between the parties and the requests, submissions or reliefs sought by the parties.

3. Is the Power Classified As One under the Substantive Applicable Law or the Procedural Law of the Arbitration?

Although Thai law does not expressly classify the power of an arbitral tribunal to grant post-award interest as one under substantive or procedural law, the authors are more inclined to view that the power can be classified as one under the substantive law. This is because the provisions relating to post-default interest and the power of an arbitral tribunal to determine or reduce a contractual penalty are stipulated in the CCC, which is a code of substantive civil and commercial law. Moreover, the AA does not contain any provision concerning post-award interest, or, in fact, any interest at all.

II CHOICE OF LAW

4. What is the Law That Applies to the Determination of What Post-award Interest Should Be? Would This Be the Governing Law of the Dispute or the Law of the Seat?

The law that applies to the determination of post-award interest can be the governing law of the dispute or the law of the seat (as the case may be). For an arbitral tribunal seated in Thailand, the governing law of the dispute must be determined in accordance with section 34 of the AA, which in essence, includes the governing law chosen by the parties, and, if the parties fail to designate the governing law, then Thai substantive law (as the law of the seat) or Thai conflict of law rules (if any) shall govern.[10]

Under the Act on Conflict of Laws B.E. 2481 (1938) Criminal Law Amendment Act (*the CLA*), section 13 provides that the applicable law of a contract is determined by the intention of the parties, and, if such intention cannot be ascertained, then the law common to the parties (if they are of the same nationality) or the law of the place where the contract has been made (if they are of different nationalities).[11] However, under the CLA, the rules determining the substantive applicable law of the dispute vary

10. *See* section 34 of the AA states that, "*The arbitral tribunal shall decide the dispute in accordance with the governing law chosen by the parties. Any designation of law or legal system of a country shall be construed, unless otherwise expressed, as directly referring to the substantive law of the country and not to its conflict of laws rules. Failing any designation by the parties, the arbitral tribunal shall decide the dispute in accordance with Thai laws, save where there is a conflict of laws, the arbitral tribunal shall apply the law determined by the principle of conflict of laws it considers appropriate. The parties may expressly stipulate that the arbitral tribunal shall determine the dispute ex aequo et bono. The arbitral tribunal shall decide in accordance with the terms of the contract and shall take into account the trade usage applicable to the transaction.*"
11. Section 13 of the CLA states that, "*The question as to what law is applicable in regard to the essential elements or effects of a contract is determined by the intention of the parties to it. If such intention, express or implied, cannot be ascertained, the law applicable is the law common to the parties when they are of the same nationality, or, if they are not of the same nationality, the law of the place where the contract has been made. When the contract is made between persons at a distance, the place where the contract is deemed to have been made is the place where notice of acceptance reaches the offeror. If such place cannot be ascertained, the law of the place where the contract is to be performed shall govern. A contract shall not be void when made in accordance with the form prescribed by the law which governs the effects of such contract.*"

depending on the nature or the subject matter of the dispute.[12] Moreover, it is worth noting that, under the CLA, if the governing law is a foreign substantive law, such law shall be applied within the scope of Thai public policy.[13]

III DO THE COURTS TAKE INTO ACCOUNT INTERNATIONAL STANDARDS WHEN FACING CHALLENGES ON POST-AWARD INTEREST?

Despite the AA being based on the UNCITRAL Model Law and Thailand being a party to many international conventions, including the 1958 New York Convention, which incorporates international standards on, among other things, arbitral proceedings and enforcement of arbitral awards, Thailand adopted these international standards by enacting the AA with some adjustments. The AA does not expressly provide that Thai courts must consider international standards, for instance, in determining the enforceability of arbitral awards.

IV SUBSTANTIVE LAW ISSUES

5. How Are Contractual Provisions on Late or Non-payment Interest Relevant to Post-award Interest? Will These Be Considered By the Arbitral Tribunal?

As discussed in response to Question 1, post-award interest under Thai law is, in most, if not all, cases post-default interest. Moreover, according to section 224 of the CCC, the default position under Thai law is that post-award interest shall be applied at the statutory rate of 5% per annum unless the award creditor has legitimate grounds to demand a higher interest rate (e.g., by means of contract). Thus, contractual provisions on late or non-payment interest are relevant since they would provide legitimate grounds for the prevailing party to demand, and for the arbitral tribunal to grant, post-award interest at a rate higher than 5% per annum.

6. How Do the Procedural Rules of the Substantive Law Apply?

The procedural rules of the substantive law do not apply by virtue of section 34 of the AA, which states that "*the arbitral tribunal shall decide the dispute in accordance with the governing law chosen by the parties. Any designation of law or legal system of a country shall be construed, unless otherwise expressed, as directly referring to the substantive law of the country and not to its conflict of laws rules.*" Where a foreign law is to be applied, only its substantive law, not its conflict of law rules or its procedural rules, is to be applied. Procedural matters are to be governed by *lex fori* or the

12. For example, section 15 of the CLA states that, "*An obligation arising out of a wrongful act is governed by the law of the place where the facts constituting such wrongful act have taken place. The foregoing provision does not apply to the facts which, having taken place in a foreign country, are not wrongful according to the [Thai] law. In no case can the injured party claim compensation or remedies other than those allowed by the [Thai] law.*"
13. Section 5 of the CLA states that, "*Whenever the law of a foreign country is to govern, it shall be applied in so far as it is not contrary to the public policy of [Thailand].*"

procedural law of the seat of arbitration, namely the AA, and not the procedural rules of the substantive law.

7. Whether the Award of Interest Can Be Subjected to Public Policy Objections, and if So, What Are They?

Pursuant to sections 40 and 43 of the AA, an award on interest can be set aside and/or enforcement of an award on interest can be resisted if there are legitimate grounds to do so. The grounds for setting aside an award and/or resisting the enforcement of an award include that "*the [recognition and] enforcement would be contrary to public policy [of Thailand].*"[14] Previous cases in which the Supreme Court has set aside or resisted the enforcement of an award on interest include the following:

(i) *Compound interest*—the Supreme Court has, on several occasions, refused to enforce arbitral awards on interest, as such enforcement would be contrary to the second paragraph of section 224 of the CCC, which prohibits setting interest on post-default interest. The Supreme Court has expressly referred to this issue as a public policy issue, which the court could use as grounds to refuse the enforcement according to section 44 of the AA.[15]

(ii) *Awarded interest rate exceeding statutory post-default interest rate without legitimate grounds*—if Thai law is the applicable substantive law and the tribunal awards an interest rate exceeding 5% per annum without legitimate grounds, pursuant to the first paragraph of section 224 of the CCC (e.g., no provisions in the contract allow the calculation of interest exceeding 5% per annum), the Supreme Court may set aside such a tribunal award based on public policy grounds in accordance with section 40 (2)(b) of the AA.[16]

---

14. *See* sections 40 (2)(b) and 44 of the AA.
15. Supreme Court Decision No. 6292/2561 in which the Supreme Court decided that "*...[T]he fact that the Arbitral Tribunal ordered the two Respondents to be liable for daily compound interest, which meant to allow the Petitioner to claim for interest on interest, is in violation to Section 224 paragraph two, and the recognition and enforcement of such award is considered against public policy and good morals. Therefore, the award may not be enforced. Thus, the Respondent shall be liable for simple interest.*" Supreme Court Decision No. 2611/2562 in which the Supreme Court decided that "*[according to the arbitral award] with regard to damages from the breach of contract in which it was ordered that the Respondent must be liable for interest on the principal of USD 4,451,041.19 together with interest at the rate of 4.25% per annum from 18 September 2013 until the payment is fully made to the Petitioner, [the Court] found that, as paragraph 13 of the arbitral award stated that USD 4,451,041319 was the sum of the difference between the contract price of the goods and the market price and the interest calculated based on such difference according to each sale contract at the rate of 7.5% per annum from 4 October 2011 until 28 August 2013, which was the date on which the award was rendered, this constituted an award granting interest on interest during the period of default since the default interest was included in the principal for the default interest calculation. This is thus in violation of Section 224 paragraph two. The Court is entitled to refuse the request for enforcement of the award in this respect pursuant to Section 44 of the AA since it is considered a question of public policy.*"
16. Supreme Court Decision No. 8265/2559 in which the Supreme Court decided that "*[T]he adjudication of the Arbitral Tribunal must be subject to the law. The award for default interest must be subject to Section 224 paragraph one of the Civil and Commercial Code ... Since the fire insurance contract does not provide that the Petitioner shall be liable for interest in the event of default more than 7.5% per annum, the Respondent had no legitimate ground to claim for the*

V PROCEDURAL LAW ISSUES

8. What Are the Main Procedural Law Issues When Considering Post-award Interest? How Are the Arbitration Laws and Other Laws or Regulations of the Seat Relevant?

Although it is rather difficult to draw the line between substantive law and procedural law issues, there are some occasions in which the Supreme Court refuses to enforce awards on interest beyond the scope of such awards. These may be categorized as procedural law issues, which an enforcing party must bear in mind when enforcing an award on interest before the Thai courts. For example, if a claimant in arbitration proceedings did not include post-award interest in the reliefs sought during the arbitration proceedings and the Tribunal did not grant any post-award interest to the claimant in the award as a consequence, then such claimant cannot reconsider and request post-award interest in the enforcement proceedings before the relevant Thai court, as this would give rise to enforcement beyond the scope of the award granted by the tribunal.[17] This is derived from the general principle reflected in section 41 of the AA, which states that "*...an arbitral award, irrespective of the country in which it was made, shall be recognized as binding on the parties, and upon petition to the competent court, shall be enforced.*"

VI EFFECT OF ENFORCEMENT ORDERS ON INTEREST ON THE AWARD ON BOTH THE SEAT AND ELSEWHERE

Legal Effect of "Enforcement" Orders By Thai Courts

As a general principle, any judgments or orders issued by the Thai courts will only be effective or enforceable within Thailand and/or against Thai persons or assets located in Thailand (as the case may be). Unless the law of the state in which the party wishes to enforce the Thai court's orders or judgments provides otherwise, the Thai court's judgments or orders would not be effective or enforceable outside of Thailand. It is also worth noting that Thailand is not a party to any international treaties or agreements relating to the recognition and enforcement of foreign judgments. Thus, foreign

interest at the rate of 15% per annum. ... There was no legitimate ground for the Arbitral Tribunal to order the Petitioner to be liable for interest at the rate of 15% per annum. Therefore, the Arbitral Tribunal's award ordering the Petitioner to pay for interest at such rate is unlawful and is deemed the case where the recognition and enforcement of the award is contrary to public policy or good morals. The Court was thus entitled to revoke the arbitral award on the part where it ordered the Petitioner to pay for default interest at the rate exceeding 7.5% per annum pursuant to Section(40)(2)(b) of the AA."

17. *See* Supreme Court Decision No. 9477/2558, in which the Supreme Court decided that "*[E]ven though the debt under the sale agreement on which the award is based on is a monetary debt, whereby the law permits calculation of interest to be made from the default date onwards, the arbitral award however must be in accordance with the claims and the request for arbitration. As the request for arbitration of the petitioner does not include a claim for post award interest, and the arbitral tribunal adjudicated on the interest only as requested. When the petitioner requested for enforcement of the award, the petitioner thus shall not request for enforcement beyond the scope of the arbitral award....*"

judgments or orders are not recognized or enforceable by the Thai courts, and *vice versa*.

However, unlike with respect to foreign court judgments, the Thai court is bound to enforce an arbitral award rendered by an arbitral tribunal seated in a foreign country, given that it is subject to an international treaty or agreement (on the enforcement of arbitral awards) to which Thailand is a party[18] and to the conditions under which foreign arbitral awards can be enforced in Thailand.[19]

What if Post-award Interest Is Not Explicitly Stated in the Award?

As aforementioned, the Thai courts are not authorized by law to order post-award interest if it is not explicitly specified in the award. In other words, the Thai courts cannot grant relief beyond what has been expressly granted by the arbitral tribunal, and, if the arbitral tribunal does not explicitly grant a post-award interest in the award, the Thai court (as the court having jurisdiction over the seat or the court with which a petition to enforce has been filed) cannot grant a post-award interest to the enforcing party.

VII POWERS OF THE COURT TO ORDER OR ADJUST POST-AWARD INTEREST

9. Does a Thai Court Have the Power to Order or Adjust Post-award Interest, Assuming It Is Either the Seat Court or the Enforcing Court?

When the enforcing court is a Thai court, such a court does not have the express power to adjust arbitral awards, including parts relating to post-award interest, as the enforcing court is only authorized by law to set aside an award or refuse to enforce an award. However, as the court may partially set aside an award or refuse to enforce some parts of an award, in practice, the court can, to some extent, adjust or revise post-award interest granted by an arbitral tribunal. For example, if an arbitral tribunal grants default compound interest in its award (which is contrary to Thai public policy and therefore cannot be enforced before the Thai courts), the court may allow enforcement of the award on simple interest without giving effect to the interest on interest.[20]

18. *See* section 41 of the AA.
19. *See* sections 43 and 44 of the AA.
20. *See* Supreme Court Decision No. 6292/2561 in which the Supreme Court decided that "*…[T]he fact that the Arbitral Tribunal ordered the two Respondents to be liable for daily compound interest, which meant to allow the Petitioner to claim for interest on interest, is in violation to Section 224 paragraph two, and the recognition and enforcement of such award is considered against public policy and good morals. Therefore, the award may not be enforced. Thus, the Respondent shall be liable for simple interest.*" Supreme Court Decision No. 2611/2562 in which the Supreme Court decided that "*[according to the arbitral award] with regard to damages from the breach of contract in which it was ordered that the Respondent must be liable for interest on the principal of USD 4,451,041.19 together with interest at the rate of 4.25% per annum from 18 September 2013 until the payment is fully made to the Petitioner, [the Court] found that, as paragraph 13 of the arbitral award stated that USD 4,451,041319 was the sum of the difference between the contract price of the goods and the market price and the interest calculated based on*

such difference according to each sale contract at the rate of 7.5% per annum from 4 October 2011 until 28 August 2013, which was the date on which the award was rendered, this constituted an award granting interest on interest during the period of default since the default interest was included in the principal for the default interest calculation. This is thus in violation of Section 224 paragraph two. The Court is entitled to refuse the request for enforcement of the award in this respect pursuant to Section 44 of the AA since it is considered a question of public policy."

United Arab Emirates

Hassan Arab & Mosaab Th. Aly

INTRODUCTION

The United Arab Emirates (*UAE*) is a federation of seven emirates (Abu Dhabi, Dubai, Sharjah, Ajman, Umm Al Quwain, Ras Al Khaimah and Fujairah). The Provisional Constitution is the founding constitutional document of the UAE, which was signed by six of the emirates on December 2, 1971. The seventh Emirate, Ras Al Khaimah, joined the federation shortly afterwards in February 1972. The Provisional Constitution was initially valid for a period of five years, and it has been renewed every five years since 1971. The Constitution was declared permanent by Federal Decree on December 2, 1996.

The UAE is generally considered a civil law jurisdiction with limited exceptions.[1,2] Although there is no formal system of judicial precedent in the UAE, lower courts respect and generally follow the precedents of higher courts.

The UAE Constitution reserves to the individual emirate's sovereignty over their own territories and territorial waters in all matters in so far as they are not within the jurisdiction of the Federation, as reserved to it by the Constitution. Where the Federal Government is yet to legislate on a particular matter within its competence, the matter remains within the competence of the individual emirate. For example, each emirate

1. Both emirates of Dubai and Abu Dhabi have established their own financial free zones, within which the DIFC Courts and ADGM Courts are based. The DIFC Courts is a common law and English speaking court system that operates in the Dubai International Financial Centre (DIFC). DIFC Courts is a judicial authority that is different from the Dubai onshore courts. The DIFC Courts does not, in principle, apply federal laws or other onshore Dubai laws but will essentially apply the DIFC laws. Similarly, ADGM Courts is a common law and English speaking court system that operates in the Abu Dhabi Global Markets (ADGM). ADGM Courts is judicial authority that is different from the Abu Dhabi onshore courts.
2. The reference in this chapter to the UAE laws shall include all local and federal laws in the UAE except DIFC and ADGM laws. Similarly, the reference to the UAE courts shall include all courts in the emirates of the UAE except to the DIFC and ADGM Courts.

has its own laws on matters pertaining to rent, and these cases are usually dealt with by Special Committees.

In June 2018, the UAE Federal Law No. 6 of 2018 concerning Arbitration came into effect to replace the arbitration chapter in the UAE Civil Procedures Law (*the CPL*). The UAE Arbitration Law no. 6 of 2018 (*the UAL*) is generally an UNCITRAL-modelled law that is in line with modern arbitration trends.

I POWER TO GRANT POST-AWARD INTEREST

1. Does an Arbitral Tribunal Have the Power to Grant Post-award Interest Under the UAE law?

The brief answer is "*yes.*" This is essentially based on Article 37.1 of the UAL, which reads as follows: "*The Parties are free to choose the law which the arbitrators shall apply to the subject matter of the dispute. Any designation of the law of a given State shall be construed, unless otherwise expressed, as directly referring to the substantive law of that State and not to its conflict of laws rules, provided there is no conflict with the public order or morality of the State.*"

It follows that an arbitral tribunal has the power to grant post-award interest as long as (i) the substantive law that applies to the arbitration proceedings permits so and (ii) the interest awarded does not contradict the UAE public policy.

Nevertheless, the mere contravention to the substantive applicable law does not render the award of such interest void, unless this also constitutes a contravention to the UAE public policy.[3]

That said, it is important to consider when the post-award interest could be in conflict with the UAE public policy. We deal with this in two aspects, as follows:

(i) *Simple or compound*: It is generally settled in the rulings of the UAE Federal Supreme Court[4] and the Abu Dhabi Court of Cassation[5] that compound interest is prohibited and against the UAE public policy. Nevertheless, the Dubai Court of Cassation does not generally consider the compound interest against the UAE public policy if it was awarded in the context of banking facilities.[6] As such, we believe that to avoid a risk of having the post-award interest set aside (or rendered unenforceable) in the UAE, a tribunal should not decide post-award interests on accrued interests.

(ii) *The Decision of the General Circuit of Dubai Court of Cassation No. 1 of 2021 ("the Decision"):* on June 9, 2021, the General Circuit of Dubai Court of Cassation decided that the legal interest on the principal debt should be 5 %

3. *See* Dubai Court of Cassation Judgment no. 1128 of 2021, commercial issued on November 21, 2021.
4. *See* Federal Supreme Court Judgment no. 67 of 2004, civil issued on May 23, 2004.
5. *See* Abu Dhabi Court of Cassation Judgments no. 17 of 2016, commercial issued on February 1, 2016 and no. 591 of 2016 commercial issued on January 31, 2017.
6. *See* Dubai Court of Cassation Judgment no. 870 of 2016, commercial issued on April 9, 2017. However, we are yet to see the impact of introducing a new article in Federal Decree law no. 14 of 2018 that apparently prohibits the compound interest by general terms.

per annum until full settlement in case of lack of agreement by the relevant parties. In our view, we do not believe the 5% interest rate decided by the above Decision is a matter of public policy in the Emirate of Dubai. As a result, arbitral tribunal may decide post-award interest that exceeds 5%. Nevertheless, we have noted a recent judgment issued by the Dubai Court of Cassation where a party challenged the enforceability of a foreign International Chamber of Commerce (ICC) award on the basis that such award decided an interest rate of 10% per annum, exceeding the rate decided by the Decision. The Dubai Court of Cassation ruled that this challenge shall be dismissed because "*the foreign award had been issued on 10 December 2020 while the Decision [of the General Circuit of the Dubai Court of Cassation] was issued later on 9 June 2021.*"[7] This judgment may therefore lay some doubt on the nature of the Decision and whether the Dubai Court of Cassation considers the 5% interest rate (as decided by its General Circuit] as a matter of public policy.

2. Is the Power Exercisable Without a Request or Submission, or Is Such a Submission Required?

As a matter of UAE law, it is generally prohibited for any court or arbitral tribunal to grant relief that is not sought or pleaded. This applies as well to an award of post-award interest.

Granting post-award interest without a request would likely be deemed a ground to set aside such interest (in case of a domestic award) pursuant to Article 53 of the UAL because this may well be considered as a "*breach to the fundamental principles of adjudications*"[8] and/or a "*breach to the UAE public policy.*"[9] Similarly, a foreign award which granted a post-award interest without a request could be rendered unenforceable (to the limit of such interest) pursuant to Article V of the New York Convention on the Recognition and Enforcement of Foreign Arbitral Awards 1958 ("*the NYC*")

3. Is the Power Classified As One under the Substantive Applicable Law or the Procedural Law of the Arbitration?

The post-award interest is a substantive issue by nature. It is thus subject to substantive applicable law rather than procedural arbitration law. This is also supported by Article 37.1 of the UAL.[10]

7. *See* Dubai Court of Cassation judgment no. 64 of 2022, civil issued on March 31, 2022
8. *See* Article 53.1(d) UAL.
9. *See* Article 53.2(b) UAL.
10. Article 37.1 of the UAL reads as follows, "*The Parties are free to choose the law which the arbitrators shall apply to the subject matter of the dispute. Any designation of the law of a given State shall be construed, unless otherwise expressed, as directly referring to the substantive law of that State and not to its conflict of laws rules, provided there is no conflict with the public order or morality of the State.*"

II CHOICE OF LAW

4. What is the Law That Applies to Determine What the Post-award Interest Should Be? Would This Be the Governing Law of the Dispute or the Law of the Seat?

As explained above, the substantive law chosen by the parties to govern the dispute (or as decided by the tribunal according to Article 38[11] of the UAL as may be the case) should apply to determine the issues related to the post-award interest.

Nevertheless, as a matter of UAE law, this shall not contradict the UAE public policy as discussed in answer to Question 1 above. Otherwise, the arbitral award may be at risk of being set aside or unenforceable in the UAE, depending on whether it is a domestic or foreign award.

III DO THE COURTS TAKE INTO ACCOUNT INTERNATIONAL STANDARDS WHEN FACING CHALLENGES ON THE POST-AWARD INTEREST?

5. Do the Courts Take into Account International Standards When Facing Challenges on Post-award Interest?

There is no reference to such "*international standards*" in the UAL. The arbitral tribunal is required, however, to consider (while deciding the dispute including the post-award interest) "*the terms of the contract, subject of the dispute, the customary practice of the relevant transaction and past practices between the parties*" under Article 38.2 of the UAL.

IV SUBSTANTIVE LAW ISSUES

6. How Are Contractual Provisions on Late or Non-payment of Interest Relevant to Post-award Interest? Will These Be Considered By the Arbitral Tribunal?

Pursuant to Article 38.2 of the UAL, the arbitral tribunal is required to consider (while deciding the merits of the dispute including the post-award interest) "*the terms of the contract, subject of the dispute, the customary practice of the relevant transaction and past practices between the parties.*"

It follows that, irrespective of the interest rate that could be determined by the substantive law, the arbitral tribunal shall in principle give effect to the parties' agreement, i.e., contractual provisions on the late or non-payment interest rate,

11. Article 38.1 of the UAL reads as follows: "*Failing designation by the Parties of the legal rules applicable to the substance of the dispute, the Arbitral Tribunal shall apply the substantive rules of the law it deems most closely connected to the dispute. 2. In deciding the dispute, the Arbitral Tribunal shall take into account the terms of the contract, subject of the dispute, the usages of the trade applicable to the transaction and past practices between the Parties. 3. The Arbitral Tribunal may, if it has expressly been authorized to do so or to act as an amiable compositor by agreement of the Parties, decide ex aequo et bono rather than on the basis of law.*"

provided that there such contractual provisions do not contradict the UAE public policy.

This is also supported by Article 77 of the UAE Federal Law No. 18 of 1993 concerning Commercial Transaction ("*the Commercial Code*") which provides that "*Where the contract stipulates the rate of interest and the debtor delays payment, the delay interest shall be calculated on basis of the agreed rate until full settlement.*"

How Do the Procedural Rules of the Substantive Law Apply?

According to Article 2 of the UAL, the UAL "*shall apply to:*

(a) Any Arbitration conducted in the State, unless the Parties have agreed that another law should govern the Arbitration, provided there is no conflict with the public order and morality of the State.
(b) Any international commercial arbitration conducted abroad, if the Parties have chosen this Law to govern such Arbitration.
(c) Any arbitration arising from a dispute in respect of a legal relationship, whether contractual or not, governed by State law, save as excluded by special provision.

As such, UAL shall apply to the arbitration proceedings in any of the circumstances set out in Article 2 above as the relevant procedural law.

As to the substantive law chosen by the parties to govern the dispute, such law would apply with exception to:

(1) Its procedural provisions which shall be replaced by the UAL as long as any of the cases set out in Article 2 of the UAL is established;
(2) Its rules related to conflict of laws unless agreed otherwise;[12] and
(3) Its rules that contradict the UAE Public Policy.[13]

3. Whether the Award of Interest Can Be Subjected to Public Policy Objections, and if So, What Are They?

In addition to the public policy concerns set out in our answers to Question No. 1, which essentially applies to the delay interest, there is another concern that needs to be considered in relation to award of interests on loans, which are different in nature from delay interest.[14]

Award of interest on loans is essentially governed by several provisions in the UAE laws, as follows:

12. *See* Article 37.1 UAL.
13. *See* Article 37 UAL.
14. Payment of delay interest arises when a breach is committed and, as a matter of UAE law, is legally considered as a compensation against the damages sustained. However, payment of interest on loan is part of the contractual obligations agreed by the parties at the execution of the contract and is not legally considered as a compensation against damages that result from any breach.

(i) Article 76 of the UAE Commercial Code provides that "*A creditor is entitled to receive interest on a commercial loan as per the rate of interest stipulated in the contract. If such rate is not stated in the contract, it shall be calculated according to the rate of interest current in the market at the time of dealing, provided that it shall not exceed 12% until full settlement.*"

(ii) Article 714 of the UAE Civil Code also provides that "*If the contract of loan provides for a benefit in excess of the essence of the contract otherwise than a guarantee of the rights of the lender, such provision shall be void but the contract shall be valid.*"

(iii) Article 458 of the UAE Penal Code provides that "*Punishment by detention for at least one year and by a fine of at least 50,000 Dirhams shall be inflicted upon any natural person who lent another natural person with interest in exchange for delaying the payment, in any kind of civil or commercial transaction, whether the interest was express or latent. Latent interest shall include any commission or benefit stipulated by a creditor, if such a commission or benefit has no corresponding real legal benefit or service provided by the creditor as a consideration. A principal debt and implied interest may be proved by all means available.*"

In light of the above legal provisions, we may summarize the conclusion as follows:

(i) In principle, it is legally permitted to charge interest on commercial loans as long as such transaction is not between two natural persons.

(ii) It is, in principle, legally prohibited from charging interest on civil loans whether such transaction is between two natural persons or otherwise.[15]

(iii) It is a criminal offense to charge interest on a loan between two natural persons whether in the context of commercial or civil transactions.[16]

We, therefore, believe that any award seated in the UAE or sought to be enforced therein should consider and comply with the above conclusions in relation to any interest awarded on loans in order to not risk the validity and/or enforceability of such award.

V PROCEDURAL LAW ISSUES

4. What Are the Main Procedural Law Issues When Considering Post-award Interest? How Are the Arbitration Laws and Other Laws or Regulations of the Seat Relevant?

As a matter of UAE law, we do not believe that there are many procedural law issues that need to be considered in relation to post-award interest. This is essential because post-award interest is a matter of substantive law rather than procedural law.

15. *See* Dubai Court of Cassation judgment no. 204 of 2015, labour issued on June 21, 2016.
16. *See* Dubai Court of Cassation judgment no. 119 of 2017, commercial issued on May 14, 2017

Nevertheless, we may again highlight that the post-award interest, as a matter of UAE law, may only be granted on the application of the interested party. In other words, the post-award interest shall not be decided by the arbitral tribunal by its own motion.

VI EFFECT OF ENFORCEMENT ORDERS ON INTEREST ON THE AWARD ON BOTH THE SEAT AND ELSEWHERE

5. Legal Effect of "Enforcement" Orders By UAE Courts

Article 52 of the UAL provides that "*An arbitral award made in accordance with this Law shall be binding on the Parties, shall constitute res judicata, and shall be as enforceable as a judicial ruling, although to be enforced, a ratification order must be obtained from the Court.*"

As a member of the New York Convention ("*the NYC*"), it is established in the rulings of the UAE Courts that each member state in the NYC, including the UAE, shall recognize foreign arbitral awards pursuant to the provisions of the NYC and enforce them in accordance with the procedures of the state where the award is sought to be enforced.[17]

In terms of procedural requirements of enforcement, the rules applicable to domestic awards are quite similar to those applied to foreign awards, as follows:

(i) *Domestic Awards:* The enforcement proceedings seeking to ratify and enforce the domestic award may officially commence by filing a petition before the Chief Justice of Court of Appeal. Such a petition would be dealt with as an *ex parte* petition (without service) and would be usually decided within one to two weeks only. The enforcement order, if issued, would be subject to challenge by way of grievance (before the Court of Appeal) within 30 days from the date it is served on the opposing party. Nevertheless, such an order would still be enforceable (i.e., execution/recovery stage may commence) even if it is challenged by way of grievance to the Court of Appeal (*the CA*) unless the CA issues an order to stay the enforcement. The CA judgment, once made, would also be subject to a second appeal before the Court of Cassation.

(ii) *Foreign Awards:* The enforcement proceedings seeking to enforce the foreign award may officially commence by filing a petition before the Execution Judge. Such petition would be dealt with as an *ex parte* petition (without service) and would be usually decided within one to two weeks only. The Execution Judge will generally be guided by the New York Convention to make his decision unless other international treaty applies. The enforcement order, if issued, would be subject to appeal (before the Court of Appeal) within 30 days from the date it is served on the opposing party. Nevertheless, such order would still be enforceable (i.e.,

17. *See* Dubai Court of Cassation judgment no. 881 of 2016 issued on 26 March 26, 2017.

execution/recovery stage may commence) even if it is appealed to the CA unless the CA issues an order to stay the enforcement. The CA judgment, once made, would also be subject to a second appeal before the Court of Cassation.

Generally, the UAE Courts' decisions to enforce a domestic or foreign award shall not affect, in any manner, the post-award interest which shall remain as decided in the award itself. As a matter of UAE law, the courts cannot amend the tribunal's decision in relation to the post-award interest. The UAE Courts may, however, set aside (partially or fully) the post-award interest (in case of domestic award) or render that part of the award (partially or fully) unenforceable (in case of foreign award) if the relevant court is satisfied that:

(i) One of the cases set out in Article 53 of the UAL[18] (by which a domestic award may be set aside) is established; or
(ii) One of the cases set out in Article V of the NYC[19] (by which an enforcement of a foreign award may be declined) is established.

---

18. Article 53 of the UAL provides that "*1. An arbitral award can only be challenged by an action for setting aside before the Court or during the pendency of an application to confirm the award. The party seeking to set aside the award must establish any of the following circumstances: (a) that no Arbitration Agreement exists or such agreement is void or has lapsed under the law to which the Parties have subjected it or, failing any indication thereon, under this Law. (b) that a party, at the time of conclusion of the Arbitration Agreement, was incompetent or under some incapacity under the law governing his capacity. (c) that a person does not have the legal capacity to dispose of the disputed right under the law governing his capacity, as provided for in Article 4 of this Law. (d) that a party to the Arbitration fails to present its case because it was not given proper notice of the appointment of an Arbitrator or of the arbitral proceedings or because the Arbitral Tribunal breached due process or for any other reason beyond his control. (e) that the arbitral award excludes the application of the Parties' choice of law for the dispute. (f) that the composition of the Arbitral Tribunal or appointment of any Arbitrator was not in accordance with this Law or the agreement of the Parties. (g) that the arbitral proceedings were marred by irregularities that affected the award or the arbitral award was not issued within the specified time frame. (h) that the award contains decisions on matters not falling within the terms of the submission to arbitration or beyond its scope, provided that, if the decisions on matters submitted to Arbitration can be separated from those not so submitted, only that part of the award which contains decisions on matters not submitted to Arbitration may be set aside. 2. The Court shall, on its own initiative, set aside the arbitral award if it finds that: (a) The subject-matter of the dispute is not capable of settlement by Arbitration. (b) The arbitral award is in conflict with the public order and morality of the State.*"
19. Article V of the NYC provides that "*1. Recognition and enforcement of the award may be refused, at the request of the party against whom it is invoked, only if that party furnishes to the competent authority where the recognition and enforcement is sought, proof that: (a) (a) The parties to the agreement referred to in article II were, under the law applicable to them, under some incapacity, or the said agreement is not valid under the law to which the parties have subjected it or, failing any indication thereon, under the law of the country where the award was made; or (b) The party against whom the award is invoked was not given proper notice of the appointment of the arbitrator or of the arbitration proceedings or was otherwise unable to present his case; or (c) The award deals with a difference not contemplated by or not falling within the terms of the submission to arbitration, or it contains decisions on matters beyond the scope of the submission to arbitration, provided that, if the decisions on matters submitted to arbitration can be separated from those not so submitted, that part of the award which contains decisions on matters submitted to arbitration may be recognized and enforced; or (d) The composition of the arbitral authority or the arbitral procedure was not in accordance with the agreement of the parties, or, failing such*

6. What if Post-award Interest Is Not Explicitly Stated in the Award?

As previously explained, the UAE Courts are not authorized to reconsider the ruling of the award, except to the limits of Article 53 of the UAL (in case of a domestic award) or Article V of the NYC (in case of a foreign award). It is also decided the Tribunal's omission to decide on a certain claim may not be a ground to set aside the arbitral award.[20]

As such, if the post-award interest is not decided in the award, the UAE Courts may not add or supplement the ruling of the award by deciding additional post-award interest.

VII POWERS OF THE COURT TO ORDER OR ADJUST POST-AWARD INTEREST

7. Does a UAE Court Have the Power to Order or Adjust the Post-award Interest Awarded By the Tribunal, Assuming It Is the Seat Court or the Enforcing Court?

The UAE Courts do not have such power whether under the UAL (in case of a domestic award that is seated in the UAE) or under the NYC (in case of a foreign award that is sought to be enforced in the UAE). This is in line with the relevant case laws that provide that the UAE judge, while deciding on the annulment claim, is not legally entitled to reconsider or adjust the assessment of the tribunal's ruling in the award in any manner, except to the limits of Article 53 of the UAL which sets out the exclusive grounds under which an arbitral award may be set aside in the UAE.[21]

---

agreement, was not in accordance with the law of the country where the arbitration took place; or (e) The award has not yet become binding on the parties, or has been set aside or suspended by a competent authority of the country in which, or under the law of which, that award was made. 2. Recognition and enforcement of an arbitral award may also be refused if the competent authority in the country where recognition and enforcement is sought finds that: (a) The subject matter of the difference is not capable of settlement by arbitration under the law of that country; or (b) The recognition or enforcement of the award would be contrary to the public policy of that country."

20. *See* Dubai Court of Cassation judgment no. 1192 of 2018 commercial issued on 28 April 2019. *See also* Abu Dhabi Court of Cassation judgment no. 115 of 2018 commercial issued on 27 February 2018.
21. *See* Dubai Court of Cassation judgment no. 38 of 2022 civil issued on 26 May 2022.

Vietnam

Do Khoi Nguyen & Pham Minh Thang

INTRODUCTION

Since Vietnam opened its doors in the early 1990s to pursue the establishment of a multi-sectoral market economy that is integrated into the global economy, the legal system has undergone a major overhaul.

Vietnamese laws have been reorganized and harmonized based on a Civil Code elaborated with the assistance of French legal experts. A Vietnamese Civil Code first emerged in 1995, which states in the plainest terms in Article 4 that the Civil Code 2015 is "*the general law governing civil relations*" in its 2015 revision.[1] Since civil relations, as defined in Article 1 of the Civil Code 2015, are all encompassing, it can be said without hesitation that Vietnam is now a civil law jurisdiction like France, Germany, Thailand, Korea or Japan. In addition, the Supreme People's Court (*the SPC*) has chosen to designate some of its decisions as binding precedents on par with SPC resolutions, which also have the force of law.

For commercial arbitration, the primary national legislation is Law No. 54/2010/QH12 on Commercial Arbitration passed by the National Assembly on June 17, 2010, effective from January 1, 2011 (*the LCA*). The LCA is largely based on the United Nations Commission on International Trade (UNCITRAL) Model Law. The government of Vietnam and the SPC have issued implementing regulations for the LCA.[2]

1. Civil Code No. 91/2015/QH13 passed by the National Assembly on November 24, 2015, effective from January 01, 2017 ("*the Civil Code 2015*").
2. E.g., Decree 63/2011/ND-CP dated July 28, 2011, providing guidance on a number of articles of the LCA, as amended by Decree 124/2018/ND-CP dated September 19, 2018, and Resolution 01/2014/NQ-HDTP of the Judicial Council of the People's Supreme Court dated March 20, 2014, providing guidance on the LCA ("*Resolution 01/2014*").

I POWER TO GRANT POST-AWARD INTEREST

1. Does an Arbitral Tribunal Have the Power to Grant Post-award Interest under Vietnamese Law?

The LCA is silent on the award of post-award interest by an arbitral tribunal.

The LCA is silent on the power to award post-award interest. The LCA only requires that an arbitral award must be in writing and cover certain key matters. As specified in Article 61.1 of the LCA, these key matters are:

a) the date, month, year and place of issuance of the arbitral award;
b) the name(s) and addresses of the claimant and the respondent;
c) the name(s) and addresses of the arbitrators;
d) a summary of the request for arbitration and the matters in dispute;
e) the reasons for making the arbitral award unless the parties have agreed that no reasons need be given;
f) the outcome reached by the tribunal;
g) the period of time for the implementation of the arbitral award;
h) the allocation of the costs of arbitration and other relevant expenses; and
i) the signatures of the arbitrators.

In other words, Article 61.1 of the LCA does not mandate that an arbitral award must say anything about post-award interest.

Institutional arbitration rules in Vietnam are also silent on the issue of whether a Tribunal may grant post-award interest. For example, the current 2017 Rules of Arbitration issued by the Vietnam International Arbitration Centre (*the VIAC*) simply require a VIAC arbitral award to cover the same matters as those listed in Article 61.1 of the LCA.[3] The VIAC Rules make no mention of the Tribunal's powers in relation to either pre- or post-award interest.

Provisions of Vietnamese Law Concerning Post-judgment Interest in Court Judgments

As the LCA is silent on an arbitral tribunal's power to grant post-award interest, provisions of Vietnamese law concerning post-judgment interest award in the context of domestic litigation may be applicable by analogy to an arbitral tribunal.[4] In particular, the Judicial Council of the SPC provided guidance on interests, interest rates

3. *See* VIAC Rules of Arbitration, effective from March 1, 2017, Article 32.1 which provides: "*An Arbitral Award shall be in writing and contain the following main information: a) Date, month, year and place of making the Arbitral Award; b) Names and addresses of the Claimant and the Respondent; c) Names of the Arbitrators or the name of the Sole Arbitrator; d) Summary of the Request for Arbitration and matters in dispute; summary of the Counterclaim and matters in dispute, if any; dd) Reasons for making the Arbitral Award unless the parties have agreed that no reasons are to be given; e) Determination of the dispute resolution; g) Period of time for implementing the Arbitral Award; h) Allocation of the costs of arbitration and other relevant expenses; i) Signatures of the Arbitrators or the signature of the Sole Arbitrator.*"

4. *See* Gary B. Born, *International Commercial Arbitration* (3rd edn, Kluwer Law International 2021) Chapter 23: Form and Contents of International Arbitral Awards (Updated August 2022), at pp. [3259]-[3368]: "*Interest can be awarded by an international arbitral tribunal on a variety of legal grounds. Applicable substantive law may permit the award of interest as an element of compensatory damages. Alternatively, statutory provisions of national law concerning pre-judgment or*

and penalties in Resolution No. 01/2019/NQ-HDTP, dated November 11, 2019, and effective from March 15, 2019 ("*Resolution 01/2019*"). Formulated with input from the Chief Prosecutor and the Ministry of Justice, Resolution 01/2019 was an attempt to provide comprehensive guidance on post-judgment interest, and it may be an applicable analogy. An SPC resolution, such as Resolution 01/2019, is by law a legal document having the force of law.[5]

Article 13 of Resolution 01/2019 expressly requires a Vietnamese court to include post-judgment interest in its first-instance judgment, as follows:

> (1) When resolving criminal, administrative, civil, marriage and family, business, commercial or labour cases, together with deciding the amount which a person having asset-related liability must pay to the judgment creditor, the Court must [also] include a decision in its judgment or decision (in the Decision section) as follows:
>
> a) With respect to the situation where there is a delay in performing a contractual obligation that the parties have agreed on payment of interest, then [the Court shall] decide that from the date following the date of first-instance trial[6] to the date the judgment enforcement is completed, the judgment debtor must bear the interest accrued on the outstanding judgment debt at the agreed interest rate but [such rate] must be in accordance with the applicable laws; if there is no agreement on the interest rate, then [the Court shall] decide based on the interest rate provided under Article 468.2 of the Civil Code 2015.
>
> b) With respect to the situation where there is an amount payable to the State budget and the laws require an obligation to pay interest on it; or for non-contractual damages; or in case there is a delay in performing an asset-related obligation under a contract or a different non-contractual asset-related obligation which the parties have not agreed on payment of interest, then [the Court shall] decide that from the effective date of the judgment or decision (if the judgment-enforcement authority has the power to enforce the judgment on its own accord) or from the date the judgement creditor submits its request for judgment enforcement (with respect to the amount payable to the judgment creditor) to the date the judgment enforcement is completed, the judgment debtor must bear the interest accrued on the outstanding judgment debt at the interest rate provided under Article 357, Article 468 of the Civil Code 2015, unless otherwise provided by laws.
>
> (2) "The agreed interest rate" referred to in clause 1 of this Article is the late-payment interest rate agreed upon by the parties under the contract or at

post-judgment interest, typically designed for application in litigations in the arbitral seat, may be held applicable or applicable by analogy by an arbitral tribunal."

5. Article 4.7 of Law No. 80/2015/QH13 on the Promulgation of Legal Documents passed by the National Assembly on June 22, 2015, effective from July 1, 2016, as amended and supplemented by Law No. 63/2020/QH14 amending and supplementing a number of articles of the Law on Promulgation of Legal Documents passed by the National Assembly on June 18, 2020, effective from January 1, 2021.
6. While there is no definition of "*the date of first-instance trial,*" there is a definition of "*the time of first-instance trial*" under Article 6 of Resolution 01/2019. "*The time of first-instance trial*" is defined as "*the date on which the Court issues the decision recognizing the parties' settlement or the date on which the Court declares the judgment after hearing the case at first-instance or at retrial.*" In our view, the reference to "*the date of first-instance trial*" should be understood as the reference to "*the time of first-instance trial.*"

> the Court. Where the parties have no agreement on the late-payment interest rate, the late-payment interest rate shall be 150% of the ordinary interest rate.

Under the above provision, it is mandatory for first-instance court judgments to include a post-judgment interest decision against the judgment debtors whether or not there is a request from a party.[7]

In addition, the reference to Articles 357 and 468 of the Civil Code 2015 further indicates that post-judgment interest is also a matter of Vietnamese substantive law, specifically the Civil Code 2015.

Article 357 of the Civil Code 2015 provides:

> (1) If the obligor delays on a payment, then it must pay interest on the overdue amount corresponding to the overdue period.
> (2) Interest rate on the overdue payment is determined based on the agreement between the parties but shall not exceed the interest rate prescribed in Article 468.1 of this Code; if there is no agreement [on the interest rate], then Article 468.2 of this Code shall apply. (Emphasis added)

Reading Article 357 in the context of Resolution 01/2019, as far as post-judgment interest is concerned, the SPC presumably takes the view that once there is a judgment against the judgment debtor, the judgment debtor must pay interest if it delays on paying the judgment debt. When the clock starts and at what interest rate will depend on the circumstances, including whether the parties have a contractual agreement on payment of interest and whether the judgment-enforcement authority has the power to enforce the judgment on its own accord. For example, if the relevant contract provides for an obligation to pay late-payment interest and an agreed late-payment interest rate, then the post-judgment interest will accrue from the date following the date of first-instance trial and accumulate at the late-payment interest rate contractually agreed by the parties. If there is no agreement to pay interest whatsoever, the clock may start from the date the judgment creditor submits its request for judgment enforcement and the post-judgment interest will accumulate at the statutory rate provided under Article 468 of the Civil Code 2015. In all cases, the clock will stop when the judgment enforcement is completed, i.e., the judgment debt is paid in full. For the discussion on

7. It should be noted that Resolution 01/2019 does not impose a mandatory requirement for awarding pre-judgment interest. Presumably, the determination on pre-judgment interest amount is part of the court's determination on the overall judgment debt owed by the judgment debtor to the judgment creditor. The court will make such determination (on the pre-judgment interest, if any) based on the applicable substantive law. For example, if there is a late-payment interest claim arising out of a commercial contract and the Vietnamese Commercial Law (Law No. 36/2005/QH11 passed by the National Assembly on June 14, 2005, effective from January 01, 2006) applies, then the aggrieved party will have the right to claim late-payment interest under Article 306 of the Commercial Law which provides: "*Article 306. Right to claim late-payment interest. Where the breaching party delays in making payment for goods or services and other reasonable costs, the aggrieved party will have the right to claim interest on such delayed payment at the average late-payment interest rate in the market at the time of payment and for the delayed period, unless otherwise agreed or provided by law.*" In such case, the pre-judgment interest will be awarded based on the Commercial Law while the post-judgment interest will be awarded based on Resolution 01/2019 and the Civil Code 2015.

the formula of post-judgment interest, please refer to "*[f]ormula for post-award interest under Vietnamese laws*" below.

Power of an Arbitral Tribunal to Grant Post-award Interest Under Vietnamese Law

While the LCA is silent on the power of an arbitral tribunal to grant post-award interest, there should be little doubt concerning the power of an arbitral tribunal to grant post-award interest under Vietnamese law given the SPC's guidance on post-judgment interest under Resolution 01/2019 (which is a Vietnamese legal document having the force of law) and its reference to the Civil Code 2015 as the substantive law. In fact, there should even be a strong argument that this power can be exercised based upon the arbitral tribunal's discretion, i.e., without a party's specific request. However, given the lack of authority on this point, an arbitral tribunal in a Vietnamese domestic arbitration may refrain from awarding post-award interest unless a party specifically asks for the relief. This conservative approach may make sense if the arbitral tribunal would like to protect the award from any challenge in the Vietnamese courts that the grant of post-award interest is a matter not claimed by the parties and thus such portion of the award must be set aside.[8] Of course, the easy answer is for the claimant to always seek post-award interest.

Domestic Arbitral Awards Often Include a Decision Granting Post-award Interest and Local Courts Have Recognized Such Decision As a Matter on Merits

While an arbitral award is subject to confidentiality in Vietnam, excerpts of certain awards can be found in court decisions where the court conducts a review to determine whether the award should be set aside or not. Those court decisions can be made available in the public domain. Based on the published court decisions, it appears that granting post-award interest is not uncommon in domestic arbitral awards, presumably based on the claimants' request. The typical language used in a domestic arbitral award regarding post-award interest is:[9]

> Within 30 days of the issuance date of this Award, the Respondent is obligated to carry out the payment obligation toward the Claimant as stated in section [...] of this Award. If the Respondent fails to fulfill its payment obligation stated in section [...] above, the Respondent shall pay the Claimant the interest on the overdue amount at an interest rate of ten percent (10%) per annum as prescribed under Article 357 of the Civil Code 2015.

Vietnamese courts have accepted domestic arbitral awards in which the arbitral tribunals granted post-award interest. First, several published court decisions show that Vietnamese courts rejected petitions to set aside domestic arbitral awards in which

8. *See* the LCA, Article 68.2(c) which provides: "*An arbitration award will be set aside if it belongs to one of the following circumstances: [...] (c) The dispute is not within the jurisdiction of the tribunal; if a part of the award concerns matters not within the jurisdiction of the tribunal then such part shall be set aside.*"
9. *See* Decision No. 03/2019/QD-KDTM dated April 10, 2019, of the People's Court of Hanoi rejecting the petition to set aside VIAC Award 15/18 dated September 12, 2018.

the arbitral tribunals granted post-award interest.[10] Second, for those published court decisions in which Vietnamese courts agreed to set aside domestic arbitral awards, the determination to set aside was not based on the arbitral tribunal's decision to grant post-award interest.[11]

Recently in 2021, in rejecting a respondent's complaint against a VIAC arbitral tribunal's decision on interest calculation in the respondent's petition to set aside a domestic arbitral award, the People's Court of Ho Chi Minh City opined that the court would not review the merits of the case which has been decided by the arbitral tribunal.[12] This confirms the view that an arbitral tribunal's determination on interest, including post-award interest, is a decision on merits, not on procedure.

Vietnamese Courts Have Also Accepted Foreign Arbitral Awards in Which the Arbitral Tribunal Granted Post-award Interest

Vietnamese courts have also accepted foreign arbitral awards in which the arbitral tribunal granted post-award interest.[13] Where the courts reject recognition for enforcement of an arbitral award, post-award interest was not the reason for rejection.[14]

10. *See* Decision No. 08/2017/QD-KDTM dated August 24, 2017, of the People's Court of Hanoi rejecting the petition to set aside VIAC Award 01/17 dated May 11, 2017, in which the arbitral tribunal decides that "*[...] 3. Within 30 days from the issuance date of this Award, the Respondent shall pay the Claimant the amounts stated [in this Award]. In the event the Respondent delays the payment of the amounts stated [in this Award], the Respondent shall pay the Claimant interest on the overdue amount in accordance with Vietnamese laws. [...]*"; Decision No. 09/2017/QD-PQTT dated September 28, 2017, of the People's Court of Hanoi rejecting the petition to set aside VIAC Award 07/17 dated September 26, 2017, in which the arbitral tribunal decides that "*[...] [The party seeking to set aside the Award] shall pay [the other party] the amounts stated [in this Award] within 30 days from the issuance date of the Award. In the event [the party seeking to set aside the Award] delays the payment, such party shall also pay interest as prescribed under Article 357 of the Civil Code 2015 at the rate of 10% per annum on the total overdue amount. [...]*"; Decision No. 755/2018/QD-PQTT of the People's Court of Ho Chi Minh City rejecting the petition to set aside Arbitral Award 75/17 HCM dated February 19, 2018, in which the arbitral tribunal decides that "*[...] the Respondent shall pay the Claimant in full the amounts stated [in this Award] within 30 days from the issuance date of this Award. In the event the Respondent delays the payment, the Respondent shall continue to pay the Claimant interest in accordance with Article 357 of the Civil Code 2015, at the rate of 10% per annum, incurred on the overdue amount during the late payment period [...]*" and Decision No. 12/2018/QD-KDTM dated November 9, 2018, of the People's Court of Hanoi rejecting the petition to set aside VIAC Award 04/18 dated August 9, 2018, in which the arbitral tribunal decides that ("*[...] 6. Within 30 days from the issuance date of this Award, the Respondent is liable to pay the Claimant the amounts stated [in this Award]. In the event the Respondent delays payment, the Respondent shall pay the Claimant interest on the overdue amount at the rate of 10% per annum as prescribed under Article 357 of the Civil Code 2015 [...].*"
11. *See* Decision No. 07/2019/QD-PQTT, dated July 18, 2019, of the People's Court of Hanoi setting aside VIAC Award 19/18, dated February 23, 2019, on the ground of unfair treatment contrary to the fundamental principles of Vietnamese laws and on the ground of procedural violation relating to notice and evidence review; and Decision No. 08/2019/QD-PQTT dated July 25, 2019, of the People's Court of Hanoi setting aside VIAC Award 85/16 HCM dated February 20, 2019, on the ground of unfair treatment contrary to the fundamental principles of Vietnamese laws.
12. *See* Decision No. 300/2021/QD-PQTT of the People's Court of Ho Chi Minh City, dated 9 March 9, 2021, rejecting the petition to set aside Arbitral Award 13/20 HCM dated November 14, 2020.
13. *See* Decision No. 05/2017/QDKDTM-ST of the People's Court of Hanoi dated July 21, 2017, in which the Court recognized for enforcement a Singapore International Arbitration Centre (SIAC)

2. Is the Power Exercisable Without a Request or Submission, or Is Such a Submission Required?

As stated above, there is a strong argument that an arbitral tribunal's power to grant post-award interest can be exercised based upon the arbitral tribunal's discretion, i.e., without a party's specific request. However, given the lack of authority on this point, an arbitral tribunal in a Vietnamese domestic arbitration may refrain from awarding post-award interest unless a party specifically asks for the relief. This conservative approach may make sense if the arbitral tribunal would like to protect the award from any challenge in the Vietnamese courts that the grant of post-award interest is a matter not claimed by the parties and thus such portion of the award must be set aside. Accordingly, it would be a good practice for the claimant to always seek post-award interest in its submission.

3. Is the Power Classified As One under the Substantive Applicable Law or the Procedural Law of the Arbitration?

As stated above, while the LCA is silent on the power of an arbitral tribunal to grant post-award interest, given the SPC's guidance on post-judgment interest under Resolution 01/2019 and Decision No. 300/2021/QD-PQTT of the People's Court of Ho Chi Minh City, our view is that the power to grant post-award interest is a substantive law issue under Vietnamese law.

Formula for Post-award Interest Under Vietnamese Laws

To the extent that Resolution 01/2019 and the Civil Code 2015 are relied upon by an arbitral tribunal when granting post-award interest, the formula for post-award interest is summarized below.

(i) *For an obligation on which the parties agree to pay interest.*

When the contract provides for an obligation on which the parties agree to pay interest (e.g., paying interest on a loan), then the formula for post-award interest applicable to the award debt on such obligation will depend on whether the contract also provides for late-payment interest rate.

If the answer is "*Yes*" (e.g., the parties agree that any overdue amount of the principal will subject to a late-payment interest rate), then the post-award interest rate for the award debt on the obligation (i.e., on the overdue amount of the principal) shall be the agreed late-payment interest rate.[15] The agreed late-payment interest rate should

arbitral award granting a post-award interest with the interest rate at USD 220.89 per day (or 2.66% per annum) until payment is completed.

14. *See* Decision No. 84/2017/KDTM-PT dated March 30, 2017, of the High-level People's Court of Hanoi in which the Court review an arbitral award issued by the arbitral tribunal for recognition for enforcement in Vietnam. The arbitral tribunal in this award granted a post-award interest at 7.5% per annum. Although the High-level Court did not recognize the award for enforcement in Vietnam, it was not due to the interest issue but due to the arbitration agreement and notice issues.
15. *See* Decision No. 300/2021/QD-PQTT of the People's Court of Ho Chi Minh City rejecting the petition to set aside Arbitral Award 13/20 HCM dated November 14, 2020, in which the arbitral

comply with the applicable law. For example, if the contract is a civil contract, then the maximum rate is 20% per annum, pursuant to Article 468.1 of the Civil Code 2015.[16]

If the answer is *"No"* (e.g., the parties have no agreement on late-payment interest applicable to any overdue amount of the principal), then the next question is whether there is any agreement on the ordinary interest rate (the interest rate for a payment obligation for which the performance is not overdue). If there is an agreed ordinary interest rate, then the post-award interest rate for the relevant award debt shall be 150% of the agreed ordinary interest rate.[17] If there is no agreed ordinary interest rate, then the post-award interest rate shall be 10% per annum, in accordance with Articles 357.2 and 468.2 of the Civil Code 2015.

(ii) *For an obligation on which the parties have no agreement to pay interest.*

For any obligation, whether arising out of a contract or outside the contract which lacks the parties' agreement to pay interest, the post-award interest rate applied to the relevant award debt shall be 10% per annum, in accordance with Articles 357.2 and 468.2 of the Civil Code 2015. Domestic arbitral tribunals in Vietnam have consistently applied this 10% post-award interest rate where the parties have no agreement on the obligation to pay interest.[18]

(iii) *Illustration on the formula for post-award interest.*

Party A lends 1 million VND to Party B for one year. Party B then defaults on the loan, paying nothing for two years, counting on the date of the award.

---

tribunal applied 12% per annum post-award interest rate, accrued on the outstanding unpaid amount. Presumably, this rate was based on the parties' contractual agreement on late-payment interest rate.

16. Article 468 of the Civil Code 2015 provides: "*1. The interest rate of a loan shall be as agreed upon by the parties. The interest rate of a loan as agreed by the parties shall not exceed 20% per annum, unless otherwise prescribed by law. Based on the actual situation and at the proposal of the Government, the Standing Committee of the National Assembly will decide to adjust the above interest rate and report to the National Assembly at the next meeting session. If the agreed interest rate exceeds the maximum interest rate prescribed in this clause, the interest rate in excess shall be invalid. 2. Where the parties agree upon the payment of interest without specifying the interest rate and have dispute over the interest rate, the interest rate shall be 50% of the maximum interest rate prescribed in clause 1 of this Article at the time of repayment.*"
17. If the lending rate is subject to a 20% per annum cap under Article 468.1 of the Civil Code 2015, the applicable cap to the post-award interest in this case would be 30%.
18. *See* Decision No. 08/2019/QD-PQTT dated July 25, 2019, of the People's Court of Hanoi setting aside VIAC Award 85/16 HCM dated February 20, 2019; Decision No. 07/2019/QD-PQTT dated July 18, 2019, of People's Court of Hanoi setting aside VIAC's Award 19/18 dated February 23, 2019; Decision No. 04/2019/QD-PQTT dated May 21, 2019, of the People's Court of Hanoi rejecting the petition to set aside VIAC Award 03/18 dated December 21, 2018; Decision No. 03/2019/QD-PQTT dated April 10, 2019, of the People's Court of Hanoi rejecting the petition to set aside VIAC Award 15/18 dated September 12, 2018; Decision No. 12/2018/QD-KDTM dated November 9, 2018, of the People's Court of Hanoi rejecting the petition to set aside VIAC Award 04/18 dated August 9, 2018; Decision No. 755/2018/QD-PQTT of the People's Court of Ho Chi Minh City rejecting the petition to set aside Arbitral Award 75/17 HCM dated February 19, 2018; Decision No. 09/2017/QD-PQTT dated September 28, 2017, of the People's Court of Hanoi rejecting the petition to set aside VIAC Award 97/17 dated September 26, 2017, and Decision No. 08/2017/QD-KDTM dated August 24, 2017, of the People's Court of Hanoi rejecting the petition to set aside VIAC Award 01/17 dated May 11, 2017.

Scenario 1: The parties have no agreement on ordinary interest rate and no agreement on late-payment interest rate. At the date of the award, the unpaid principal is 1 million VND and no unpaid interest.

The post-award interest rate will be 10% as there is no agreement on paying interest.

Scenario 2: The agreed ordinary interest rate is 4% per annum but the parties have no agreement on compound interest and no agreement on late-payment interest on the unpaid interest amount. At the date of the award, the unpaid principal is 1 million VND, and the unpaid interest is 80,000 VND (i.e., 40,000 VND x 2 years).

The post-award interest rate will be.

For the unpaid 1 million VND principal amount: 6% per annum post-award interest rate (i.e., 150% x 4% per annum ordinary interest rate) as there is no agreement on late-payment interest rate.

For the unpaid 80,000 VND interest amount: 10% per annum post-award interest rate, as the parties have no agreement on paying interest on the unpaid interest amount.

Scenario 3: The agreed ordinary interest rate is 4% per annum. The parties also agree that late-payment interest rate on any overdue amount of the principal shall be 5% per annum, but there is no agreement on compound interest and no agreement on late-payment interest on the unpaid interest amount. At the date of the award, the unpaid principal is 1 million VND, and the unpaid interest is 90,000 VND (i.e., 40,000 VND for the first year plus 50,000 VND for the second year).

The post-award interest rate will be.

For the unpaid 1 million VND principal amount: 5% per annum post-award interest rate, as per the parties' agreed late-payment interest rate.

For the unpaid 90,000 VND interest amount: 10% per annum post-award interest rate, as the parties have no agreement on paying interest on the unpaid interest amount.

(iv) *What happens if a domestic arbitral tribunal applies a post-award interest rate different from the formula provided by Resolution 01/2019 and the Civil Code 2015?*

In Decision No. 300/2021/QD-PQTT, the People's Court of Ho Chi Minh City viewed that interest rate is an issue on merits, not subject to review by the court. This is presumably the prevailing view of Vietnamese courts when reviewing petitions to set aside domestic arbitral awards. However, we must note that an arbitral award may be set aside if it is contrary to the fundamental principles of Vietnamese laws.[19] If an arbitral tribunal applies a post-award interest rate higher than either the rate agreed by

19. *See* the LCA, Article 68.2(dd) which provides: "*An arbitration award will be set aside if it belongs to one of the following circumstances: [...] (dd) The arbitral award is contrary to the fundamental principles of the Vietnamese laws.*"

the parties or, without such agreement, a 10% per annum rate, it may be possible that a Vietnamese court could set aside the award based on the public policy ground.[20]

(v) *What happens if a foreign arbitral tribunal applies a post-award interest rate different from the formula provided by Resolution 01/2019 and the Civil Code 2015?*

The recognition for enforcement of a foreign arbitral award in Vietnam is governed by Law No. 92/2015/QH-13 on civil procedure passed by the National Assembly on November 25, 2015, effective from July 1, 2016 (*the CPC*).[21] Article 458 of the CPC provides that Vietnamese courts shall not retry the dispute over which the foreign arbitral tribunal has issued an award.[22] The courts, however, will not recognize a foreign arbitral award for enforcement in Vietnam if such award falls within one or more circumstances provided under Article 459 of the CPC.[23]

20. *See* Resolution 01/2014, Article 14.2(dd) which provides: "*'The arbitral award is contrary to the fundamental principles of Vietnamese laws' means the arbitral award violates the fundamental behavioural principles that have the overall effect on formulation and implementation of Vietnamese laws. When considering a request to set aside an arbitral award, the Court must determine whether the arbitral award violates one or more fundamental legal principles, and such principle relates to the dispute resolution of the Arbitration. The Court only sets aside an arbitral award after indicating that it contravenes one or more fundamental principles of Vietnamese laws, which are not adhered to by the arbitral tribunal when issuing the arbitral award, and the arbitral award seriously infringes upon the interest of the State, the lawful rights and interests of a party or the parties or third person(s).*"
21. *See* Articles 424-430, CPC, at pp. [451]-[463].
22. *See* Article 458.4, CPC, which provides: "*When considering a petition for recognition and enforcement, the [adjudication] Council shall not retry the dispute over which the Foreign Arbitration has issued an award. The Court may only check and compare the Foreign Arbitration award and the documents and materials accompanying the petition in accordance with the provisions in Chapters XXXV and XXXVII of this Code, other relevant provisions of Vietnamese laws and international treaties to which Vietnam is a party, as the basis for issuance of a decision recognizing or not recognizing such award.*"
23. *See* Article CPC 459.1 which provides: "*1. The Court shall not recognize a Foreign Arbitration award when it finds the evidence provided by award debtor to the Court to challenge against the petition for recognition has a basis, is legal, and the arbitral award falls within one of the following circumstances: a) The parties of the arbitration agreement do not have capacity to sign such agreement according to the laws applicable to each party; b) The arbitration agreement is not valid according to the laws of a country which the parties have chosen to be applied or according to the laws where the award is issued in case the parties do not choose the governing law to such agreement; c) The award debtor being agencies, organizations and individuals were not promptly and properly notified of the appointment of arbitrator, of the procedures for resolution of the dispute by the Foreign Arbitration, or, for other legitimate reasons, they were not able to exercise their litigation rights; d) The Foreign Arbitration award was issued on a dispute which was not requested by any parties to be resolved or outside of the request of parties to the arbitration agreement. If it is possible to separate the part of the award on the issues requested and the part of the award on the issues which were not requested to be resolved by the Foreign Arbitration, the part of the award on the issues requested may be recognized and enforced in Vietnam; dd) Compositions of Foreign Arbitration tribunal, procedures of the Foreign Arbitration proceeding are not conforming to the arbitration agreement or to the laws of the country where the Foreign Arbitration award has been issued, if the arbitration agreement does not provide for such matters; e) The Foreign Arbitration award has not taken compulsory legal effect on the parties; g) The enforcement of the Foreign Arbitration award has been annulled or terminated by a competent government agency of the country where such award is issued or of the country whose law has been applied. 2. A Foreign Arbitration award will also be denied recognition and enforcement if*

The non-recognition ground of "*the recognition and enforcement in Vietnam of the Foreign Arbitration award are contrary to fundamental principles of Vietnamese laws*" is vague enough to give the courts broad discretion in applying this ground to set aside an award if the court deems it necessary.[24] To date, it appears that Vietnamese courts would not invoke this ground if the post-award interest is equal to or lower than the late-payment interest rate provided under Article 468 of the Civil Code 2015 (i.e., applying the rate agreed by the parties or, if no agreement is available, then 10% per annum rate).[25] However, if the post-award interest rate granted is higher than the rate agreed by the parties or higher than the 10% per annum rate (in the circumstances of no agreement by the parties), there could be a possibility that the reviewing courts may consider such decision to be "*contrary to the fundamental principles of Vietnamese laws*" as a ground for non-recognition.

II CHOICE OF LAW

4. What Is the Law That Applies to Determine What the Post-award Interest Should Be? Would This Be the Governing Law of the Dispute or the Law of the Seat?

In general, the law that applies to determine post-award interest is the governing law of the dispute to the extent that the question is one of substantive rather than procedural law. At least one Vietnamese court has taken the view that an arbitral tribunal's determination on interest, including post-award interest, is a decision on merits rather than procedure.[26]

Having said that, the answer is not so clear-cut where Vietnamese law is the law of the seat while the governing law of the dispute is foreign law and the award can be considered either as a domestic or a foreign arbitral award under Vietnamese law.[27] If

---

Vietnamese courts find that: a) According to Vietnamese laws, the dispute must not be resolved by arbitration; b) The recognition and enforcement in Vietnam of the Foreign Arbitration award are contrary to fundamental principles of Vietnamese laws."

24. *See* Article 14.2 (dd, Resolution 01/2014.
25. *See* Decision No. 05/2017/QDKDTM-ST of the Peoples Court of Hanoi dated July 21, 2017, the Court recognized for enforcement of a SIAC arbitral award granting a post-award interest with the interest rate at USD 220.89 per day (or 2.66% per annum) until payment is completed; and Decision No. 84/2017/KDTM-PT dated March 30, 2017, of the High-level People's Court of Hanoi in which the Court review an arbitral award issued by the arbitral tribunal for recognition for enforcement in Vietnam. The arbitral tribunal in this award granted a post-award interest at 7.5% per annum. Although the High-level Court did not recognize the award for enforcement in Vietnam, it was not due to the interest issue but due to the arbitration agreement and notice issues.
26. *See* Decision No. 300/2021/QD-PQTT of the People's Court of Ho Chi Minh City dated March 9, 2021, rejecting the petition to set aside Arbitral Award 13/20 HCM dated November 14, 2020.
27. This uncertainty arises out of the "*foreign arbitration*" definition under Article 3.11 of the LCA which provides: "*A foreign arbitration is an arbitration formed under provisions of a foreign law on arbitration which the parties agreed to select to settle the dispute outside or within the territory of Vietnam.*" *See* N. T. Hien et al., *Legal Handbook on Arbitration and Mediation* (2017), at pp. [23]-[24], where the authors take the view that an arbitral award is a foreign arbitral award if the dispute is referred to a foreign arbitral institution established under a foreign law on arbitration, regardless of whether the seat is Vietnam or not. The Handbook provides an example that if the dispute is referred to an ICC arbitration seated in Vietnam, the arbitral award of such arbitration

the award is considered to be a foreign arbitral award, then recognition and enforcement under the New York Convention, as codified in the CPC, is required. In this context, post-award interest can be challenged by a Vietnamese award debtor as violating a fundamental principle of Vietnamese laws to the extent the post-award interest rate is higher than the judgment interest rate provided by Resolution 01/2019. In our view, this is an argument that cannot be easily dismissed.

If enforcement of the award is sought as a domestic arbitral award, then the arbitral tribunal probably consisted of mostly Vietnamese-qualified lawyers. It is hard to imagine an arbitral tribunal, consisting of mostly or all foreign arbitrators, issuing an award that seeks enforcement as a domestic arbitral award, especially if the governing law is not Vietnamese law. Thus, in the case of an arbitral tribunal consisting of mostly Vietnamese-qualified lawyers, the arbitral tribunal will most likely apply Resolution 01/2019, including any applicable limitations or cap to protect the award from being set aside under Article 68 of the LCA.

III DO THE COURTS TAKE INTO ACCOUNT INTERNATIONAL STANDARDS WHEN FACING CHALLENGES ON THE POST-AWARD INTEREST?

It is unlikely that Vietnamese courts would consider international standards when facing challenges on the post-award interest, especially when such international standards are not moored to the laws of a specific jurisdiction.

IV SUBSTANTIVE LAW ISSUES

5. How Are Contractual Provisions on Late or Non-payment of Interest Relevant to Post-award Interest? Will These Be Considered By the Arbitral Tribunal?

As stated above, contractual provisions on late or non-payment of interest must be considered in determining a post-award interest rate.

6. How Do the Procedural Rules of the Substantive Law Apply?

If the arbitration is seated in Vietnam while the substantive law applicable to the dispute is foreign law, then the foreign procedural rules would not apply to resolve the dispute.

V PROCEDURAL LAW ISSUES

7. What Are the Main Procedural Law Issues When Considering Post-award Interest? How Are the Arbitration Laws and Other Laws or Regulations of the Seat Relevant?

must be considered as a foreign arbitral award under Vietnamese laws and must be recognized for enforcement in accordance with the CPC and the New York Convention.

If the award contains a post-award interest computation error or mistake, a party may, within 30 days of receipt of the award or within a different time period agreed by the parties, request the arbitral tribunal to correct the error or mistake.[28] However, that party must immediately notify the other party of such request.[29] If the arbitral tribunal considers that the request is legitimate, then the arbitral tribunal will make the correction within 30 days from the date of receipt of the request or within the time limit extended by the arbitral tribunal.[30] The arbitral tribunal can also, on its own initiative, correct the error within 30 days from the date it issues the award and notify the parties.[31]

If the award does not contain a determination on a post-award interest claim already presented during the arbitration proceedings, a party may, within 30 days of receipt of the award or within a different time period agreed by the parties, request the arbitral tribunal to make an additional award and must immediately notify the other party of such request.[32] If the arbitral tribunal considers that the request is legitimate, then the arbitral tribunal will issue the additional award within 45 days from the date of receipt of the request or within the time limit extended by the arbitral tribunal.[33]

If the award is a domestic arbitral award, then within 30 days of receipt of the award, a party can petition a competent Vietnamese court to set aside the award based on one of the grounds provided under Article 68.2 of the LCA.[34] As stated above, one of the grounds is the public policy ground.

If the award is a foreign arbitral award, then within three years from the date on which the award takes legal effect, the judgment creditor may submit an application to the Vietnamese Ministry of Justice (if provided so under the international treaty to which Vietnam is a signatory) or to a competent Vietnamese court (if the relevant international treaty does not specify or if there is no relevant international treaty) to request for recognition and enforcement of the award.[35] The court shall not recognize the award if the court determines that the award falls within one of the circumstances stipulated under Article 459 of the CPC.[36] As stated above, one of the grounds for not recognizing a foreign arbitral award is the public policy ground.

VI EFFECT OF ENFORCEMENT ORDERS ON INTEREST ON THE AWARD ON BOTH THE SEAT AND ELSEWHERE

Domestic awards are enforced under the law on enforcement of civil judgments. In other words, a domestic award can be enforced like a court judgment.[37] Similarly, a

28. *See* Article 63.1 LCA.
29. *See* Article 63.1 LCA.
30. *See* Articles 63.1 and 63.5 LCA.
31. *See* Article 63.3 LCA.
32. *See* Article 63.4 LCA.
33. *See* Articles 63.4 and 63.5 LCA.
34. *See* Article 69 LCA.
35. *See* Article 451 CPC.
36. *See* Article 459 CPC.
37. *See* Article 67 LCA.

foreign arbitral award which has been recognized for enforcement in Vietnam shall have the same legal effect as an effective decision of a Vietnamese court and can be enforced under the law on enforcement of civil judgments.[38]

VII POWERS OF THE COURT TO ORDER OR ADJUST POST-AWARD INTEREST

8. Does the Vietnamese Court Have the Power to Order or Adjust Post-award Interest, Assuming It Is Either the Seat Court or the Enforcing Court?

A Vietnamese court (either as the seat court or the enforcing court) does not have the power to order or adjust post-award interest. If an award debtor in a domestic arbitration case petitions a competent Vietnamese court to set aside the award, then the reviewing court can only decide to either set aside or not set aside such award.[39] If an award creditor in a foreign arbitration case petitions a Vietnamese competent court to recognize the award for enforcement, then the reviewing court can only decide to either recognize or not recognize such award.[40]

38. *See* Article 427.2 CPC.
39. *See* Article 71.5 LCA.
40. *See* Article 458.5 CPC.

www.ingramcontent.com/pod-product-compliance
Lightning Source LLC
LaVergne TN
LVHW021727021026
849161LV00004BA/755